THE KAW
The Heart of a Nation

RIVERS OF AMERICA BOOKS

(already published are:)

THE ALLEGHENY by Frederick Way, Jr.
THE ARKANSAS by Clyde Brion Davis
THE BRANDYWINE by Henry Seidel Canby
THE CHAGRES by John Easter Minter
THE CHARLES by Arthur Bernon Tourtellot
THE CHICAGO by Harry Hansen
THE COLORADO by Frank Waters
THE CONNECTICUT by Walter Hard
THE DELAWARE by Harry Emerson Wildes
THE EVERGLADES by Marjory Stoneman Douglas
THE FRASER by Bruce Hutchison
THE GILA by Edwin Corle
THE HOUSATONIC by Chard Powers Smith
THE HUDSON by Carl Carmer
THE HUMBOLDT by Dale L. Morgan
THE ILLINOIS by James Gray
THE JAMES (New Revised Edition, 1945)
by Blair Niles
THE KAW by Floyd Benjamin Streeter
KENNEBEC by Robert P. Tristram Coffin
THE KENTUCKY by T. D. Clark

THE
RIVERS OF AMERICA

Present Editors

CARL CARMER

JEAN CRAWFORD, *Associate*

Former Editors

CONSTANCE LINDSAY SKINNER

RUTH E. ANDERSON, *Art*

THE KAW

THE HEART OF A NATION

by

FLOYD BENJAMIN STREETER

Illustrated by
ISABEL BATE *and* HAROLD BLACK

RINEHART & COMPANY
INCORPORATED
New York *Toronto*

IN MEMORY OF

MY PARENTS

WHO WERE PIONEER SETTLERS

IN KANSAS

Contents

THE KAW
The Heart of a Nation

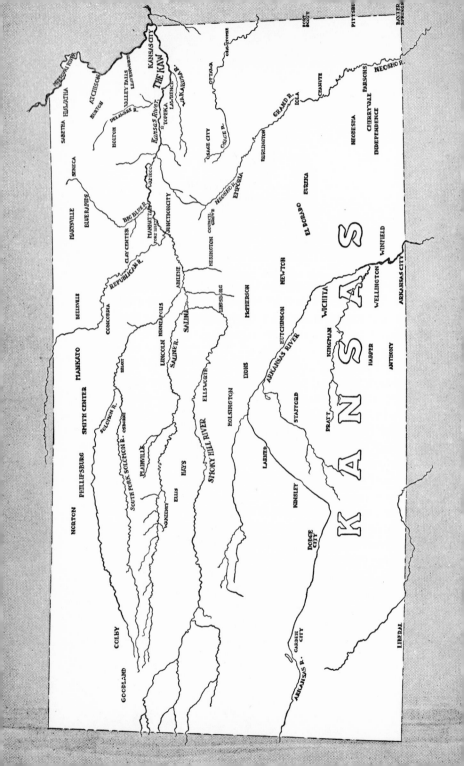

I

The River

I N THE heart of the Great Plains, where so much of the dramatic history of the West has been made and where countless folk tales have originated, flows the Kaw River, a wide, shallow stream about seven hundred miles long from the source of its farthest tributary to its mouth. Each season enacts a new drama on its banks, adds a new chapter to the folk-say of the plains.

Its tributaries rise in the short-grass country of Colorado, rush madly into Kansas during the spring, meander lazily in the dry heat of summer or sometimes disappear altogether, leaving only damp and treacherous sand to mark their passing. In Kansas these same tributaries unite into rivers, wind through the short- and tall-grass prairies to the hills of eastern Kansas where they empty into the Kaw itself, a broad, silt-laden, saffron-hued river, which joins the Missouri at Kansas City.

These streams pass through a rich agricultural empire. The valley of the Kaw and its tributaries is a vast tapestry patterned by ranches that number their acreage in the thousands, seas of wheat, green oases of corn, millet, canes and kaffirs, fruit and vegetable tracts, hundreds of wooded hills, unnumbered salt mines, miles of oil derricks, hamlets, villages, and small cities, the whole crossed and recrossed by roads and railroads, and always streams, blue waters, gray waters, yellow waters.

If one is seeking wooded heights, these will be found by driving the river roads of eastern Kansas in the spring when the redbud vies with the white plum to dominate the bluffs, on the one hand, while below the blue-green of new willow loses itself in the diaphanous mists rising from the river. If in search of the unusual, then travel along the winding river roads of central Kansas in autumn when the flaming sumac, russet oak, brown elm, hackberry, and golden cottonwood flaunt their colors against a background of rock-crowned hills. It is on the western plains that the most haunting beauty is found. These plains are a world of pastels where skies are not just blue, but azure, where clouds are never white or gray but tinted masses, where thunder and lightning are not just thunder and lightning but majestic battles of the elements. In April, the plains are a jade world; in June, a pale-green world; in August, a seared world; in autumn, a rose world.

The river was named for the Kansa, or Kaw, tribe of Indians which lived on its banks from an early date. The tribe was of the Siouan linguistic stock; and Kansa, or Kansas, is a Siouan word which means Wind People or People of the South Wind.

The word "Kansa," or "Kansas," has passed through modifications but has changed little in sound. The Siouans and the Kansa tribe generally pronounced it känsa or kä-sa. The early traders changed the Indian form of pronunciation. They gave the *a* the sound of *au* or *aw*. From this corruption came the word "Kau" or "Kaw." The explorers and early mapmakers called the tribe and the river Cans, Causa, Kansa, Kances, Kanza, Konza, Quans, etc. Eventually the stream was named Kansas River, though it is commonly called the Kaw.

The story of the Kaw goes back into the dim past. Before white men came, the Indians made their home on the banks of the stream, and they have a long legendary history. Then, seventy years before the founding of Jamestown, the first white man, Francisco Vasquez de Coronado, came to the territory now included in Kansas which was known as Quivira. A half century after Coronado's journey, two other Spaniards, Antonio de Humana and Don Juan de Onate, led expeditions to Quivira. In the eighteenth century, French traders and trappers came to the Kaw country. One of them, Etienne de Bourgmont, went up the river to the headwaters of the Smoky Hill in 1724 for the purpose of establishing trade relations with the Comanche Indians. Finally, in the nineteenth century, the American pathfinders, General Zebulon M. Pike, Major Stephen H. Long, and John C. Frémont, led exploratory expeditions along the banks of the Kaw or its tributaries.

The geographical location of the Kaw made it the main path of travel between the Mississippi Valley and the Far West. The traders bound for Santa Fe, the Mormons for Deseret, the emigrants for Oregon, the gold seekers for California, the soldiers of Kearny and Doniphan for the Mexican frontier, all began their westward journey by way of the Kaw. Approximately ninety thousand persons started across the plains from the mouth of the Kaw in 1849 and 1850. This river was the route of important stage and freight lines; and is now the route of three transcontinental railroads, three national highways, and bus and truck service.

The first settlers located along this river. When Kansas was admitted as a state in the Union, Topeka on the banks of the Kaw was made the state capital. The

State University and the State Agricultural College were established in river towns.

In an ever-changing panorama the various phases of Kansas development passed on its banks—the struggle between free and slave forces; the era of the cowboy, when river towns were busy markets for the never-ending herds of cattle brought from the plains of the Southwest; and the quieter but no less dramatic conquest by the settler who made the prairie wilderness "blossom as the rose."

The citizens of the Kaw are a wide-awake, progressive lot of people. For many years they were classed as radicals and reformers. Maybe they were more puritanical on moral issues and quicker to fight economic and social injustice than some of their neighbors. If so, it was because of the character of the early settlers and their life on a cruel frontier.

Life on the frontier was hard. It was doubly hard in Kansas. The pioneers had to endure not only the ordinary hardships of the frontier but also a succession of reverses and disasters. There were border wars, droughts, grasshoppers, floods, prairie fires, blizzards, and dust storms. Yet they stuck it out, though some are unkind enough to say their continued residence in the state was due more to lack of finances than to unusual staying qualities. This is expressed in a popular folk song:

> We do not live but only stay,
> And are too poor to get away.

It was out of the crucible of these years that the true Kansas spirit developed. Having conquered seemingly unsurmountable obstacles, Kansans learned to speak lightly of reverses, learned to rise above the trials of the hour, and developed that rare sense of humor which enabled them to laugh at themselves and the foibles of men. Their children have inherited that sense of humor. Most of the "Kansas stories" have originated in Kansas, and some of these stories are whoppers.

Out of this background came a code of ethics which banned injustice and called for a rigid moral standard. It is quite natural that Kansans should have taken a leading part in all progressive movements and political revolts—the antislavery crusade, woman suffrage, equal rights, the Populist party, Prohibition, and Bryan and free silver.

These disciples of reform waged such a vigorous and spectacular campaign that Kansas became the byword of the nation and was referred to as the source of every radical idea and crackpot theory. Many of the measures urged by these militant leaders have been written into the statute books and are now the accepted law of the land. The present generation does not see much wrong with these laws or with their pioneer sponsors.

The aggressive radicalism of pioneer times has largely disappeared. In its place has come a saner and more conservative attitude toward social and political issues. The people are still up and coming and sufficiently influenced by the past to support progressive measures; but they are not swept off their feet by new isms, nor do they follow the old just because it is old.

Men and women trained in the Kansas spirit have gone and are going to the far corners of the earth, where they are taking their places and leaving the stamp of their indomitable spirit, their courage, their optimism.

Kansans have had and still have enduring faith in their state. Like St. Augustine, they have their City of God. It is the Kansas of their dreams—the Kansas of the future, free from droughts, grasshoppers, dust storms, and "mortgage fiends." Many of the pioneers who helped build this prairie empire are still living. The present may be hard and discouraging, but they and their children know that reverses have come and gone, good years have followed lean years. These people cannot be whipped. They continue to carry on, looking hopefully to the next harvest, confident that better times are ahead. In fact, Kaw folk, old and young, much of the time talk and think in terms of the future. As they often put it when reference is made to an older section of the country, "They've been where they're going. Out here we've only started on our way."

2.

The Wagon Trails

IN THE early days of western travel the man bound for the Rocky Mountains or the Pacific Coast reached the edge of civilization when he arrived at the mouth of the Kaw. Ahead was the bleak prairie, six hundred miles wide and uninhabited except by roving bands of Indians and buffalo.

This prairie wilderness was cut by trails which started near the mouth of the Kaw and spread out as they advanced into the plains. No highway engineers built these primitive roads; they just grew. No one knows who blazed the first trail. Maybe buffalo wore a path and man followed the tracks of the animals. Perhaps the Indians made the path, and the white men followed it, first on horseback, then in wagons and stagecoaches. Anyway, down through the years, an endless procession of men and vehicles crawling up the trail kept wearing the tracks deeper and wider until a muddy wagon road developed.

If the traveler was headed southwest he took the Santa Fe Trail which entered Kansas on the south side of the Kaw, and then he followed its twisted pathway to arrive at his destination. If he was bound for California or Oregon, he traveled the road which ran along

9

the south bank of the Kaw about seventy miles, crossed the river, and followed the Big Blue River out of Kansas and went west along the Platte. If he wanted to reach the gold fields of Colorado, he used the Leavenworth and Pikes Peak Express route through northern Kansas, or took the Butterfield Trail along the Kaw and Smoky Hill rivers.

Jones, Russell and Company of Leavenworth organized the Leavenworth and Pikes Peak Express line in 1859 to carry passengers and freight to and from the gold fields of Colorado. The line, equipped with fifty-two coaches, went into operation in April. The first two westbound coaches left Leavenworth on the 18th and arrived in Denver on May 7th. The route they traveled ran west from Leavenworth to Indianola, a town situated two miles north of Topeka, followed the north bank of the Kaw to Junction City, and then continued west along the divide between the Republican and Solomon rivers. The whole length of the road, as first laid out, was 687 miles; later, this distance was shortened.

Owing to the scarcity of fuel and water on the high plains, the company abandoned this route a few weeks after the line went into operation, and moved the stock and coaches to the Platte, where they ran the stages on a weekly schedule.

During the rush to the gold field in the spring of 1859, circulars and cards, issued in eastern Kansas, urged the gold seekers to follow the Smoky Hill route, that is, travel by way of the Kaw and Smoky Hill rivers, and represented it as a "good, plain road with good camps and 250 miles shorter than any other route."

An immense "foot," "handcart," and wagon emigration rushed up the Kaw valley. Some travelers got discouraged and returned home. Others went on. Many of them, even those with teams, lost their way. Some died on the plains or were picked up along the way too weak to travel. Others traveled for miles without water and subsisted on the flesh of dead animals or on prickly pears, managing to reach Denver in a starved condition.

Graves, bleaching bones on the prairie, deserted wagons, an occasional cookstove, scattered mining tools, and a few names carved on the walls of cliffs marked this ill-advised attempt to reach the gold fields. All these signs of failure, excepting the names on the rocks, have long since disappeared.

The Smoky Hill route was abandoned, except for freight and express, until 1865 when David A. Butterfield, a pioneer businessman of Denver and later of Atchison, organized a company to open a freight and passenger line between Atchison and Denver known as the Butterfield Overland Despatch.

The first coach left Atchison on September 11th and reached Denver in the morning of the 23rd. Butterfield and other officials accompanied the coach. All Denver turned out to see it arrive. The local paper gives the following account of the event:

The coach was met about four miles up Cherry Creek, when Col. Butterfield was taken into the carriage with his honor the Mayor and other distinguished citizens, and escorted to the Planter House, through several of the principal streets, the band playing lively and patriotic airs in its most lively and inspiring style.

The procession was made up of carriages filled with the business men of the city, and a cavalcade of horsemen preceded by the First Colorado Band. A banner was borne in one of the leading carriages, with the following inscription: "The energy of our old townsman Col. D. A. Butterfield proves him the Hercules of Expressmen. Welcome Dave and your Express!"

On another banner was represented a train of cars headed West, and a coach filled with passengers leaving it toward the mountains in the distance. . . .

After a short respite was given to the Colonel, during which time many of his old friends availed themselves of the opportunity to shake him by the hand, and to congratulate him upon the successful opening up of his great route, he was loudly called for by the crowd which had gathered in front of the hotel. . . .

When Col. Butterfield appeared upon the veranda, he was received with such a salvo of cheers as must have told him that the people stood with their hearts in their hands . . . He said the enterprise was a child of Colorado, and he had no misgivings upon the score of its being well taken care of by its mother. He illustrated the feasibility of the route by stating that he came through from Fort Ellsworth, 380 miles, without a change of stock, in seven days.

The old trails were used by many people for many purposes, but chiefly for overland trade. The Santa Fe Trail was the oldest, since its trade really began in 1821. Prior to that date several attempts were made to reach Santa Fe, but few were successful. In 1821 William Becknell and four companions made a successful trip from Missouri to Santa Fe and sold their goods at a large profit. About that time two other parties from Missouri, one led by Thomas James and the other by Hugh Glenn, arrived in Santa Fe. They sold everything they had, and the New Mexicans wanted more.

Prior to 1824, goods were transported on the backs of horses and mules. In 1824 a company of traders left Independence, Missouri, with a large outfit of pack animals and vehicles. They carried a shipment of goods valued at more than $25,000. From this time, wagon trains became the usual mode of transportation. The wagons used in this trade were manufactured in Pittsburgh. Their capacity was about a ton and a half, and they were drawn by eight mules or the same number of oxen. Later larger wagons were employed.

Congress recognized the importance of the Santa Fe trade in 1824. That year Senator Thomas H. Benton of Missouri introduced a bill authorizing the president to appoint three commissioners to survey a road from the

Missouri River to the boundary line of New Mexico, and from there to Santa Fe, with the consent of the Mexican government. President Monroe signed this bill, making it a law, at the close of his term of office. President John Quincy Adams put it into effect by appointing the three commissioners, who made satisfactory treaties with the Indian tribes and marked the trail with stones and earth mounds.

In the early days Council Grove, about a hundred and fifty miles west of Independence, was the frontier outpost. Wagon trains usually assembled here and organized by electing a captain and other officers and adopting a code. The animals were permitted to rest a day or so while the men procured timber for axletrees and other repairs; beyond this grove there was no serviceable timber near the trail.

When the train stopped for the night, the captain assigned certain men to guard duty. There were usually eight watchers, each standing a fourth of every alternate night. The train broke camp early in the morning. Josiah Gregg, the historian of the trail, describes the scene:

Catch up! Catch up! is now sounded from the captain's camp and echoed from every division and scattered group along the valley. The woods and dales resound with the gleeful yells of the light-hearted wagoners who, weary of inaction and filled with joy at the prospect of getting under way, become clamorous in the extreme. . . . Each teamster vies with his fellows who shall be soonest ready, and it is a matter of boastful pride to be the first to cry out, "All's set."

The uproarious bustle which follows, the hallooing of those in pursuit of animals, the exclamations which the unruly brutes call forth from their wrathful drivers, together with the clatter of bells, the rattle of yokes and harness, the

jingle of chains, all conspire to produce an uproarious confusion. . . .

"All's set!" is finally heard from some teamster—"All's
set," is directly responded from every quarter. "Stretch
out!" immediately vociferates the captain. Then the "heps!"
of the drivers, the cracking of whips, the trampling of feet,
the occasional creak of wheels, the rumbling of the wagons.
. . . "Fall in" is heard from head-quarters, and the wagons
are forthwith strung out upon the long inclined plain. . . .

After this manner the wagon train proceeded day
after day across the prairie until it reached Santa Fe.
When the caravan was about a hundred miles from the
city, the owners would ride ahead to arrange with the
customs officials and local merchants for the disposal of
the goods. The residents of the old capital eagerly
awaited the arrival of the wagons. Dr. Gregg gives a
vivid picture of the long train rolling into town:

The arrival produced a great deal of bustle and excitement among the natives. "Los Americanos!" . . . "Los car-
ros!" . . . "La entrada de la Carvana!"—the Americans,
the wagons, the arrival of the caravan—were to be heard
in every direction; and crowds of women and boys flocked
around to see the newcomers; while crowds of *leperos* hung
about as usual to see what they could pilfer. The wagoners
were by no means free from excitement on this occasion.
Informed of the "ordeal" they had to pass, they had spent
the previous morning in "rubbing up"; and now they were
prepared with clean faces, sleek combed hair, and their
choicest Sunday suits, to meet the "fair eyes" of glistening
black that were sure to stare at them as they passed. There
was yet another preparation to be made in order to "show
off" to advantage. Each wagoner must tie a bran new
"cracker" to the lash of his whip; for on driving through

the streets and *plaza publica*, every one strives to outvie his comrades in the dexterity with which he flourishes this favorite badge of his authority.

By 1826 wagons had completely supplanted pack animals. Sixty wagons carried goods to Santa Fe that year, and the trade amounted to $91,000. A steady increase followed until 1846, when four hundred fourteen wagons made the trip with merchandise valued at $1,752,250.

Overland freighting on the western trails was an enormous business from 1859 to 1869, that is, from the discovery of gold in Colorado to the completion of the Union Pacific Railroad across the continent. An eyewitness says that he counted 888 wagons between Fort Kearney and Julesburg in one day in the sixties, and that frequently a train a mile long might be seen on the road. Many times a number of trains traveled together, and the string of white canvas-covered wagons extended for miles. Probably the largest six-mule wagon train that ever strung out on the plains transported supplies for General Custer's command during his winter campaign against the Indians in 1868. It comprised over eight hundred army wagons and was four miles long in one column.

The firm of Russell, Majors, and Waddell did a large part of the freighting on the western trails. This firm was one of the oldest and most widely known of the freighters on the plains. For many years they were the government contractors for transporting military supplies to all the posts on the frontier. In their outfit the number of wagons in a train was twenty-five, officered as follows: a captain, who was wagonmaster; an assistant wagonmaster; a night herder; a driver who

looked after the extra horses; and a driver for each
wagon.

The drivers of the ox teams, known as bullwhack-
ers, were experts at whip-throwing and swearing. The
heads of the firm stipulated that any one of their teamsters who whipped cattle unmercifully or uttered an
oath should forfeit his wages. One day a bullwhacker
entered Alexander Majors's office and asked for a job.

"Can you drive oxen?" asked Majors.

"Yep," replied the man, "I can drive oxen to hell
and back."

"Well, well," replied the freighter, "I can't use you
because our firm doesn't make that point."

The admonition against profanity proved ineffective when a wagon train got stuck in the mud. Somehow
swear words and mudholes went arm in arm along the
Kaw.

The headquarters of this firm were located outside
of Leavenworth between the fort and the city. Horace
Greeley, who visited the headquarters in 1859, left this
description:

. . . Such acres of wagons! such pyramids of extra
axletrees! such herds of oxen! such regiments of drivers and
other employees! No one who does not see can realize how
vast a business this is, nor how immense are its outlays as
well as its income. I presume this great firm has at this hour
two millions of dollars invested in stock, mainly in oxen,
mules and wagons. (They last year employed six thousand
teamsters and worked forty-five thousand oxen) . . .

When the freighting business was at its height, this
firm owned more than 6,200 wagons, each built to
carry from 5,000 to 7,000 pounds of merchandise, and
worked 75,000 head of oxen. If the oxen were yoked

together and hitched to the wagons, this would make a train approximately forty miles long.

The line of mail stages established from St. Louis to Santa Fe in 1849 was one of the earliest routes in the West. The stages ran once a month. As the line became more popular, the owners moved the eastern terminus to Independence, Missouri.

The first mail stage ran from the Missouri River to Salt Lake City on July 1, 1850, as a monthly service.

In a few years the service on both Santa Fe and Platte routes was changed from monthly to weekly, and in the early sixties a daily system was instituted on both trails.

The fare to Santa Fe was $250, the allowance of baggage was limited to forty pounds. It required about two weeks to make the trip. The fare from Atchison to Placerville on the Overland line was $225, and the trip was made in seventeen or eighteen days.

The stations on the stage routes were ten to fifteen miles apart, though some out on the plains were twenty-five to fifty miles apart. At these points animals and drivers changed, and meals were served. About every thirty miles there was a ranch selling hay to the trains of emigrants and freighters. Every fifty or a hundred miles there was a small grocery store and blacksmith shop; and in the sixties about as frequently a military post for protection against the Indians.

The stage stations were quite similar in construction—plain, nearly square, one-story structures of one to three rooms—and were made of logs or prairie turf. The roofs consisted of logs on which were placed some willows, then a layer of hay covered with earth or sod, and over all a sprinkling of coarse gravel. The floors were usually the natural soil.

The eating houses, called "home stations," were

twenty-five or thirty miles apart. A number of these were two or three times larger than the stations at which no meals were served, and they were provided with sheds, outbuildings, and other conveniences. Julesburg was one of the oldest of the stations. The buildings were constructed of cedar logs and were the largest between Fort Kearney and Denver.

The meals at the stage stations were a subject of varying comment. The fare on the Santa Fe stages included the travelers' meals, which consisted chiefly of hardtack, bacon, and coffee, and at times antelope and buffalo meat.

The meals at the stations along the Overland route consisted of bacon, eggs, hot biscuits, coffee, dried peaches and apples, and pies; beef was occasional; buffalo, elk, and antelope steaks in season; and canned fruit and vegetables at least half the time.

Some of the eating places were quite dirty. At one station out on the plains a passenger sat down at the table with a half dozen others and began complaining about the lack of cleanliness. The landlord, overhearing his remarks, at once spoke up:

"Well, sir, I was taught long ago that we must all eat a peck of dirt."

"I am aware of that fact, my dear sir," responded the passenger, "but I don't like to eat mine all at once."

At another station one of the drivers refused to eat, explaining that he had a weak stomach. He had watched the landlady fondle the dogs and cats, and without washing thrust her hands into the flour and mix up a pan of biscuits. Those who knew nothing about the dogs and cats declared that she beat any woman on the line making delicious biscuits.

One time for weeks nothing was served for dessert excepting dried-apple pies. The drivers, stock tenders, and passengers, becoming tired of this article of diet, all rebelled. As some of the drivers expressed it, they had "dried-apple pies from Genesis to Revelation." Finally a verse was distributed up and down the line, and had the desired effect:

Dried Apple Pies

I loathe! Abhor! Detest! Despise!
Abominate dried-apple pies;
I like good bread; I like good meat,
Or anything that's good to eat;
But of all poor grub beneath the skies
The poorest is dried-apple pies.
Give me a toothache or sore eyes
In preference to such kind of pies.

The farmer takes his gnarliest fruit,
'Tis wormy, bitter, and hard, to boot;
They leave the hulls to make us cough,
And don't take half the peelings off;
Then on a dirty cord they're strung,
And from some chamber window hung;
And there they serve a roost for flies
Until they're ready to make pies.
Tread on my corns, or tell me lies,
But *don't* pass to *me* dried-apple pies.

The early stagecoaches were built in Concord, New Hampshire, and were known as Concord coaches. They cost $1,000 each. A writer in the *Missouri Commonwealth*, published at Independence, July, 1850, describes the coaches:

. . . The stages are got up in elegant style, and are each arranged to convey eight passengers. The bodies are beautifully painted and made water tight, with a view of using them as boats in ferrying streams. The team consists of six mules to each coach. The mail is guarded by eight men, armed as follows: Each man has at his side, fastened in the stage, one of Colt's long revolving rifles, and in a holster below, one of Colt's long revolvers, and in his belt a small Colt's revolver, besides a hunting-knife; so that these eight men are ready, in case of attack, to discharge one hundred and thirty-six shots without having to reload . . .

The stages ran on a definite schedule along the entire line. A few minutes before the time for departure, the coach drawn by four horses drove up in front of the station. A crowd gathered to see it start.

The driver was a rough-and-ready young plainsman who knew all the dangerous spots between Atchison and Placerville and could dash over a winding trail at a lively gait and keep the coach right side up. He carried a six-shooter and a knife in his belt and was versed in the ways of the Indian.

While the hostler stood at the head of the lead team, the driver distributed the baggage in the boot behind and under the driver's feet so that the load was evenly balanced. With no load on top, the coach would be less top-heavy for mudholes and hillsides.

The passengers climbed in and made themselves comfortable. Then the driver mounted the box-seat, picked up the lines, and nodded to the hostler. Amid ejaculations of "Write as soon as you get there" . . . "Tell Henry to visit us the next time he comes East" . . . "Better have your hair cut so the Cheyennes can't scalp you" and "good-bye John," the driver cracked his whip and the coach rolled away, leaving a gray cloud of dust behind. The horses were fresh, and the first mile or two the driver had to hold them down.

The trail crossed a level prairie and then wound through low hills where a recent storm had damaged the road. When the stage came to the rough stretch it began to pitch, much to the discomfort of the passengers. It struck a chuckhole, throwing the lady passenger against the side. She scowled and said:

"I wonder where that fellow learned to drive. It's 'nough to kill a person."

Then the stage hit another hole. This time the woman landed against the fat salesman on her left. She didn't say anything, but looked as if she could slaughter both the driver and Ben Holladay, the owner of the stage line.

They soon reached smooth road. The horses gradually wore off the wire edge and settled down to a steady trot. An hour later they were in sight of the next station. When they were a half mile from it the driver cracked his whip. The horses plunged forward and raced up the trail, the driver bringing them to an abrupt stop in front of the station, as a cheer went up from the little group awaiting the arrival of the stage.

This was a "swing station," where they changed horses. The hostlers performed this feat in three minutes, and the coach bounded away.

The stage traveled over a good road the remainder of the day, and the ride became monotonous. The passengers passed the time telling stories and singing songs. The driver became drowsy, and to keep awake he sang the "Song of the Overland Stage Driver," which had been written by Nathan Stein, an employee of the Overland line, and was popular among the army of stage boys.

I sing to everybody, in the country and the town
A song upon a subject that's worthy of renown;
I haven't got a story of fairy land to broach,
But plead for a cause of sticking to the box seat of a
    coach.

Statesmen and warriors, traders and the rest,
May boast of their profession, and think it is the best;
Their state I'll never envy, I'll have you understand,
Long as I can be a driver on the jolly "Overland."

They reached the "home station" late in the afternoon. The day's travel was about seventy miles.

The following morning in a driving rain they rode over the prairies and passed numerous freight and emigrant wagons stalled in the mud. The drivers were cracking their whips over the backs of the oxen and were shouting and swearing in their attempt to get the wagons out. It required nine or ten yoke of oxen to move some of the large wagons.

About noon they came to a creek swollen to a torrent, which compelled them to spend the afternoon and night at a station. Scores of emigrants camped along the stream, and two coaches filled with passengers spent the night on the opposite side. At daybreak the creek had fallen, so the coach and other vehicles could cross and travel on up the trail.

At the larger stations the travelers often spent the evening dancing. The landlord prepared the floor by moving the furniture from the center of the room and placing it along the wall. Everybody in the neighborhood came to the dance, and in those parts the "neighborhood" covered quite an area; some of the guests traveled fifty miles or more.

The first dance was a quadrille. The musician took

his fiddle out of the case and tuned it. Then he shouted "Fill up the floor!" and the dancers took their places. He played "Irish Washerwoman," and the dance began. A waltz followed, and the dancers circled and whirled about the room to the strains of "Chamois O'brine."

The waltz over, they formed for another square dance. Set after set danced. Every couple took part. There were no wallflowers. The fiddler played his instrument joyously and endlessly. They danced on and on to the tunes of "Arkansas Traveler," "Fisher's Hornpipe," "Devil's Dream," and other old favorites until one o'clock, when the hostess served cake and coffee. After this lunch they danced a short time and then the fiddler played "Home, Sweet Home." The guests departed and the travelers retired and dreamt of Indian attacks and other unpleasant incidents on the lonely trail.

The old trails and stage roads were of vital importance in the settlement of the Kaw and other sections of the West. Many of the forty-niners were favorably impressed with the Kaw country and later became residents of Kansas. Among them were five governors of Kansas. The first settlers in Douglas and Shawnee counties located along the California Trail. The colony which founded Lawrence came from Kansas City over this highway. The founders of Topeka used the same road to reach the site of the capital city. When the emigrant route, known as the Jim Lane Trail, was opened in 1856, no white men resided along it from Nebraska City to Topeka. The first train over this highway numbered five hundred persons and sixty wagons. After passing the northern line of Kansas, parties dropped off and formed settlements along the route, the last being at Holton. The remainder of the train reached Topeka on August 13th, ate their supper in the Garvey House, and were given a public reception in the evening at Constitution Hall. The early settlers at Ellsworth and points west used the Butterfield Trail. Scores of similar instances could be cited. A seemingly endless procession of emigrant wagons going toward the setting sun went up the trails those days, and numerous settlements sprang up along the roadside. The trails were also the main avenues of communication between the pioneer settlements. Towns on the trail flourished, while those off the beaten way had a real struggle for existence and often had to move or die.

When the railroads were built westward up the Kaw and Platte rivers, the trails lost much of their importance. By 1870 the main line of the Union Pacific had been opened to the west coast; the Kansas Pacific was completed to Denver that year; and the Santa Fe was being pushed southwest through Kansas. These railroads became the chief carriers of passengers and freight. Then the stage and freight lines were used as feeders and to carry passengers and freight beyond the end of the railroad.

A few of the stage stations have been preserved; the ruins of others remain. In pastures and other places where the soil has not been disturbed the trails can be followed, the wheel tracks and the ruts made in muddy weather being quite distinct. Some of these rough places are a hundred feet or more wide. When the road became too rough or muddy, the drivers turned out and made new tracks. Pits in the banks or in the ground mark the sites of dugouts and other buildings along the way.

3

The First Families of the Kaw

THE historians say that Francisco de Coronado and his party were the first men with European blood in their veins to visit the Kaw country. No one has come forward to dispute this, so the conquistador's name heads the roll.

He was searching for gold. His rainbow, minus the pot of gold, ended at the Quivira Indian village in central Kansas. Here he visited for about a month. The natives told him that beyond Quivira, to the northeast, was the Kingdom of Harahey. From the stories he concluded that the ruler of Harahey was a white man.

The general sent a letter by a Quiviran messenger asking the ruler to meet him on the border. The conference was probably held on the south bank of the Smoky Hill River southwest of the present city of Lindsborg. If so, Coronado feasted his eyes on the Smoky Hill, one of the two rivers which form the Kaw, and saw in the distance the smoky hills which he mistook for mountains.

Maybe the honor of being the first white man to see the Kaw should go to a Frenchman. There is reason to believe that about the year 1700 French adventurers from Canada ascended the Missouri River until they arrived at the Grand Kansa Village on or near the site of Doniphan in northeastern Kansas, where they presented steel knives and cloth to chiefs who had never seen such things. On the way they passed the mouth of the Kaw and may have taken time to explore the stream for at least a short distance.

Etienne Veniard de Bourgmont, a French officer, was on or near the Kaw in the early eighteenth century. One of his contemporaries states that he was in these parts as early as 1703. That date is too early, for at that time he was an officer in Quebec. He was commandant at Detroit in 1706, where he got into a peck of trouble with his superiors and fled. He probably came west. For a time all trace of him was lost. No one knows how extensively he explored the Kaw region. In some way he acquired a lot of knowledge of the prairie tribes before he made his official expedition up the Kaw in 1724.

Bourgmont and his party were undoubtedly the first white men to travel up the Kaw to its source. He visited the Kansa Indians in the villages on the Missouri River in 1724 and persuaded them to go with him to visit the Comanches on the headwaters of the Smoky Hill for the purpose of making a treaty of peace and establishing trade relations. With a retinue of nineteen French soldiers, more than a thousand Indians, including women and children, and three hundred dogs to drag the provisions, he traveled westward up the valleys of the Kaw and the Smoky Hill. He was so pleased with what he saw that he pronounced the country the "most beautiful land in the world."

The commandant returned to France in 1725, taking with him eight warriors and the daughter of a Missouri chief. These natives had the time of their lives. They were received by royalty, danced at the opera and the theater, and hunted in the Bois de Boulogne. But they thought that the highly perfumed Parisians "smelled like alligators."

A century later Frenchmen were trading with the Indian tribes in the Kaw country. When France ceded Louisiana to the United States, the Chouteau family were leading fur traders in this area. Pierre and Auguste Chouteau and ten others organized the Missouri Fur Company in 1808. This company established posts among the Indians of Missouri, Nebraska, Kansas, and Arkansas, but was unfortunate and went out of business in 1812. The following year the American Fur Company was formed, and the elder Chouteaus and Pierre Jr. and his brother Francis became members.

This company occupied the posts of the Missouri company and made an effort to monopolize the trade of the Southwest. The officials sent Francis Chouteau to Kansas, and he became the leading trader in the Kaw valley. In 1820 he built Four Houses, a trading post on the north bank of the Kaw near the site of Bonner Springs, so called from its being built on the four sides of an open square. He lived here with his family. A year later he founded Chouteau's Landing at the mouth of the Kaw. In 1825 Cyprian Chouteau joined his brother Francis, and they established a house on the south side of the Kaw opposite the present site of Muncie. In 1830 Frederick Chouteau opened a trading post on Mission Creek, two miles south of the Kaw in Shawnee County.

Probably the first English-speaking white man to see the Kaw was Daniel Morgan Boone, son of the famous frontiersman. With two Frenchmen as companions, he visited the mouth of the Kaw in 1795. Later he was appointed by the government to teach Kansas Indians better methods of farming. He and his

family built a log house at the mouth of Stonehouse
Creek in Jefferson County in which a son named Napo-
leon was born in 1828.

About that time the missionaries came to the Kaw.
In 1829 the Methodists established a mission among the
Shawnees in Johnson County and placed the Reverend
Thomas Johnson of the Missouri Conference in charge.
Two years later the Baptists, under the leadership of
the Reverend Isaac McCoy, opened a mission about two
miles to the northwest, and in 1834 the Friends started
a mission in these parts. The Catholics established a
mission on the Wakarusa near the Kaw at an early date.

The passage of the Kansas-Nebraska Bill in May,
1854, opened Kaw lands to settlement. The people residing in the territory were to decide whether or not
they would have slavery, and as a result settlers made a
grand rush from both sides of Mason and Dixon's line
to stake claims along the Kaw and other streams.

Even before the president signed the bill creating
Kansas Territory, Missourians entered and selected
choice farms. Some of the earliest settlers along the
Kaw in Douglas and Shawnee counties were from Missouri and other slaveholding states. A company organized at Weston, Missouri, founded Leavenworth in
June, and parties from Platte City founded Atchison
in July.

Leaders in both the North and the South founded
emigrant aid societies and town companies to populate
the new territory. The chief agency for the North was
the Massachusetts Emigrant Aid Company chartered in
Massachusetts in April, 1854, and later called the New
England Emigrant Aid Company.

In June this company sent Dr. Charles Robinson
and Charles H. Branscomb to explore the territory and
select a site for a colony. Dr. Robinson was a forty-

niner who had gone west over the California Road. On that occasion he and his party climbed "Mount Oread," the hill southwest of Lawrence, and noted the beauty of the spot. Dr. Robinson remembered the magnificent view and selected for the colony the site on which Lawrence now stands.

Meantime Eli Thayer, president of the company, had completed the first colony. He made fifty speeches and found only twenty-nine men willing to emigrate to the prairie frontier, be neighbors to Indians, and fight slaveholders. Most of these bold spirits lived in Massachusetts. They represented the leading vocations and professions. In the group were ten mechanics, five farmers, two merchants, an architect to plan the homes, a banker to care for their money, two doctors to keep them well, and a lawyer to get them out of trouble.

The colony left Boston on July 17th. Thayer, himself, described it:

Immense crowds had gathered at the station to give them the parting godspeed and the pledge of their future cordial care. They moved out of the station amid the cheering crowds who lined the tracks for several blocks. The fact of this intense public interest impelled others to prepare to join the colony, intending to go one month later. . . .

The emigrants remained in Worcester the first night and received a suitable ovation. . . .

The next day I took charge of the party, and we were met in the evening at Albany by a good number of citizens, who welcomed us with great cordiality. The next day we were cheered at all the principal stations as we passed on our westward journey, until we reached Rochester. Here a very large crowd had gathered to welcome and cheer our party. . . .

The colonists arrived at Kansas City in the evening of the 27th. Here they purchased an ox team to transport the baggage, and at ten o'clock the next morning started on foot for their destination forty miles across the prairie. They arrived August 1st and ate their first meal on Mount Oread. The next few days were spent in claim hunting around the proposed townsite. Then about half the group went back east with the intention of bringing their families in the spring.

The second colony, consisting of men, women, and children, left Boston at the end of August. In the party were four musicians from Hartford, Vermont. Their names were Joseph and Forest Savage and Azro and N. Hazen. They had their instruments with them. Before starting they assembled in the Boston and Worcester station in Boston and played and sang Whittier's "Hymn of the Kansas Emigrant" which became the "national hymn" to the colonists. Then they played and sang a hymn written for the occasion. The first stanza is given here:

> We'll seek the rolling prairie,
> In regions yet unseen,
> Or stay our feet unweary,
> By Kansas flowing stream;
> And there with hands unfettered
> Our altars we will raise,
> With voices high uplifted
> We'll sing our Maker's praise.

The colony arrived at Lawrence on September 9th. The musicians were the nucleus of the Lawrence Band, a famous pioneer musical organization.

There were no sawmills in Kansas, and consequently no lumber could be procured. The first winter the settlers lived in tents, log cabins, houses in the construction of which "shakes" were used as a substitute for clapboards, and in "hay tents." A hay tent was made by setting up two rows of poles, then bringing the tops together and thatching the sides with prairie hay.

In October Cyrus K. Holliday, a young Pennsylvanian, arrived at Lawrence and the following month, in company with Dr. Robinson, went up the Kaw valley to locate townsites for the fast-coming emigrants. They selected the site for Topeka on a beautiful rise of ground on the south bank of the Kaw.

In November Enoch Chase and three others arrived from the East. After remaining in Lawrence a week, they started up the Kaw for the purpose of locating farms and of founding a town if they discovered a suitable site. They arrived at the present site of Topeka on the 29th, and being pleased with the location they each filed on a quarter section of land.

Three days later another party, consisting of nine men, arrived at Lawrence looking for a place to locate. Holliday and Robinson spoke so highly of the site of Topeka that they decided to send four of their number, accompanied by Robinson, Holliday, and M. C. Dickey, to examine and report on the advantages of the location. The party went up the Kaw the next morning, which was Monday, December 4th. Arriving that evening, they found Chase and his companions erecting a log house at the foot of what is now Kansas Avenue. The entire party stayed in the house that night.

The next morning the committee examined the proposed townsite and were entirely satisfied with it. The men organized a town company and staked out the town. They planned on the town's becoming the state capital, and with that in mind laid out broad avenues and spacious parks. Holliday was chosen president of the town company. The first parties who had located on the townsite surrendered their claims and selected tracts adjoining the town.

At a subsequent meeting held for the purpose of naming the town, they considered several names and finally decided to call it Topeka. No one appears to know the real meaning of the word. Some writers say Topeka is an Indian word meaning "potatoes." In territorial days satirists translated it "small potatoes," which made Topeka folks indignant, especially when the writers called them "small potatoes."

The second house built on the townsite was a sod hut. During the winter thirty-six persons joined the settlement, six of the number being women. One settler built a log house and a blacksmith shop in the rear. Before spring several sod huts and shake cabins were constructed, besides a board shanty which was the first boardinghouse in town.

In the summer of 1854 settlers found their way to the junction of the Republican and Smoky Hill rivers, which form the Kaw. Near that point Fort Riley had been established in 1853.

In November, 1854, Colonel W. P. Montgomery and other officers at the fort, most of them Free Staters, formed a town company and located the town of Pawnee on the north bank of the river not far from the fort. At that time it was supposed that the Kaw was navigable, at least as far west as the confluence of the Republican and Smoky Hill. Steamboats plied the Kaw when there was water enough, waiting for a rain when the river was low. The town company believed they were locating Pawnee at the head of navigation and set to work on the townsite in December. Trouble arose with the settlers on the site. Montgomery settled the dispute in a summary manner; a squad of his men drove the settlers off in January.

Governor Andrew Reeder notified the association that if they would erect the necessary buildings he would convene the first territorial legislature at Pawnee. At that time there were two houses on the townsite, but men were put to work erecting a stone building designed for occupancy by the legislature.

The Executive Office was established at Pawnee early in 1855, and in July the territorial legislature met at that place. Unfortunately Asiatic cholera made its appearance at Fort Riley at that time and spread from the fort to Pawnee, the first case in town occurring on July 4th. The legislature, just convened, became alarmed and passed a bill for adjournment to Shawnee Manual Labor School, in Johnson County. The governor vetoed the bill, but the territorial court sustained the measure and Pawnee lost the capital.

At that time Jefferson Davis was secretary of war and decided to destroy the place. By his order the boundaries of the fort were so enlarged as to absorb Pawnee. The officers did not execute the order until September, when they drove the inhabitants from the town and destroyed most of the buildings. They left the stone capitol building, and it still stands a short distance from Highway 40.

In the fall of 1854, Colonel George S. Park of Parkville, Missouri, laid out a townsite on the present site of Manhattan and called it Poleska. Later in the season Samuel D. Houston, of Illinois, and others located a townsite at the mouth of the Big Blue River and called it Canton. On March 6, 1855, a committee of the New England Company left Boston and reached Canton on the 25th. They decided to consolidate the two town companies with their own and make one good town. Accordingly, they organized the Boston Town Association and named the town Boston. Then they erected several rough claimhouses and took steps to hold them against claim jumpers.

On April 27th a colony left Cincinnati, Ohio, on the steamboat *Hartford* bound for central Kansas via the Ohio, Mississippi, Missouri, and Kaw. They planned to found a town and name it Manhattan, believing that it might bear some comparison to its namesake. Misfortune followed this group. At St. Louis the colony numbered eighty. The authorities at that place, believing the *Hartford* was an abolition boat, delayed her some days. A pilot was hired at fancy wages, and the boat started for Kansas City. Cholera broke out on the way, resulting in the death of several persons. At Kansas City low water on the Kaw delayed the steamer a week. When the craft reached Lecompton, she ran aground. Another rain raised the river, and there was no further delay until the boat reached a point a half mile beyond the mouth of the Big Blue, where it grounded and was forced to land its passengers and freight.

This was June 1st. Three members of the company hired a wagon and drove up the Kaw to the site of Junction City, where they laid out a town. During their absence other members of the party interviewed the Boston Association. The latter offered half their townsite to the Cincinnati Company if they would locate on it. The Cincinnati colony accepted the offer, and they changed the name of Boston to Manhattan.

The early settlers lived in hay tents, log cabins, and shake houses. Sod houses and dugouts also were common.

Unless the roofs were steep, the clapboards would leak. Construction against rain was possible, but keeping snow out was another matter. Fine dry snow would drift in through the cracks no matter how carefully the lumber was laid. One lady writes: "It was no uncommon thing to wake up on a winter morning and find our beds covered with a white sheet of snow." The winter of 1855-56 was exceptionally severe. It often snowed for three days at a time and completely covered some of the cabins.

The settlers lacked matches, so they started fires by means of flint and steel. Since it was difficult to start fires, they placed large backlogs in the fireplace to hold the fire. Neighbors borrowed fire by transporting live coals.

Their clothing was heavy, and for the most part they wore homemade fabrics. If they purchased cloth, they generally bought calico, and paid forty or fifty cents a yard for it. They made all garments by hand. Needles were scarce and high priced. Thread was rarely available, most of it being spun at home.

The ordinary diet in the homes for winter consisted of a preponderance of corn products, as corn was the "sod crop" of the Kaw pioneers. They ate corn bread, parched corn, hominy, and corn-meal mush and milk, with perhaps a vegetable that would keep through the winter. Milk was an important food item. Beef and pork were plentiful. Hogs did well on corn and on the acorns which were abundant in eastern Kansas. The farmers grew sorghum and used it in place of sugar, which was scarce. They pressed out the juice by a crude press and distilled it to draw off the dregs. Salt was rare and hard to get, and pepper was in heavy demand. Coffee was almost unobtainable, so the pioneers devised a substitute. They dried sweet potatoes in the sun, shelled and dried green okra, and browned wheat in the iron skillet over a fire. Then they ground these together to form a concoction which served for coffee.

There was fun, and folks had a good time. When a settler built a house, it was the custom to have a house-warming. The guests usually danced and passed the little brown jug around. Sometimes they changed the customary program for these occasions and called in a circuit rider, who preached a sermon, after which a generous meal was served.

The hotels sponsored dances, at which there was usually plenty of liquor and riotous fun. The men had to buy tickets that cost as much as five dollars.

Singing schools were numerous. The singing teacher usually held his groups together more through the entertaining nature of his personality than through any training he may have had for the job.

The arrival of covered-wagon trains gave Kaw folks, especially the boys, a thrill. These caravans usually had with them someone who played the fiddle and could spin yarns. The settlers gathered around the campfires to listen to the entertainment and hear the news from the outside world. Newspapers were scarce on the frontier, and when available were literally "read to pieces." The boys were delighted to get permission from the drivers to crack the whip over the beasts of burden as the train moved through town.

Camp meetings were a regular part of the summer's activities. Everyone took a week off and attended. It did their souls good to see the evangelist snatch some hardened sinner from the brink of the flaming pit or to have a good brother get the power and kick the lights out. One writer says, "On a fair day a preacher of average ability could be heard a mile or more."

Probably the first sermon preached to a white congregation was that of the Reverend S. Y. Lum, Congregational minister from Middletown, New York, on October 1, 1854, in a hay tent in Lawrence. Two weeks

later the Congregationalists of the town organized
Plymouth Church. The congregation held services in
the hay tent until a fire destroyed it during the winter.
After that they held services wherever place could be
found until 1857, when they put up a church built of
stone. The Baptists organized in June, 1855, their first
house of worship being at Atchison. The Kansas-
Nebraska conference of the Methodist Episcopal Church
held its first meeting at Lawrence in October that year.
At the time there were twelve Methodist churches with
a total white membership of 661, besides 66 proba-
tioners.

The first families yearned for education and established schools almost as soon as they built churches. The
earliest schools were supported by private subscription.
In January, 1855, five months after the first colony
arrived, funds were subscribed to start a school in Lawrence. On the 16th, Edward P. Fitch of Hopkinton,
Massachusetts, opened the school in the room back of
Dr. Robinson's office in the Emigrant Aid Building.
The school opened with twenty pupils, and a week later
the enrollment was thirty-five. Fitch taught for three
and a half months. That spring Miss Kate E. Kellogg
arrived with a party of emigrants from Massachusetts
and opened a school in the Emigrant Aid Building, with
a "very respectable number of students" in attendance.

In Topeka, Miss Sarah Harland taught a private
school during the summer of 1855, and on January 2,
1856, James Cowles opened "The Topeka Academy." A
month later the Town Association solicited subscriptions and made plans to erect a school building.

Private schools were opened in other places, a total
of over a hundred being organized in territorial Kansas.
The following is a description of one of the earliest
schools:

The school house was improvised from an old residence building built of logs from the oak timber near by. It had one three-light and two two-light windows, glass, size eight by ten inches. The floor was of puncheons and the roof of clapboards weighted with poles. The furniture consisted of seats made of slabs, with no backs, and four pegs for legs. Boards were fastened to the walls near the windows; here the pupils did their writing. The teacher's stool was a block sawed from the end of a log about eighteen inches in diameter, and his desk a board fifteen inches wide and three feet long, fastened to the wall in the corner.

Pupils attending these schools brought the old books used in the states or new ones purchased by the parent from the local book dealer. The question of textbooks was left wholly to the judgment of the parent. When Miss Kellogg opened her school in the summer of 1855 she adopted the books used by Edward Fitch the previous winter. Maybe this was a compliment to the quality of the texts. More likely it meant that the parents were too poor to buy others.

The first territorial legislature, which met in July, 1855, passed an act providing for a system of free common schools for all white citizens between the ages of five and twenty-one. Owing to the political situation, little was done until 1858 when additional legislation was enacted for the organization, supervision, and maintenance of the common schools. In 1860 there were 222 school districts in sixteen counties.

The settlers also made provision for higher education. The territorial legislature chartered eighteen colleges and universities. The oldest is Highland College, which began as an Indian school under the direction of the Presbyterian Church. It was chartered as a school for white students in 1858. The Methodists founded

Baker University at Baldwin, a few miles south of the Kaw, in territorial days, and it has been in continuous operation since 1858.

The Methodists also formed an association to build a college at or near Manhattan on the Kaw in 1857. They called the school Bluemont Central College. The legislature granted a charter the following year. When the legislature accepted the Congressional grant to aid in establishing an Agricultural College in 1863, the trustees of Bluemont College offered their land and building to the state. The latter accepted the offer, took over the campus and endowment, and opened school on September 2nd. The faculty consisted of a president and five instructors. Fifteen students enrolled in the college and ninety-four in the preparatory department.

In 1856, Amos A. Lawrence of Boston, for whom the town of Lawrence was named, made plans for a college on the north end of Mount Oread, the hill southwest of Lawrence, and gave notes and stock amounting to $10,000 for the foundation of a Free State College. An imperfect title to the property caused a cessation of plans, and the money was held in trust at interest.

When the question of the location of the State University came before the legislature in 1863, there were several contestants, chief among which were Lawrence and Manhattan, on the Kaw, and Emporia, on the Neosho River to the south of the Kaw. Manhattan received the Agricultural College and withdrew from the contest. There was a hard fight between the other two competitors, which was transferred to the legislative halls. Lawrence promised forty acres of land and $15,000 to secure the institution. After a heated battle Lawrence won by one vote, which was cast by the presiding officer. The act designated Lawrence as the seat

of the university if that place would give the state forty
acres of land and $15,000 in money. Should the town
fail to comply with these provisions and should Emporia donate eighty acres of land adjacent to town, then
the university was to be located at the latter place. By
an exchange of real estate with Dr. Robinson, Lawrence
secured forty acres on Mount Oread for the campus,
and by using the fund donated by Amos Lawrence the
town kept the school from going to Emporia.

In 1864 the legislature passed a law providing for
the organization. The charter of the University of
Michigan was the model. The government of the institution was vested in a board of regents to be appointed
by the governor. There were to be six departments—
liberal arts, law, medicine, theory and practice of elementary instruction, agriculture, and normal training.

On the tract ceded to the state was a foundation,
fifty feet square, laid by the trustees of Lawrence University in 1859. In the fall of 1865 the regents contracted for a building to be erected on this foundation.
The building, known as North College, was completed
a year later. It was constructed of brick and stone, and
was three stories high.

Early in 1865 the regents elected the Reverend R.
W. Oliver, rector of the Protestant Episcopal Church
of Lawrence, as chancellor. In July of the following
year they employed a faculty of three professors: Elial
J. Rice, professor of belles-lettres and mental and moral
science; David H. Robinson, languages; and Francis H.
Snow, mathematics and natural science. Rice was a
gray-haired man of much experience, while Robinson
and Snow were young fellows just out of college.

The two young instructors arrived in Lawrence
early in September. Says Professor Robinson:

Having established ourselves in an excellent boarding house on Kentucky street, conveniently near the University, Professor Snow and I started out to call upon our worthy Chancellor. We desired from the official head of the University definite instructions in relation to opening the institution the coming week. Greeting us very kindly the Chancellor invited us to his study. The air was thick with tobacco smoke. Regent Starrett was present, smoking a pipe with a stem about six feet long. Six or eight similar pipes and a large pouch of tobacco were lying on the table. The men were evidently "hail fellows well met," and were having the jolliest kind of time. Our coming had broken off one of Starrett's best stories—and he could tell good ones. Politely declining to join in the smoking, farther than was absolutely necessary, we tried to state our business. But no; that interrupted story must first be finished. It was a good story, and so well told that we had to have another to match it. The fun then grew fast, if not furious, one story provoking another in rapid succession, and the air all the time growing thicker and bluer, until we, poor fellows, half sick, finally insisted that we could stay no longer, and asked what preparations we should make for the opening of the University. I think we expected, in rather a vague way, some general instructions about the reception of students from high schools upon examination, and from other institutions upon certificates. Our genial Chancellor, after considering a moment, kindly gave us our instructions—the most unique, I presume, ever given by the head of a great institution to his colleagues. Speaking with a strong Scotch accent, which I shall not try to indicate, he said: "I would advise you, young gentlemen, to go to Mr. Jaedicke's gun shop and hire some guns, and to Mr. O'Conner's livery stable and hire some saddle horses, and go away back on the hills and hunt prairie chickens. You may be gone two or three days. This will be as good preparation for your work next week as you can make." Saying this he dismissed us.

School was scheduled to open September 12th. The faculty were on duty early in the morning of that day, but no one else, except some carpenters who were building the stairs, came for some time. Then the boys and girls came in, a few at a time. After the devotional exercises, the students were sent to the several instructors for examination. Professor Robinson says they "examined, in all forty students," and "instead of the expected college classes, we had a few candidates for the lower forms of a rather indifferent high school."

The work ran along smoothly until spring, when the students began to drop out of school. By the middle of April more than half the number had quit; then the instructors became worried and looked for the cause. Some of the students had gone home to help with the farmwork; others had severe cases of spring fever. The teachers saw that something must be done or they would be lecturing to empty chairs. A strong appeal to the patrons and students averted the threatened disaster, and they closed the year with twenty-two students.

Professor Snow, who achieved quite a reputation as a scientist, used to work late at night in the laboratory.

One dark, rainy night about midnight Snow and Robinson started home. Guided by an occasional flash of lightning they reached Tennessee Street, which recent rains had gullied to the depth of seven or eight feet. Just as they were about to cross the street it began to rain hard and they had started to run when a flash of lightning showed Snow disappearing in a deep gully. Robinson says, "Stopping short on the brink, I waited developments. Hearing nothing, I called. No answer.

Then came a sort of muffled, splashing, sputtering noise, followed by a call for help. Reaching down as far as I could, and catching hold of a muddy hand, I drew out the most forlorn, woebegone, bedraggled-appearing professor ever seen in Lawrence."

Fourscore years have passed since the first families settled along the Kaw. Few of the original settlers are left to tell the story. They built the foundations of an economic and cultural empire which doubtless surpasses even the fondest dreams of the most optimistic of the founders.

4

Bleeding Kansas

"WE ARE in favor of making Kansas a 'Slave State' if it should require half the citizens of Missouri, musket in hand, to emigrate there, and even sacrifice their lives in accomplishing so desirable an end," declared the *Democratic Platform*, a newspaper published at Liberty, Missouri.

To this the *Western Chronicle* responded: "Them's our sentiments."

The occasion of this journalistic outburst was the passage of the bill opening Kansas Territory to settlers and allowing the residents to decide whether slavery would be permitted.

The introduction of this bill in Congress had started a sectional controversy. The friends and foes of the measure engaged in a prolonged battle of words. As the oratory grew louder, the sectional animosity became stronger. When the opposing forces saw that Congress was certain to pass the bill, they prepared to send colonists to Kansas for the purpose of winning the fight through the ballot box. If this failed, the settlers could settle the issue with Sharps rifles.

The territory, prized so highly in 1854 that men were willing to shed blood, was a vast "prairie ocean" extending from the Missouri border to the Rocky Mountains and was inhabited mainly by Indians. The entire white population consisted of only seven hundred soldiers located at Forts Leavenworth and Riley, and at Walnut Creek Post Office on the Santa Fe Trail; and an equal number of civilians living at the Indian missions, the stage stations, and the trading posts along the rivers.

As soon as Kansas Territory was organized, settlers from the free and slave states rushed to the Kaw to get the choice lands. In this real estate race the Missourians usually won first place. Even before Congress passed the organic act, residents of Missouri crossed the boundary line and spotted the best claims, then pre-empted them before the Northerners arrived.

When the first colony sent out by the New England Emigrant Aid Company was ready to start for Kansas, a southern paper wished "them the utmost success their hearts can desire, for the hardy pioneers of Kansas will doubtless have tar and feathers prepared in abundance for their reception." The tar and feathers committee wasn't on hand to "receive" them, but they did run into trouble with Missourians who claimed the land the company had selected for the townsite of Lawrence.

The New England Company "bought out" two of the claimants, but a third man refused to sell. He occupied a tent on the north side of a ravine which ran through the townsite, while the New Englanders occupied a tent on the south side, in proof of ownership. Dr. Robinson, the company's agent, proposed that the matter be referred to the Land Office or the courts for arbitration. The claimant rejected this proposal and insisted on the removal of the New England tent.

Each party continued to occupy their tent and

scowl defiantly at the other, but neither tried to cross the ravine until the afternoon of October 5th when a party of armed men, in a wagon, drove up to the New England tent. While the men stood guard, the claimant's sister loaded the tent into the wagon, and they started off. At that moment the city marshal, Joel Grover, who was unarmed, followed by a townsman carrying a revolver, rushed up. The latter seized the horse by the bridle and demanded the surrender of the property. Other settlers having reached the scene, the men gave up the tent, but said as they left:

"We'll be back in a short time with two hundred men and then we'll move that tent."

That night the Yankees organized a "Regulating Band" to be ready for the next day's battle.

The following afternoon eighteen armed men on horseback assembled in the vicinity of the aggrieved man's tent. The Lawrence citizens went for their guns, and in a short time thirty armed Yankees stationed themselves near the contested tent and awaited the attack.

At four o'clock the Missourians sent the following note to Robinson:

"If the tent is not moved within one-half hour, we shall take the trouble to move the same."

"If you molest our property, you do it at your peril," was Robinson's curt reply.

Then, in full view of the enemy, the Lawrence men went through a variety of "drills," marching and countermarching, in single file and by platoons.

The half hour passed, then three-quarters of an hour. By this time the Missourians were arguing among themselves.

"Give 'em a little more time. Let's not start shooting unless we have to," said a coolheaded man.

"I'm not going to make a fool of myself. Give 'em hell and give it to 'em now," exclaimed a fire-eater.

"That's the talk," cried an unwashed, bewhiskered fellow, who was spoiling for trouble.

Others took part in the debate which almost resulted in a fight among friends when one or two of them called some of the others "cowards." It was nearly sundown before the wrangle terminated, and it did so then because the fire-eaters became disgusted and left. Soon the rest began to break up and leave.

In time the company got clear title to the townsite.

Early in 1855 the governor ordered an election to be held on March 30th for the purpose of electing members of the territorial legislature. Since this legislature might establish or exclude slavery, each party felt that it must win the election. For weeks before election day, residents of the border counties of Missouri held meetings and made plans. On election day hundreds of Missourians, "with rifles upon their shoulders, six shooters in their belts, and a liberal supply of whisky in their wagons," entered Kansas and voted at the polls.

The invaders didn't usually disturb election officials, who meekly accepted all the votes offered. Those who objected were promptly overawed. An illustration of the latter procedure occurred at Lawrence. One of the judges insisted that the first Missourian who presented himself should swear that he was a resident of Kansas. The man hesitated. The leader of the group ordered the fellow to the rear and presented himself.

"Are you a resident of Kansas?" asked the judge.

"I am," was the reply.

"Does your family live in Kansas?" inquired the judge.

"It is none of your business. If you don't keep

your impertinence to yourself, I'll knock your damned head from your shoulders."

The judge decided it was time to retire, and the voting continued without "impertinence" from the election officials.

All of the proslavery candidates, excepting one, were elected.

This legislature, known as the "bogus legislature," met in July and passed a set of enactments, among which was the Missouri slave code for the protection of slavery in Kansas.

The Free Staters protested against this legislation, but finding their protests were of no avail they ignored the laws as far as possible. The proslavery men formed a law and order party and waited for evidence of "rebellion."

During the summer and early fall there was little disturbance. Each side waited for the other to make the first move. Trouble broke in November and resulted in the Wakarusa War. It grew out of a claim dispute. Charles W. Dow, a Free Stater, and Franklin M. Coleman, a Proslavery man, lived on adjoining claims at Hickory Point, about ten miles south of Lawrence. Coleman, a native of Virginia, was a "rather good-looking man of genteel appearance, with dark hair and beard"; was about five feet eleven in height; and had a wife and two small children. Dow was a large, powerful fellow who had come from Ohio and was unmarried. They had quarreled a number of times over the boundary line of their claims. The sympathy of the neighbors ran according to political predilections. In the forenoon of November 21st, the two men walked down the road toward Coleman's place together and exchanged words on the controversial subject with more heat than usual. Coleman was armed with a shotgun loaded with buckshot, while Dow carried an iron bar some two feet in length. The former claimed that when they were opposite his cabin, Dow advanced upon him with the bar raised ready to strike, and that he fired in self-defense. Dow fell dead in the road. That night Coleman fled to Westport.

The murder aroused Dow's Free State neighbors. They held a meeting a day or two later to devise means of bringing the fugitive to justice. Among those present was a peaceable old man named Jacob Branson, who had come from Indiana. He and his wife lived on a claim adjoining Coleman's farm and Dow boarded with them. Usually a quiet man, but now stirred with indignation, Branson was outspoken at the meeting.

Harrison Buckley, one of Coleman's friends, who had egged on the murder, was present and expressed alarm at the violent tone of the meeting, especially at Branson's words. He quoted the old man as saying:

"If I could draw a bead on Buckley he would not breathe the pure air of this planet another minute."

He said that his life was in danger and swore out a warrant for Branson's arrest. The warrant was put in the hands of Samuel J. Jones, who had been appointed sheriff of the county by the "bogus legislature." Jones was postmaster of Westport, Missouri, at the time and not a resident of Kansas. He is described as a handsome fellow, twenty-eight years old.

On the night of November 26th Sheriff Jones left Franklin, a proslavery settlement four miles from Lawrence, with fifteen or sixteen men on horseback, to arrest Branson. It was as beautiful a moonlight night as ever smiled on the Kaw. The moon was about full, the sky was clear, and the air was mild for November. The party went along the Wakarusa until they reached Blanton's bridge. There they stopped to refresh the "inner man" and then started toward Hickory Point, reaching Branson's cabin about ten o'clock.

The old gentleman and his wife were asleep. A noise awakened him. There was a knock at the door.

"Who's there?" inquired Branson.

"Friends," was the reply.

"Come in."

At that moment they forced the frail door open and rushed in, Jones in the lead. Drawing a pistol and pointing it at Branson, who had got out of bed, the sheriff said:

"You're my prisoner!"

"What for—and what authority?" stammered Branson.

"I'm sheriff of Douglas County. You must go with us."

"You wouldn't hurry me. If I have to go, I shall go when I get ready."

"I'll blow you to hell if you don't get ready in a hurry."

Branson dressed hastily, and in the excitement put an old straw hat on his head. They took him out, placed him on a sharp-backed mule, and started for Lecompton by way of Lawrence.

As soon as they were gone, a lad who was staying with the Bransons set out to alarm the neighbors. Meantime Samuel F. Tappan, a young newspaper correspondent from Lawrence, who had seen the sheriff's posse at Blanton's bridge early in the evening, spread the word that Branson was to be arrested. The Free State men decided to rescue him. Major J. B. Abbott, who lived near Blanton's bridge, engineered the rescue. By eleven o'clock fifteen men had gathered at Abbott's house. Three were residents of Lawrence: Samuel F. Tappan; Samuel C. Smith, secretary to Charles Robinson; and

Samuel N. Wood, who had come from the same section of Ohio as the murdered man. The rest of the party
were Branson's neighbors. They were armed with all
sorts of weapons. Some carried Sharps rifles, one a shotgun, a few had pistols, and one man clutched a large
rock in each hand.

The rescue party didn't know what road the sheriff
and his posse would take, and in the night it was impossible to see them any distance. While they were discussing the next step, someone burst into the house and
said, "They are coming."

The men rushed out pell-mell and got into the road
ahead of the posse. The latter halted within two rods
of the rescue party. A moment passed in silence when
Jones said:

"What's up?"

"That's what we want to know," said one of the
rescue party.

"Is Branson there?" asked Abbott.

"Yes, I am here, a prisoner."

"If you want to be among your friends come over
here," said Wood.

"If you move we will shoot you," came from one
of the sheriff's party.

"Come on, let them shoot if they want to. If you
shoot, not a man of you will leave alive," was Wood's
retort.

Branson rode the mule over to his friends.

"Who's mule is that?" asked several.

"Belongs to them," said Branson.

"Then get off and drive it back."

Branson dismounted and turned the mule toward
its owners, but it hesitated. Wood stepped up to it and
expedited its movements by a couple of kicks.

"Gentlemen, if you don't give Branson up we will fire," said Jones.

"We have nothing to do with it," replied the Free State men.

Both parties raised their guns and began cocking them.

Jones then rode up on horseback and announced that he had a warrant for Branson's arrest and must serve it. When asked to show the warrant the officer did not do so. He was told that until he produced the warrant the old man could not go with him. After parleying for some time, the sheriff and his party rode away.

The rescue party proceeded to Lawrence, realizing that to take a prisoner from the hands of an officer was a serious offense. The people of Lawrence were concerned over the situation. They expected the town would be held responsible for the act, though only three of her citizens were involved. Early next morning the drum was beaten on the streets as a signal for the citizens to assemble. They met in the School House Hall, heard the story of the rescue, and appointed a committee of safety empowered to defend the town in case of an attack.

Sheriff Jones went to Franklin and sent a message asking the governor to call out the militia. An exaggerated report reached the governor, which led him to believe that an armed force was in open rebellion at Lawrence and that three thousand men were needed to suppress it. He issued a proclamation calling out the militia.

In response to this proclamation, some fifteen hundred men gathered at Franklin and along the Wakarusa River in the next day or two. They surrounded Lawrence, guarded the roads, and searched every vehicle.

The Free Staters were not idle. Hearing of the

situation, various military companies came to Lawrence. The committee of safety appointed Charles Robinson commander in chief and Jim Lane second in command. Altogether about five hundred men came in. They threw up earthworks at the most exposed points and made other preparations for defense. They lacked artillery, and when this seemed least likely to be supplied, a messenger came to town with the news that a twelve-pound howitzer, bought by Free State men, had arrived at Kansas City, and that this was stowed away in a Kansas City warehouse.

Captain Thomas Bickerton, a son of the Kennebec who was living on a claim near Lawrence, volunteered to go after the cannon. The captain was accompanied by two young men, David and Robert Buffum; all three had the appearance of plain citizens. As soon as they reached their destination, the captain hunted up the warehouse and sauntered in with a nonchalant air, remarking that he was returning with a wagon that was almost empty, so thought that he might as well take a box or two along with him, which he understood had been stored there for a friend of his, one Mr. John Smith of Lawrence, who had requested him to bring them along with him if he could conveniently do so.

The agent was a rabid proslavery man, but as his customer appeared to be all right he pointed out the two boxes, one containing the gun, and the other the carriage. The captain receipted for these and was about to place them in his wagon when the warehouseman, becoming suspicious, said:

"Look hyar, stranger, thar's somethin' mighty dubersome about them boxes. They say you Lawrence folks air gittin' all manner of curious traps up thar, to wipe out our boys with, and I'll jest allow to hev a squint into them goods afore they roll out of Kansas City."

"Waal I guess, mister, there ain't nothin' extra in 'em no how. I don't know for certin, but John Smith says he's expectin' a buggy-wagon, along with some other notions, which his folks are a sendin', and I shouldn't wonder if it wan't them. But I guess they might hev bought it a tarnation sight cheaper in Saint Louie, and saved payin' freight, besides, don't yeou?" was the captain's comment.

"I don't kear nothin' fur that, but I'll be dog-gauned ef I don't think it's about reasonable to hist a lid off of them thar boxes, and see what's inside fur myself. Well I do, stranger."

"Waal, I kinder sorter expect that ef yeou'r willin' tu take the risk, it won't make no *great* difference to Mister Smith anyway ef yeou du, so here goes; hand us that axe, will yeou, Sam?"

At this stage in the conversation, David Buffum seized the axe and knocked up one side of the lid of the larger receptacle, which, as he well knew, contained the wheels, and then threw down the instrument. The captain looked in and called out triumphantly:

"There, mister, didn't I tell yeou, just look for yeourself. Guess yeou'll say I'm right another time: ef that ain't a buggy-wagon it ain't nothin' at all. Don't yeou see the wheels."

The agent peeped in and saw what he supposed, in the dim light of the building, to be a pair of wagon wheels. He acknowledged his mistake and permitted Bickerton to load the boxes into the wagon.

On the return trip Bickerton and the boys traveled all night without any sleep. As they neared Lawrence, a troop of cavalry was sent out to escort them in. They mistook these for the enemy and got their guns ready.

But in a few minutes the captain recognized some of the horsemen, and knew that they were Free State troopers. The party reached town safely.

About this time the defenders discovered that their supply of ball and powder was exhausted. Mrs. George W. Brown and Mrs. Samuel N. Wood devised a plan which, with the approval of the Free State generals, they were determined to put into execution.

They knew that both powder and lead, together with a large quantity of Sharps rifle caps and cartridges, were deposited with friends of freedom at two separate points south of Lawrence: at the homes of Major J. B. Abbott, just beyond the Wakarusa, and of Samuel Gleason, Mrs. Brown's father, who lived about twelve miles south of town at a place called Mud Springs. They planned to drive to the home of these northern sympathizers, secure a quantity of these munitions, and on their return smuggle them past the enemy's picket guards.

On a bright December morning the two women hitched old Sally to the buggy. Both ladies were clothed in an eccentric fashion for the trip, Mrs. Wood wearing two dresses and a petticoat which was lined with wadding. At eight o'clock they stepped into the vehicle and started out, accompanied by a guard to the edge of town. They passed the picket guards of the Lawrence camp and continued on without any noteworthy adventure. After reaching their destination, they stowed the powder and caps and other munitions among their clothing and started home. The pickets allowed them to pass their lines, and they brought their load into town.

Free State leaders got in touch with the governor and told their side of the story. The governor saw that he had acted without investigation and was anxious to avert any further violence. He went to the Wakarusa camp and urged the officers to disband their men. Next he came to Lawrence and conferred with representatives of the committee of safety. Dr. Robinson and Jim Lane accompanied the governor to Franklin where they met a committee of proslavery men and signed a treaty of peace on Saturday, December 8th.

The weather, which had been mild, suddenly changed on the day of the treaty. In the evening a heavy sleet storm set in, turning into a regular Kaw blizzard, and the thermometer dropped to ten below zero. This bitter cold weather was an added incentive for men to cease fighting and go home.

On Sunday the Missourians, in a sullen frame of mind, started home, carrying three dead bodies—"one killed by the falling of a tree, one shot by the guard accidentally, and one killed in some sort of a quarrel."

There was one casualty on the Free State side— Thomas W. Barber, who had been shot and killed on December 6th, outside of Lawrence. Thomas W. and Robert F. Barber, brothers, and their brother-in-law, Thomas M. Pierson, had been in Lawrence. About one o'clock they started for their homes seven miles west of town. All three were mounted. Robert Barber and Pierson carried revolvers, but Tom Barber was unarmed. After they had ridden about four miles on the California trail, they took a crossroad to the left. At that point they noticed a party of a dozen horsemen on the right of the California road. Soon after they left the main road, two of the horsemen approached them on the right and came up on a trot; the trio were walking their horses. One man was a heavily built fellow with whiskers and rode a gray horse, while the other was a tall man mounted on a sorrel horse.

As the pair rode up, the brothers were riding side

by side and Pierson a little in the rear. After halting them, the rider of the gray horse asked:

"Where are you going?"

"Home," replied Tom Barber, who answered for his party.

"Where are you from?"

"Lawrence."

"What's going on in Lawrence?"

"Nothing in particular."

"Nothing in particular, hey?—We have orders from the governor to see that the laws are executed in Kansas. We arrest you," he added.

"What laws have we disobeyed?"

The rider raised his hand and pointed toward his party.

"Then turn your horses' heads and go with us."

"We won't do it," replied young Barber.

"You won't, hey?" said the man, at the same time starting his horse so as to bring him on the right side of Barber, who moved his horse slightly toward the speaker. The man drew his pistol and discharged it at Barber. After firing he rode around in the road and stopped some ten paces in the rear. Meantime, Robert drew his pistol and shot at the man; then fired at the rider of the sorrel horse, who had taken a shot at them. Pierson was so slow drawing his six-shooter that the pair were galloping down the road by the time he was ready to fire.

"Boys, let's be off," said Tom Barber, and the three started at a gallop, the brothers side by side, Pierson, whose horse was slower, again in the rear.

After they had gone a hundred yards Tom Barber said, "That fellow shot me."

"Where are you shot?" asked Robert.

He pointed to his right side.

"It is not possible, Tom."

"It is," he said with a smile. Then he dropped the reins and reeled in his saddle. Robert caught hold of him by his left shoulder, grasping his loose overcoat. He held him up about a hundred yards; but unable to hold him longer, the wounded man fell to the ground. Robert dismounted and called "whoa," stopping both horses. He walked over and, looking at his brother, said, "He is dead."

While the two consulted as to what to do, they saw the horsemen advancing upon them. Barber mounted and they started on a gallop toward home, leaving the body in the road. The news of the tragedy soon reached Lawrence, and a carriage, guarded by a party of horsemen, went out for it.

The following spring the conflict was renewed. On April 18th Sheriff Jones came to Lawrence to arrest some of the Branson rescuers. He made no arrests, but returned the next day and tried to arrest Samuel F. Tappan. The latter slapped Jones's face and escaped. The sheriff then applied for a posse and the governor supplied an officer and ten soldiers. On the 23rd Jones reappeared in town with his posse and arrested six citizens, on the charge of "contempt of court" in not assisting him to make arrests on his previous visits. He remained in town overnight in a tent with his aides. That evening someone in the darkness fired a shot at the sheriff, wounding him. The citizens of Lawrence disavowed the act and offered a $500 reward for the arrest of the guilty party.

The territorial judiciary then took a hand in the controversy. Judge Samuel D. Lecompte, chief justice of the territory, summoned the grand jury to meet at Lecompton and charged them to investigate evidences of treason. As a result, the jury indicted several Free State leaders for treason.

The United States marshal believed that an attempt to execute the writs issued by the court would "be resisted by a large body of armed men." He seemed to think that men who were armed with Sharps rifles, slapped the sheriff's face, and then shot at him in the dark were vicious individuals and that a large force would be needed to handle them. Anyway, on the morning of May 21st, the marshal with a posse of four hundred men and some pieces of artillery appeared on Mount Oread. At eleven o'clock the deputy marshal rode into town and found the streets quiet. He enlisted the aid of a number of citizens and arrested three of the men who had been indicted for treason.

The citizens invited the marshal and his men to dine at the Free State Hotel. After dinner the marshal returned to camp and said he had made all the arrests he cared to at the time and dismissed his men.

Sheriff Jones was on hand. As soon as the men were dismissed as the marshal's posse, he summoned them to act as a posse for him. The sheriff rode into town with a company of men and drew up in front of the Free State Hotel, which was the headquarters of the committee of safety. He demanded that all arms in the place be surrendered. The committee gave up the arms in their possession. Then they pulled out from under a building the cannon which Bickerton had brought to Lawrence during the Wakarusa War and turned it over to the sheriff.

Jones gave the hotel until five o'clock to move out the furniture and the personal effects of the guests. Then he turned his cannon on the building and fired. The first shot went over the roof, and the people cheered. The next shot hit the walls but did no damage. After firing at the building for a time with little effect, he attempted to blow it up with a keg of powder. This made a big noise and a lot of smoke, but the building stood. Then he applied a torch and burned the building to the ground. Meantime, his men ransacked the two newspaper offices, broke the presses, and scattered the type. They burned Dr. Robinson's house and pilfered other homes.

That summer three proslavery "forts" practically cut Lawrence off from help and supplies. These so-called forts were the log homes of leaders of the southern cause, with portholes for guns, and were supplied with provisions and ammunition for defense or siege. The three forts were as follows: one at Franklin, four miles east of Lawrence; Fort Saunders on Washington Creek, twelve miles southwest; and Fort Titus, about two miles from Lecompton. A Free State force attacked these forts and captured them one at a time.

The warfare spread from the Kaw to other streams. In fact, the whole territory was in a state of confusion. John Brown, who ended his antislavery crusade at Harpers Ferry, was in the thick of the bloodshed. He had come to Kansas in the fall of 1855 to join his sons, who were living on claims about ten miles west of Osawatomie. When trouble broke on the Wakarusa, news of the conflict reached Brown from time to time, and he was eager to get in the fray. On Thursday, December 6th, a courier from Lawrence arrived to summon him to the defense of that town. The father and four sons set out that afternoon and traveled all night, reaching the besieged city the following forenoon. An eyewitness says, "As they drove up in front of the Free State Hotel they were all standing in a small lumber wagon. To each of their persons was strapped a short, heavy broad sword. Each was supplied with a goodly number of fire arms and navy revolvers, and poles were standing endwise around the wagon box, with fixed bayonets pointing upwards." Dr. Robinson immediately organized a company of militia, consisting of Brown's sons, neighbors of the murdered Barber, and some new arrivals, and commissioned Brown as captain. The war ended on Saturday.

In the afternoon of that day the people gathered in front of the Free State Hotel, which at the time was unfinished, to hear what the governor, Dr. Robinson, and Jim Lane, fresh from signing the treaty, had to say. A box outside the door served as platform and doorsill, and planks led to the ground. The three men mounted the platform and made brief speeches, telling the crowd they had signed a treaty with the enemy and the war was over, but avoided mention of the terms. The crowd was in doubt. They had heard that the treaty was a surrender to slavery. When Robinson had finished, John Brown, fairly bursting with indignation, mounted the platform. An eyewitness says that "he got up to address the people, but a desire was manifest to prevent his speaking. Amidst some little disturbance, he demanded to know what the terms were."

"If I understand the governor's speech something has been conceded, and we will have to obey the bogus laws," he said.

"No! No! Down with the bogus laws! Lead us to fight first," cried the listeners.

"I am an abolitionist, dyed in the wool. I'll be one of ten men to make a night attack upon the Border Ruffian camp," continued Brown, and was enlarging upon his plan when friends of peace, seeing a revolution sprouting, pulled him off the box. Then Robinson mounted it and calmly assured the crowd that they had surrendered nothing; that the treaty was a "triumph of diplomacy." With this assurance, the people were satisfied and withdrew. Brown and his sons returned home.

News of the attack on Lawrence reached Brown on May 22nd of the following year. He hastily mustered two rifle companies, consisting of fifty or sixty men, and started for that place. In ᵗhe afternoon they learned that Lawrence had been destroyed the day before they left home. Accordingly, they halted and decided not to go on or return home until they received further orders. They pitched camp at Prairie City. On the following day, May 23rd, in the forenoon, Lieutenant Henry H. Williams came in from the Pottawatomie settlement and reported that in the absence of the rifle companies proslavery men had gone about the neighborhood threatening the lives of Free State settlers and ordering them to leave the country.

Anger welled in the breasts of these men as they listened to Williams's report. At the close of his narrative, Brown exclaimed:

"It is time to stop that sort of thing. It has gone on long enough. I'll attend to those fellows."

An hour later Williams walked over to a shed near the camp, under which stood a grindstone, and saw a group of men sharpening their cutlasses.

"What's up?" he asked.

"We're going down upon the Pottawatomie to take care of the ruffians who're making trouble there," replied one of the men.

"We're going down," added Brown, who was looking on, "to make an example. Want to go?"

"No."

That afternoon eight men, six of whom were members of Brown's household, climbed into a farm wagon, and amid the cheers of their comrades started for the Pottawatomie. At night the party camped in a wooded tract between two deep ravines about a mile north of the stream. They remained in the woods that night and all the next day; but at nightfall of the 24th the camp was astir. About ten o'clock the men, armed with short two-edged swords, pistols, and rifles, left camp quietly and went in a northerly direction. They went to the homes of proslavery settlers and killed five men. They cut "them down with swords," one of the party said, "to avoid alarming the neighborhood by the discharge of firearms."

This gruesome act aroused Henry Clay Pate of Westport, Missouri, to lead a force to avenge the massacre. Brown attacked Pate at Black Jack and captured the whole outfit, holding them for two weeks until they were released by federal troops from Fort Leavenworth.

In southeastern Kansas, James Montgomery, a native of Ohio, who had emigrated to Linn County in 1854, organized a band of Free State men, converted his house into a fort, and became the best known of the Jayhawkers. The Free State settlers on the Osage, the Marmaton, and other streams looked to him for protection. During the autumn General George W. Clark, at the head of a proslavery force, overran portions of Linn and Miami counties, laying waste the property of Free State men and driving obnoxious settlers out of the country. Then the invaders, or their friends, took possession of the claims. Montgomery prepared a list of the names of proslavery men residing on claims belonging to Free Staters. All these usurpers were visited and warned to leave. Those who ignored the warning were ejected.

Linn County, in that area, was the home of Captain Charles A. Hamilton, a proslavery man who had emigrated from Georgia in 1855 and had located on a claim in the Marais des Cygnes valley. Here he built a house of logs and fortified it. Hamilton had an only daughter, a cultured and attractive young woman. In the winter of 1857-58, she met Dick Northrup, a young Northerner. He called on the young lady a number of times that winter but kept at a safe distance if the father was about the fort.

One Sunday evening Dick heard that the captain was in Missouri, and came to spend the evening with the daughter. He had scarcely got comfortably seated by her side when Hamilton walked in. Dick rose to his feet and stammered:

"It—it's a fine night, sir."

The captain stepped to the door and opened it, saying in a sarcastic manner:

"Yes, I think it is rather a fine night. Suppose you walk out and try it."

There was no alternative, so Dick bowed to the young lady and left. Shortly after that she went to Missouri, and Dick joined Montgomery's force.

About this time Hamilton was charged with horse stealing by his Free State neighbors and left the community.

On the morning of May 19th Hamilton returned with twenty-five or thirty followers. They went about the neighborhood and forced Free State men in line. One of the first victims was the Reverend B. L. Reed, a Baptist minister about forty years old, a native of Connecticut, who had moved to Linn County, Kansas, the previous spring. About eight o'clock that morning Reed went to the home of a neighbor named James, a mile distant, to borrow a horse. While he was talking with James and a man named Taylor about a school and other subjects, Captain Hamilton and his followers came up and ordered the three to fall in line.

"I won't do it," said the minister.

"You won't, eh?" said Hamilton, drawing a pistol and pointing it at him.

"I am willing to do anything that is right," Reed then said.

"Hitch your horse and fall in line."

Some of the armed band went into the house and soon returned, remarking, "We couldn't find any powder."

A man driving a pair of horses came down the road. They ordered him to stop.

"Where do you live?" one of the armed men asked.

"Sugar Mound," was the reply.

"Get out and fall into line."

Then they started in a northeasterly direction with their prisoners. After marching about a mile they brought two other men into line, then a third, and a fourth.

About that time Hamilton and six followers left the main body to bring in a man called Dutch Snyder who had acquired quite a reputation for fearlessness. The armed men rode up to the blacksmith shop in which Snyder was working and shouted:

"Hallo, there!"

Snyder went to the door. Hamilton exclaimed:

"Now, by God, sir, you're my prisoner."

"Not yet," replied the blacksmith, springing back into the shop. He seized a shotgun and told his son, a lad of seventeen, to run to the house for his rifle. The dwelling was several rods distant, up a steep bank.

"Why, father, they will kill me."

"Don't be afraid; I'll protect you."

The boy went on the run.

"Stop! or we'll shoot you down in your tracks," shouted Hamilton.

"Go on," roared the father, "I'll kill the first man who takes aim at you."

Not one of the band raised his gun until the boy

had reached the house; then Hamilton fired at Snyder, missing him. The blacksmith replied with his gun, the charge hitting Hamilton's horse in the neck, but the captain dropped unharmed behind the animal.

The blacksmith jumped back into the shop, reloaded and fired, wounding one of the band. They began to retreat, so he ran for the house. Several shots were fired at him, one lodging in his hip. He dropped behind a fence to reload. As the proslavery men, believing him disabled, approached, Snyder rose up and fired.

By this time the boy came out with the rifle. Father and son, taking shelter behind trees, fired so briskly that the men left.

The prisoners and their guards heard the firing. A part of the guards started to aid Hamilton, but soon returned leading the wounded horse. The captain ordered his men and prisoners to march. After he had taken eleven prisoners, he marched them to a deep ravine at the edge of the woods adjoining his house and there he ordered them to halt and fall in line. He then ordered his men to present arms. The horses' feet were on a level with the heads of the prisoners and only ten feet distant. Hamilton's men fired, and all the prisoners fell. Five were killed, five wounded, and one was uninjured.

Some of the men dismounted and came among the prisoners to see if all were dead.

"There's old Reed, he isn't dead; give it to him," said one.

"Where is he?" asked another.

"There's the black devil; shoot him," was the reply.

"Shoot in the ear," said another.

Reed says, "I lay with my face to the ground and prevented respiration; my back was covered with blood, so they thought me dead. The man who they thought was me, was one by my side, who fell dead, but lay with his eyes open."

After shooting the dead man, they came to the man who was uninjured, kicked him over, and said:

"He's as dead as the devil."

They felt in the pockets of a man who was supposed to have $100 on his person and took a watch from another; then they mounted and rode away.

The minister's wife and others soon reached the scene. The preacher and the other four wounded men recovered.

This bloody deed brought forth a vehement outburst of feeling throughout the North and inspired John Greenleaf Whittier to write the poem "Le Marais du Cygne," which was published in the September, 1858, issue of the *Atlantic Monthly*.

In the late fifties peace gradually came to the territory and the Free State men got control of the government. The slaveowners had removed their slaves from Kansas by this time. Only two slaves were reported in the census of 1860. It is estimated that there had not been more than fifty slaveowning settlers and three hundred slaves in the territory. However, several thousand persons from slave states remained in Kansas.

Scarcely had Kaw folks begun their peaceful occupations when the nation was rent by secession and plunged into a civil war. Kansas took her stand with the Union, and in proportion to her population supplied more than her quota of fighting men.

The Civil War furnished the opportunity for bandits and guerrilla bands to make raids on unprotected communities. The most cowardly of these was Quantrill's raid on Lawrence in August, 1863.

William C. Quantrill, the leader, was born in Ohio in 1837. His father, who was a schoolteacher of good family and character, died when William was a boy. The son was not robust. He suffered from a throat trouble and was expected to develop tuberculosis, the malady which had caused his father's death. The boy prepared to be a teacher. He was a bright student, but quite a troublemaker in school. At the age of twenty he came to Kansas, and he and some friends took claims near Stanton in Miami County.

Quantrill was five feet eleven inches tall, slender but well formed. He had piercing blue-gray eyes, the upper lids of which were too low, imparting a peculiar expression which was especially noticeable when he became angry. His nose was large and was "curved," or "hooked." His forehead was high, and his hair golden in color.

The first winter Quantrill was in Kansas the neighbors suspected him of stealing. Being in bad repute, he went to Fort Leavenworth in the spring of 1858 and accompanied a provisions train bound for Utah with supplies for General Johnston's army. He assumed the name of Charlie Hart on this trip. The following year he returned to Kansas, and during the winter of 1859-60 he taught school in the Stanton neighborhood.

At the close of the school term he went to Lawrence and boarded at the Whitney House on the banks of the Kaw. The Whitney House was kept by Captain Nathan Stone. The family nursed Quantrill through a prolonged illness; the daughter, Lydia, waited on him. In return for her kindness he gave her a ring of considerable value and requested her to keep it through life in token of his friendship.

Quantrill associated with a bad lot of men who were engaged in doubtful occupations, which attracted the attention of the authorities. As a result he left town and went to Missouri, where he and four accomplices robbed the home of a wealthy slaveholder. Then he became the leader of a marauding band of tough characters, and in a short time was the most noted guerrilla chieftain on the frontier.

On August 19, 1863, Quantrill assembled 294 men at Columbus, Johnson County, Missouri, and moved over to Lone Jack, in Jackson County, where he completed the organization. They crossed over into Kansas about five o'clock in the afternoon of the 20th and halted to rest their horses and eat supper. Then they rode across the prairie toward Lawrence, reaching it at daybreak.

Quantrill raided Lawrence for revenge, and he got it. He burned homes and stores and killed men, especially Free State leaders. Most of the men "took to the woods," or followed the example of Senator Jim Lane and hid in the cornfields. The women defended the homes that day, and in several instances they outwitted Quantrill and saved the lives of their menfolks. Tales of their bravery and resourcefulness have come down to us through the historian Richard Cordley and other sources.

Near the center of the town was an outdoor cellar with an obscure entrance. A woman took her station at a convenient distance from this cellar and directed into it every fugitive who came that way. Thus eight or ten escaped from the murderers. Finally, the guerrillas, noticing that their victims always disappeared when they came into this locality, suspected this woman of aiding in their escape. They demanded that she show their hiding place. She refused. One of them drew his revolver and pointed it at her:

"Tell us, or I will shoot you."

"You may shoot me," answered the woman, "but

you will not find the men." Finding they could not intimidate her, they left.

The Reverend H. D. Fisher, pastor of the Methodist church, made a remarkable escape. For some months prior to the raid he had been chaplain of a Kansas regiment. He was at home for a few days at this time, and the raiders knew it. As he was one of the men Quantrill particularly wanted, he started for a place of safety as soon as he heard that the guerrilla chieftain was making a charge on the town. Seeing there was little chance of escape by flight, he returned to his home and hid in the unfinished cellar. Soon the raiders surrounded his house and demanded that his wife tell them where he was. When she refused to tell, they searched the house and then started for the cellar. She lit a lamp and told them to go down and see for themselves. As the cellar had been only partly excavated, Fisher had climbed upon a bank and lay in the darkness. The light of the lamp did not reveal him.

Failing to find him in the cellar they went up and declared that they would smoke him out. They began to kindle fires about the house, but Mrs. Fisher put them out as fast as they lit them. They lit too many, however, and she saw that the flames would burn the house. The raiders went out and stood along the fence waiting for the man to come out. Mrs. Fisher poured water over the spot where her husband was lying to keep the fire away as long as possible, but at last she whispered to him that she could do no more and he would have to get out in some way. The cellar had a small window by the kitchen door. Fisher crawled through this; his wife threw a carpet over him, and rolling him up in it, dragged the bundle into the yard, and threw it under a peach tree. Then she brought pieces of furniture and piled them around it. The raiders did not leave until the house was in ashes.

Al Winchell, being hard pressed, ran into the house of Dr. Charles Reynolds, rector of the Episcopal church, who, at the time of the raid, was away from home, a chaplain in the army. Mrs. Reynolds dressed Winchell in woman's clothing, shaved off his mustache with a case knife (she always kept her knives very sharp), put a nightcap and a shaker bonnet on him, and turned the pockets of his dress inside out. Mrs. Winchell, who believed her husband had been killed, at that moment came into the Reynolds home with their baby. They seated Winchell in a rocking chair with the baby in his arms and christened him "Aunt Betsy." Some of Quantrill's men searched the house, but did not disturb Aunt Betsy.

After four hours of slaughter and burning, in which one hundred and fifty citizens were killed and thirty were wounded, Quantrill and his men came together. They had learned that Major Preston Plumb was approaching from the east with a body of troops. For that reason they left town and escaped.

In the spring of 1865, Quantrill and some of his guerrillas were in Kentucky. Early in May a company of soldiers attacked them at a farmhouse, wounding Quantrill. They took him to the hospital of the military prison at Louisville, where he died on June 6th. He was buried in a Catholic cemetery in that city.

When the Civil War closed, men laid down their arms and returned to their farms. Then followed an era of railroad construction, westward extension of settlements, and the building of an agricultural empire.

5

Building the Railroads

THE first families of the Kaw realized the importance of railroads, and shortly after their arrival adopted measures to encourage the building of this mode of transportation. The first legislature of Kansas Territory, which assembled in July, 1855, chartered five railroads. One of these projects was the Leavenworth, Pawnee and Western Railroad Company which was to build a railroad from Leavenworth via Pawnee to the western boundary of the territory, at that time in the Rocky Mountains. The company organized in January, 1857, and the engineers made surveys and profiles of the road and completed the location from Leavenworth to Fort Riley that year.

At that time the settlers were struggling to make both ends meet and lacked money to build railroads, and eastern capitalists were reluctant to invest in railroads in a new country that was torn by border strife. Then came the Civil War, causing further delay.

For some years prior to the Civil War there had been agitation for the building of a transcontinental railroad. The northern states wanted the road built over a northern or central route, while the South wanted it built west from some point in that section. One pur-

pose of the Kansas-Nebraska Bill was to aid the northern
and central routes. When the South seceded, the opposition to granting government aid in the construction
of a railroad over a northern route was removed. It was
also important at that time to save California to the
Union. Therefore, in the summer of 1862, Congress
passed the Pacific Railway Act which chartered the
Union Pacific Company and made possible the building
of the Union Pacific, and of the Kansas Pacific which
took over the franchise of the Leavenworth, Pawnee
and Western.

Section 9 of the 1862 law authorized the Leavenworth, Pawnee and Western Company to construct a
railroad and telegraph line west from the mouth of the
Kaw so as to connect with the Union Pacific on the one-
hundredth meridian; and granted alternate sections of
land in a strip ten miles wide on each side of the line and
promised a subsidy of $16,000 a mile in government
bonds.

Later legislation doubled the land grants for the
Union Pacific and the Kansas Pacific. The Kansas Pacific received a total of 6,000,000 acres of land and
$6,303,000 in bonds.

Soon after the passage of the Pacific Railway Act,
a contract for the construction of the Leavenworth,
Pawnee and Western railroad was let to Ross, Steele and
Company, a Canadian firm, which began work on the
road.

Things went along smoothly until the summer of
1863. Under the superintendence of a man named Carter the contractors had expended some $50,000 on the
grades and had about a hundred men employed when
they received an order to stop all work.

General John C. Frémont, the western explorer,
and Samuel Hallett, of Steuben County, New York, had

purchased the controlling stock and had changed the name to Union Pacific Railway, Eastern Division; this name was retained until 1868, when it was called Kansas Pacific. Frémont became president of the company and lived in the East. Hallett established his office in Leavenworth where he could be in close touch with the construction.

Samuel Hallett was a hotheaded fellow who battled with someone from the day he took over the company until his untimely death a year later. Associated with him were his brothers John and Tom. John was in general charge of construction, while Tom, a large burly man, was an assistant.

The new stockholders pronounced the old contract invalid and ordered all work to cease. Carter refused, so Samuel Hallett declared war on him and by some means got the help of a company of United States dragoons and rode down on the superintendent and his construction gang. He reported to his eastern confreres that he "drove them back into the river until they cried enough." His foreman, S. S. Sharp, seized Carter by the collar and led him to the bank and would have ducked him had he not begged so earnestly.

Frémont and Hallett soon disagreed. The latter obtained control of the organization and the books and tried to get rid of Frémont. For a time there were two sets of officers, but the Hallett organization was recognized by the government, and Frémont sold his interest. Hallett brought in Thomas C. Durant, builder of the Union Pacific and other railroads, and John D. Perry, president of the Exchange Bank of St. Louis. The latter became president of the railroad in 1864.

Then the impetuous Hallett lost patience with Leavenworth. That city was the headquarters of the great overland freighting business and believed itself indispensable to the railroad builders. It demanded exorbitant prices for land and supplies and withheld the bonds that had been voted until a specified number of miles of road had been completed.

Hallett, indignant, removed everything to Wyandotte. The first ground was broken in a dense forest near that town on September 7, 1863. Among those present were Samuel Hallett; A. B. Bartlett, a lawyer; Silas Armstrong; and H. H. Sawyer, a foreman. Sawyer handed an ax to Bartlett and Armstrong, and said:

"Cut down a tree. The honor of doing the first work on the right of way will go to him whose tree falls first."

The men set to work, and the chips flew. Armstrong's tree fell first, but it remained attached. Bartlett's tree fell a few seconds later, clean cut.

The graded roadbed began at the state line and stretched westward up the Kaw valley. Since there was no railway connecting it with the East, the pioneers said it had "neither beginning nor end." A large stake was planted on the state line at the end of the roadbed, having on its eastern face, toward Missouri, the inscription "Slave State," and on its western face, toward Kansas, the words "Free State."

The first rail of this great line was laid without pomp or ceremony, April 14, 1864, in Wyandotte at the foot of Minnesota Avenue on a spur which was to be used in handling material brought up the river. In order for the company to get the government subsidy it was necessary to incorporate this spur in the system.

The company planned to build the road about three miles north of Lawrence and about two miles north of Topeka.

News of this alarmed the people of both cities. Leading citizens called upon Samuel Hallett, who refused to change his plans unless the company received a liberal subsidy. Senator Lane got the signatures of thirty-six United States senators and the endorsement of President Lincoln to a petition requesting the company to run the line to the north bank of the Kaw opposite Lawrence and Topeka. Hallett still refused to bring the road to the banks of the river without a subsidy. Then some of the businessmen of Lawrence sent John Speer, a local newspaperman, to Washington to urge Senator Lane to save their city. On reaching the nation's capital, Speer went directly to the senator, who said:

"Don't you worry! Don't you worry! I will see about this."

Lane sent for Perry and Hallett. The next day they came to his hotel room, and again they refused to change the course of the road without the subsidy. Lane was ill and was lying on his bed. His eyes flashed and he partly arose on the bed. Pointing his long, bony finger at Perry, he said:

"Before you get a dollar out of that burned and murdered town you will take up every stump and every old log you have buried in your grade to save money, and stone ballast every rod to Lawrence; and even then, when you get your first subsidies let Jim Lane know."

"Don't talk to me! Don't talk to me!" he added as Perry tried to reply.

The following day Hallett informed Lane that he would locate the line so that it would approach the Kaw at the nearest practical points opposite Lawrence and Topeka and that he would instruct his brother to make the location.

An act approved July 3, 1866, relieved the company of the obligation to connect with Union Pacific at the one-hundredth meridian and authorized the construction of the road up the Kaw and Smoky Hill to a point fifty miles west of Denver, where it was to unite with the transcontinental line. This change saved 105 miles between Fort Riley and Denver.

The railroad was completed to Manhattan in August, 1866, and to Abilene in March, 1867. A month later the screech of the locomotive was heard in the new town of Salina.

William Bell, who visited Salina while it was the terminal station, describes the place as a town of a thousand inhabitants with several broad streets marked with stakes. The main street was cut up with deep ruts and strewn with rubbish. On each side of the street were wooden buildings of "all sizes and shapes of embryonic existence." About the railroad station and on each side of the track for some distance "lay pile after pile of the munitions, not of war but of peace—iron rails, oaken ties, cradles and pins, contractors' cars, little houses on wheels, trucks innumerable both empty and full."

The road reached Fort Harker in June, 1867, and for a time Ellsworth was the end of the line. The townsite had been laid out in February that year on the banks of the Smoky Hill joining the military reservation on the west. Several parties began erecting buildings in anticipation of the arrival of the railroad. Ellsworth got nicely started when a flood in June caused the Smoky Hill to overflow and put the town four feet underwater, carrying the frail frame houses and piles of unused lumber down the stream.

Then the inhabitants moved to a site on higher ground two miles to the northwest. Here they built a new town with great rapidity. A newspaperman who visited Ellsworth on July 20th wrote:

Much has been said and written—justly too—concerning the rapidity with which towns and cities spring up along the line of the great Union Pacific Railway, but in the many instances which verify such statements, we doubt if a parallel to the new city of Ellsworth is on record. . . . Whatever may have been the oversight of the town company in their selection of the site known as the "old town," they certainly have redeemed themselves in choosing the present location. Ellsworth is the present terminus of the U.P.R.W., and is likely to be for the remainder of this year. All freighters and transportation companies, together with the Government business are located there, thus rendering it the business point along the road. . . .

As an evidence of the thrift of the place at the present time, we have only to mention the following business houses and businessmen, all of whom are doing, what is known among western men as a "smashing business" . . . (There follows a list of forty business firms, fifteen of which were dispensers of liquor.)

Ellsworth was the tough town at the end of the railroad and got a good start in wild life. Then the railroad moved on. Scarcely had the town become peaceful when the Texas drovers brought their herds there, and the wild days started all over again.

West of Ellsworth the railroad entered the Indian country, and the tribes resented this intrusion. For the purpose of obtaining the red man's consent, a council had been called at Fort Harker in 1866. The leading chiefs and warriors of all the Plains tribes were there. On the white side were a regiment of cavalry, high-up railroad officials, and scores of frontiersmen. The council continued for three days with much speechmaking, but with no concrete results. The railroad officials offered rewards and made threats by turns. On the third night, when the whites thought they were about to reach a peaceful settlement, Roman Nose, the war chief of the Cheyennes who had not hitherto spoken, strode forward and made a short speech against the railroad. Within three minutes he undid all that had been accomplished in the three days.

The council broke up. The Indians went home. The railroad men went back to their job of building the road and pushed it forward into the red man's empire.

When Roman Nose saw that the railroad would be built in spite of his opposition, he called his people together and rode on the warpath. They killed scores of settlers, destroyed numerous homes, burned stage stations, ran off hundreds of head of stock, and raided railroad camps. The railroad armed the workers, and several companies of cavalry guarded the line. Despite this protection, the Indians wiped out construction gangs and for a time stopped all work.

About the time the railroad reached Ellsworth, the grading gangs were at work near Fort Hays, and towns were being laid out along the right of way. Late in May Rome was platted on the west bank of Big Creek north of the fort. In June William E. Webb of St. Louis, representing the Big Creek Land Company, arrived for the purpose of laying out the townsite of Hays City on a tract of land about a mile east of Rome.

It was generally believed that water could not be obtained on the proposed townsite. Webb, confident that this was an erroneous notion, was ready to plat the town when a man named Lee happened along with some drive wells. Webb stopped the wagon and persuaded Lee to make the test. The latter set up his rig, while doubting Thomases from Rome looked on and made caustic remarks.

The soil yielded grudgingly to the blows of the well digger's mallet. One of the Romans remarked:

"Put your well down in a brick kiln; you'll have better luck."

"I'll send over a diamond drill," volunteered another.

"Aw, gunpowder'd be better," chimed in a third.

Lee hammered his mallet to pieces, then used up a liberal allowance of cordwood, but made little headway. As the drill sank slowly into the earth he believed the effort hopeless and said dubiously:

"Good-bye, drill; the present generation won't be able to pull you up."

The last block of wood was battered almost to pulp; the Romans stood by taunting. Lee gave a last despairing blow when the drill sent back some sort of answer which caused him to ell:

"Water, g ntlemen—there she is!"

The news of the strike flew to Rome. The owners of some wagons, who had gone into camp, moved over to the new townsite. Other families from Rome and elsewhere followed.

Soon Hays was a town of a few tents and sod shanties, one grocery store, a clothing store, three dance halls, and twenty-two saloons.

The railroad was completed to Hays in the fall of 1867. Otero and Sellar, Chick, and other Mexican traders, with their long freight trains and army of bull-whackers and mule skinners, moved in and built huge warehouses. The rough element, which followed the railroad, flocked here, and Hays succeeded Ellsworth as the tough town at the "end of the railroad."

The railroad pushed westward across the plains in 1868. Coyote was the temporary terminal that summer. It consisted of a collection of canvas saloons, sheet-iron hotels, and sod dwellings surrounded by tin cans and scattered playing cards.

In a few weeks the terminus moved to Sheridan, and house-raising began in Coyote. A month's hammering, and Sheridan was built. In less than a year it had a population of two thousand.

Sheridan was a genuine frontier town. Before one street had been surveyed the engineer was called on to locate a graveyard. He located it on a ridge overlooking town. "I'll give you a high lot" was a threat in Sheridan which meant a grave on the hillside. During the first week three of the inhabitants went with their boots on, and during the winter the number increased to thirty, not one of whom died in bed.

Financial difficulties beset the Kansas Pacific, and for a time there seemed little prospect of its being built beyond Sheridan. The officials saved th road by securing a grant of land and a loan of mone which enabled them to complete the line to Denver in 1870. In 1873 the company defaulted in the payment of interest on its bonds, and the road went into the hands of a receiver. Its affairs were reorganized in 1879. The following year the Kansas Pacific and the Denver Pacific consolidated with the Union Pacific.

The construction of another great railroad in the Kaw valley followed the launching of the Kansas Pacific. This was the Atchison, Topeka and Santa Fe, which was built from Topeka southwest through Kansas; in a few years it was extended northeast to Atchison, and connection was made with Kansas City by leasing the Kansas City, Topeka and Western, a road that had been built on the south bank of the Kaw from Topeka to that city.

Cyrus K. Holliday was the projector and founder of the Santa Fe Railroad. Born near Carlisle, Pennsylvania, April 3, 1826, Holliday spent all the early years of his life near the place of his birth, except for a short residence in Ohio. He received his education in the common schools of his home town and at Meadville College, Allegheny, Pennsylvania. Trained for the legal profession, he practiced law for a time, but wanted to engage in big business. Having cleared $20,000 in a railroad venture in his native state, he came to Kansas with this capital.

He arrived at Lawrence in October, 1854. After remaining there a month, he went up the Kaw with a party in search of a townsite. They selected the site of Topeka, and he became president of the Town Company. Next he used his influence to get Topeka made the capital. Then he made plans to build a railroad over the Santa Fe Trail from the Missouri River to Santa Fe.

Holliday was a member of the territorial legislature in 1859. In January he wrote the charter of the "Atchison and Topeka Railroad Co.," filling in the names of L. C. Challiss, a member of the legislature, and General W. C. Pomeroy as two incorporators from Atchison and his own name as a representative of the Topeka interests. He introduced the charter into the legislature, and the bill passed late in the session.

The capital stock of the corporation was to be "one million five hundred thousand dollars which could be increased from time to time, to any sum not exceeding the amount expended on account of said road, divided into shares of one hundred dollars each." It was further provided that when "fifty thousand dollars shall have been subscribed to the stock and ten per cent paid in to the grantees, they are authorized to organize the company and open books for further subscriptions."

Nothing was done toward the organization of the company for over a year and half.

On a Saturday morning in September, 1860, Holliday, accompanied by E. G. Ross, Joel Huntoon, and Milton C. Dickey, started from Topeka to Atchison, fifty miles away, to organize the company. On reaching that city, they went to Challiss's office and organized the company by subscriptions of stock and the election of officers. They selected C. K. Holliday as president, Peter J. Abell as secretary, and Milton C. Dickey as treasurer.

Holiday issued a call for a railroad convention at Topeka for the purpose of deciding on a system of land grants "to be petitioned for at the next session of Congress." The convention assembled on October 17th and adopted resolutions which were entrusted to the Kansas territorial delegate for presentation to Congress.

More years passed before the work got under way. First, the drought of 1860 caused hard times. Then came the Civil War.

The bill which made possible the building of the Santa Fe Railroad passed Congress early in 1863. The act provided for two railroads: the Santa Fe, to be constructed from Atchison via Topeka southwest through the state, and a railroad from Leavenworth south through Lawrence. For the purpose of aiding the construction of these railroads, it granted to the state alternate sections of land in a strip ten miles wide on each side of the railroads.

The Kansas legislature accepted the grants in 1864 and passed legislation empowering and authorizing each county near or through which the Santa Fe Railroad was built to issue bonds not to exceed the amount of $200,000 to help finance the construction of the road.

Eight days after the state accepted the grant and transferred it to the railroad, the stockholders met and elected the following officers: Samuel C. Pomeroy,

United States senator, president; Sam Wood, of Waka-rusa War fame, vice-president; C. K. Holliday, secretary; and D. L. Lakin, a native of Alabama, treasurer.

The officers had accomplished much, but there still remained a long period of waiting. The war and the uncertain outlook for business made people with money reluctant to invest in a railroad in Kansas, whose record for border wars and droughts stood second to none. It was hard to convince capitalists that the Santa Fe, projected into a country which looked like a desert, would be a profitable investment.

However, by 1865 the directors had disposed of enough stock and raised money otherwise in New York so that they could begin work. Two years later the people of Shawnee County, of which Topeka is the county seat, voted bonds to aid in the construction of the railroad through the county. These bonds were put on the market in financial centers but failed to attract much notice.

Holliday, anticipating financial difficulties, had secured from the government the right for his railroad to purchase a tract of 400,000 acres of land in the Pottawatomie Indian reservation just west of Topeka. These lands were well located and found ready buyers. From their sale the company realized several hundred thousand dollars, a fund badly needed in the early construction of the road.

In the fall of 1868 Dodge, Lord and Company of Cincinnati secured the contract to build the road, and arranged with Thomas J. Peter, a member of the firm, to build the first twenty-five miles, from Topeka to Burlingame.

Peter was an able engineer who produced results. At the same time he was an interesting personality. He was strictly temperate in his habits and would neither

drink, chew, nor smoke, but when aroused his profanity was simply awful. He had a remarkable memory
and did not issue written orders. The subordinate who
failed to remember his instructions three months after
they were verbally given aroused Peter's profane wrath.

The contractors broke ground early in November,
1868. A small party of people assembled to celebrate the
event. The speaker's platform was a pile of dirt. Senator E. G. Ross was the chief speaker. Colonel Holliday
mounted the pile and astonished his listeners with the
prediction that they would "live to see the road completed to Santa Fe." The crowd laughed at this prediction.

Thomas Peter pushed the construction vigorously.
By the latter part of March ten miles of roadbed was
ready for ties and rails, while rails and fastenings for
another ten miles were being shipped from St. Louis.

A month later the construction gangs had laid seven
miles of track and had completed the grade to Wakarusa, a village twelve miles out. Late in April a party,
including officials of the company, made an excursion
trip to Wakarusa, to take part in a picnic celebration.
They rode in two coaches to the end of the track and
then traveled the remaining distance in carriages.

After dinner Colonel Holliday delivered a speech
in which he made statements regarded as wild prophe-
cies even by the most optimistic spirits in the crowd.
Glenn Bradley, the historian of the railroad, says he
told his audience that in the not distant future the railroad would cross the Rockies and reach Santa Fe. This
was greeted with murmurs of doubt, but when he went
on to say that someday this band of steel would join the
Gulf of Mexico and California with the Mississippi Valley and the Great Lakes, it was too much for his listeners. Some laughed scornfully, others stared in amaze-

ment, while one young man named Tom Anderson, doubling up in laughter, flung himself down on the ground, and kicked up his heels, at the same time exclaiming:

"Oh, the damned old fool."

The close of 1869 saw twenty-eight miles of the road completed. It reached Emporia in the summer of 1870, and Newton a year later, when construction was halted for several months.

Work started from Newton about May 1, 1872. Albert A. Robinson, an able engineer, assisted by James D. Burr, had surveyed the line. James Criley, an efficient Irishman who could swear as hard as he worked, had charge of tracklaying and erection of bridges.

The construction gangs completed the road to Hutchinson, thirty-three miles west of Newton, on June 17th; to Great Bend, fifty-one miles beyond, August 5th; to Dodge City, September 19th, and to the Colorado line on December 28th.

Newton was the "end of the railroad" from July, 1871, until the following spring. In addition, it was a leading Texas cattle market. During those months it acquired a reputation for bloody gun battles equaled by few other western towns.

As the railroad advanced, the distinction for gross lawlessness and crime passed to Great Bend, Larned, and finally to Dodge City, the most notorious of them all.

Dodge City was laid out in August, 1872, just a month before the railroad reached it. It was located in the heart of the buffalo country. Scores of hunters came here each season. The first season the trade in skins and meat was the town's chief support. The town was first called Buffalo City. When the residents applied for a post office, there were two towns in Kansas by that name: Buffalo Station on the Kansas Pacific Railroad and the town of Buffalo in Wilson County. Consequently the postmaster general, in granting the post office, suggested the name Dodge City.

Several of Dodge's pioneer citizens came from Hays. One of the first was James H. Kelley, who ran a saloon and was mayor of the town. In Hays he was known as "Hound" Kelley and in Dodge as "Dog" Kelley, because he was owner of a pack of hounds. Then there were Mose Waters, another liquor dealer; Larry Deger, the three-hundred-pound city marshal; R. W. Evans, a merchant; and W. N. Morphy, one of the founders of the *Ford County Globe*.

The first man killed in Dodge was a Negro named Texas. A platform had been erected, and the black man was standing in front and below in the street. A crowd had gathered, and several shots were fired, when a gambler by the name of Denver shot the darky, killing him.

During the first winter gun battles were quite common and resulted in fourteen graves on Boot Hill. At the digging of the first grave the bystanders quarreled over the direction in which the head of the deceased should be placed, and the funeral was about to end in scandal when the justice of the peace adjusted the issue, for that day and for all time:

"What's the difference, anyhow? When Jehovay wants a man he can find him, no matter how he happens to be planted."

And he settled the question so far as the gravediggers were concerned. There was no semblance of plan or regularity in the location of the graves. Unsightly white crosses marked some of them; yellow crumbling stones stood at the head of others; and still others were merely sunken spots. Friends and relatives didn't care for the graves, and the town did little, if anything, beyond exempting the place from taxation.

In a short time the railroad moved on, and with it went a portion of the roughs. As a rail town, Dodge City saw a great deal of lawlessness, but nothing comparable to the cow-town era.

While the engineers were pushing the line westward through Kansas into Colorado, the railroad company was selling its lands to finance the construction. In 1869 the company opened an office in Topeka for the purpose of selling the land to individual purchasers. D. L. Lakin, who proved to be an efficient agent, was put in charge.

The following spring the land department began the survey and appraisement of the grant. A party of nine men began the work, the completion of which required more than four years. They traveled in a covered wagon, starting at Emporia and working westward. They surveyed and secured a description of each section; then forwarded these descriptions, together with the appraised values, to the office at Topeka, where plats were made by counties.

When they had surveyed and plotted all the land, the Topeka office devised ways of selling the tracts. They offered to sell the land on easy terms and to carry buyers and their freight at reduced rates. They started a big advertising campaign, and prepared extensive mailing lists which brought thousands of letters of inquiry. They also compiled a list of several hundred newspapers and invited the chief editor of each to come to Kansas. These invitations stated that, upon acceptance, transportation, including Pullman passes, would be provided. Three hundred editors and writers gathered at Atchison on a fixed date and started west on a special train equipped with dining and sleeping cars. At nearly every station where the train stopped a banquet was spread, and there were floats and booths upon which were displayed the products of the prairie farms. The result of this excursion was several hundred columns of reading matter that money could not have bought.

The local agents of the railroad company received no salary. For remuneration they had to depend on commissions from actual sales. Some of them used novel methods to make a sale, as illustrated by the story of the party of ten prospective buyers who got off at one of the stations. The local agent felt sure of making a sale. The leader of the group, a doctor by profession, insisted on seeing Dodge City before they made the purchase, evidently figuring that the trip could be included in the transportation furnished by the railroad. They reached Dodge early in the morning and went to Dog Kelley's saloon. The land agent had wired Kelley to have the doctor put in jail. Kelley invited the doctor to go hunting. The hounds had just captured an antelope when "Indians" came over the hill and dashed upon the horsemen, who started for town at breakneck speed. On their return the doctor was put in jail on the charge of carrying concealed weapons. While this was taking place, the land agent arrived, rounded up the remainder of the party, and took them back. Then Kelley had the doctor released.

The land-selling campaign extended to Europe and resulted in the removal of several thousand Russo-German Mennonites from southern Russia to Santa Fe Railroad lands in Kansas. These people brought the hard wheat which has made the Kaw country the nation's granary.

The panic of 1873 delayed construction for two years and disarranged the finances of the railroad.

Boston capitalists gained control in 1874, and the following year expansion began both east and west. The Santa Fe secured connection with Kansas City by leasing the Kansas City, Topeka and Western, a local railroad that ran along the south bank of the Kaw between Topeka and Kansas City, and incorporated a new company under Colorado laws for the purpose of building the road to Pueblo.

By 1889 the Santa Fe railroad was over 7,000 miles in extent with terminals at Chicago, Denver, San Diego, Los Angeles, Galveston, El Paso; and Guaymas, Mexico. Cyrus Holliday's dream was a reality. The prophecy he made at Wakarusa in 1869 was fulfilled. But it is not written in the records that the local wit who, on that April day, rolled on the ground in unrestrained mirth ever had a serious moment in which he admitted that Holliday wasn't a "damned old fool" after all.

6

An Illinoisan's Dream

WHILE Roman Nose and his savage allies were trying to stop the building of the Kansas Pacific Railroad, an Illinoisan, with imagination and farseeing vision and the courage to act, conceived and established a market for Texas cattle on this railway. The man who projected this great enterprise was Joseph G. McCoy, engaged at the time in a large livestock shipping business at Springfield. The realization of his dream made the Kaw the outlet of the cattle kingdom and ushered in the most romantic era in Kansas history.

Joseph G. McCoy was born in Sangamon County, Illinois, December 21, 1837, and was the son of David and Mary McCoy. Joseph was the youngest child in a family of six boys and three girls. His parents were pioneer settlers in Sangamon County, having moved there in 1819. In the fall of 1823 they moved on to a tract of unbroken prairie land about eight miles southwest of Springfield in what is now Cartwright township. Joseph was born and reared on this farm.

David McCoy, familiarly known as Uncle Davie, was a successful farmer and a public-spirited citizen. Starting with a small farm, he added to it as time passed until he owned quite a tract of land. At an early date he

built a gristmill and adopted a rule that grist belonging
to a widow should never be tolled. The McCoys supplied
most of the money for building the Presbyterian church
in that neighborhood. The church was often spoken of
as the McCoy church.

David and Mary reared their children well and gave
them advantages not enjoyed by many of the boys and
girls in that neighborhood. After Joseph received such
instruction as the district school afforded, he attended
the academic department of Knox College. The McCoy
boys grew up to be tall, well-dressed young men with
"nice manners."

Joseph was a frequent visitor in the Pleasant Plains
neighborhood in the northwestern part of the county
where relatives lived. He went hunting with the boys,
deer and other wild game being plentiful in that section.
He used to call on Abbie Corson, a young woman living in that vicinity, and occasionally escorted her to
parties. Once Abbie and Joseph ate a "philopena" together, a social game then in fashion in which the young
couple divided an apple, a cookie, or a piece of cake,
and ate it. At their next meeting the one who said
"philopena" first, was entitled to receive a gift from
the other. Abbie remembered to say "philopena" first,
and Joseph gave her a book of poems entitled *Friendship, Love and Truth.*

As the boys grew up, the father turned more and
more to the business of raising and shipping livestock.
Before the Wabash Railroad came to Springfield, the
McCoys and their neighbors used to drive their cattle,
sheep, and hogs to Beardstown, about forty miles northwest on the river, to be shipped. Father and sons worked
together and were known as the "big stock feeders and
shippers" of Sangamon County.

In 1861 Joseph married Sarah Epler of Pleasant

Plains and at that time, or shortly thereafter, established a firm to deal in livestock, in which he and his brothers James and William were the active partners. At least one sister, Mrs. Polly Ann Scott, invested money in the firm. The father also probably had an interest in the business as many of the cattle were fattened on the McCoy farm. By 1866 the firm was doing a large shipping business. One thousand head of native cattle, costing from $80 to $140 per head, was not an unusual week's shipment, and three shipments were generally on the road at the same time during the entire season.

Joseph McCoy became interested in the Texas cattle industry as a result of the northern drive of 1866. That year more than a quarter of a million cattle crossed the Red River. Several thousand of these were driven into Illinois. Among the drovers who brought their herds to central Illinois in search of a market was W. W. Sugg, an Illinoisan who had spent several years on the frontier and had eventually gone to Texas.

An eyewitness says that Sangamon County was alive with longhorns. These bawling critters were on the roads and in the pastures, and scared folks, especially the children, every time one started in their direction. One morning a group of school children were coming down the road with their books and dinner pails. Some herders on horseback dashed up and yelled, "Get on the other side of the fence, quick! Texas cattle are coming." The youngsters lost no time climbing over the fence, and hid in the brush and weeds. The herd was so long passing that the children were late for class. Another time two of the same children climbed through the fence into a pasture to pick berries. Some longhorns started on the run in their direction. Seeing that they would be overtaken, the larger of the two girls turned on the cattle and raised her umbrella. They stopped, and then she lowered it, and the girls went toward the fence. The cattle followed, and she again raised the umbrella. By repeating the raising and lowering process several times they reached the fence.

Northern farmers knew of the disastrous effects of Texas fever and were afraid these cattle would spread the disease among the native stock. The prevailing notion was that all Texas cattle were infected, and therefore they were as welcome as lepers would have been.

The drivers encountered the stiffest opposition in Missouri. Armed mobs met them on the border and committed all sorts of outrages. Honest fear of Texas fever prompted some of this resistance, but most of the attacks were perpetrated by armed bands of cattle thieves for the purpose of stealing the stock.

When W. W. Sugg entered Missouri with his herd, consisting of a thousand head, an armed mob seized and beat him. He finally succeeded in getting his herd through to Christian County, Illinois, and there went into winter quarters.

In the spring of 1867 Joseph McCoy purchased Sugg's herd. From him he learned about Texas' great supply of cattle for which there was no local market. At that time in Texas a man's "poverty was estimated by the number of cattle he possessed." Sugg told him the only way the owners could market their cattle was to drive them north where they encountered hostile farmers and were attacked by gangs of thieves. He related the experiences of the drovers in getting their cattle through southeastern Kansas and western Missouri.

McCoy listened attentively to the drover's story and was impressed by it. He began to wonder why a market could not be established at some accessible point to which the Texas man could drive his cattle unmolested, and there find a buyer. The more he pondered over the subject the more convinced he became that it was practicable. Men to whom he broached the subject ridiculed the idea, and some said he was crazy. Despite what others said, he believed his plan was sound.

Uncertain whether the market should be established on one of the southern rivers or at a rail town on the western prairies, he got out maps of the western states, ran his finger along the southern rivers and the western railroads, measured distances and looked for the location of the settled areas. A market on the prairies should be established beyond the settled region and on a railroad. At that time the Kansas Pacific and the Union Pacific were building west and had reached the frontier. While McCoy doesn't say so, he certainly had the Kansas Pacific in mind when he studied the maps and formulated his plans.

It was then June. If he was to open a market that season he would have to hurry He decided to visit the West and get firsthand information. He took a train to Kansas City. Here he quizzed drovers, cattle buyers, in fact, any and everybody who could give him information. Among others he talked with parties who were interested in a large herd that was expected to arrive somewhere in Kansas. Next he took a trip up the Kansas Pacific to Junction City, then called the "edge of civilization."

While stopping at the Hale House, he was introduced to Colonel J. J. Myers, of Lockhart, Texas, a veteran cattleman who knew the West. He had made his first trip into the far West with Frémont and since then had traveled extensively on the plains and in the Rockies. The colonel was a small-sized, quiet gentleman, well along in years, and was the owner of several thousand head of cattle down in Texas, so McCoy thought here was just the man before whom to lay the proposed plan.

He invited Myers to take a walk; they strolled off to a lumber pile and talked for two hours or more. The Illinoisan explained the contemplated project fully and was told by the Texan that a depot for the sale and shipment of cattle was the greatest need of the stockmen of his state, and that whoever would establish such a market and conduct it on a legitimate basis would undoubtedly be well patronized.

As a result of this conversation, McCoy decided to locate the market along the line of the Kansas Pacific. He offered to buy from a leading businessman of Junction City a tract of land adjoining town and sufficiently large to build a stockyard and such other facilities as were necessary for cattle shipping. The owner asked an exorbitant price, which amounted to a refusal to sell at any price.

Failing to obtain a location in Junction City, the Illinoisan took a train for St. Louis for the purpose of consulting railroad officials about the rates of freight and facilities for the accommodation of livestock He visited the general offices of the Kansas Pacific. The president promised that the road would handle the freight if McCoy was willing to risk his money in the enterprise and agreed to pay him one-eighth of the freight on each car of cattle shipped. Then the cattle dealer went to the offices of the Missouri Pacific to inquire about the rates of freight from the state line to St. Louis. Here he found a cold, hardheaded executive who refused to listen and ordered him out of his office. McCoy has related the incident:

Here was the first really great man engaged in the contemptible occupation of managing a railroad, that the Illinoisan ever beheld. Entering the elegant office of the President and finding that dignitary arrayed in much store clothes, quietly smoking a cigar while looking over some business papers, the Illinois "Bovine Puncher," dressed in a style that greatly contrasted with the official's garb—rough, stogy, unblacked boots, a slouch hat, seedy coat, soiled shirt, and unmentionables that had seen better days twelve months previous, when they had adorned the counter of the Jewish dealer. He timidly stated his business in modest terms, and asked what rates of freight would be charged on the stock coming to St. Louis. When he had made his statement and propounded his question, the railroad official tipping his cigar at right angles with his nose, and striking the attitude of indescribable greatness when stooping to notice an infinitesimal object, and with an air bordering on immensity, said:

"It occurs to me that you haven't any cattle to ship, and never did have any, and I, sir, have no evidence that you ever will have any, and I think you are talking about rates of freight for speculative purposes, therefore, you get out of this office and let me not be troubled with any more of your style."

McCoy left the office wondering what could have been the purpose of the Almighty in "creating and suffering such a great being to remain on earth, instead of appointing him to manage the universe." Determined to complete the arrangements, he went to the offices of the Hannibal and St. Joseph Railroad where he closed a contract giving satisfactory rates of freight from the Missouri River by way of Quincy to Chicago.

He went east to set his house in order and then returned to central Kansas where he inspected the towns west of Junction City. He found the citizens of Solomon and Salina hostile to the Texas cattle trade, so he turned to Abilene, a "small dead place consisting of about one dozen log huts." After a few days of investigation, he selected Abilene as the shipping point. He decided on that village because the country south and west of town was entirely unsettled; it was well watered and was supplied with excellent grass. Furthermore, it was the farthest point east at which a good depot could have been established.

He purchased a tract of land adjoining town for the location of the stockyards, offices, and hotel. He brought pine lumber from Hannibal, Missouri, hardwood from Lenape, Kansas, and put a force of men to work. By September 1st he had completed stock and shipping yards that would accommodate three thousand cattle and load a train of forty cars in two hours, had a ten-ton Fairbanks scale in position, and a hotel under construction. The railroad company put in a hundred-car switch at Abilene and erected transfer and feed yards at Leavenworth. The buildings, yards, and equipment at Abilene represented an investment of $35,000 on McCoy's part.

As soon as McCoy decided to locate the market at Abilene, he sent W. W. Sugg into southern Kansas and the Indian Territory with instructions to hunt up every straggling herd and tell the drovers about Abilene. Mounting his pony at Junction City, Sugg rode in a southwesterly direction, crossed the Arkansas at the site of Wichita, and went south into the Indian Territory; then he turned east until he found the trails of herds which he followed until he overtook a drove and told the owner about the new market to which he could drive his stock unmolested by irate farmers and cattle thieves.

This was joyous news, but seemed too good to be true. The fact that the messenger was a cattleman added weight to his words, but the drovers were suspicious and shook their heads in doubt. Yet they turned their lead steers north, and with the North Star by night and the sun by day to guide them, they drove their herds in the direction of Abilene.

The first herd that arrived was driven from Texas by a man named Thompson but was sold to Smith, McCord, and Chandler, northern men, in the Indian Territory, and driven by them to Abilene. However, Colonel O. W. Wheeler, a little, bewhiskered man, in company with Messrs. Wilson and Hicks, en route to the Pacific Coast, drove the first herd that came direct from Texas and broke the trail. They stopped their herd about thirty miles from Abilene for rest, and after an argument among themselves, they sold the cattle at the new market. Other herds came up the trail that fall. The total drive for the year amounted to 35,000 head, a goodly number considering the fact that the market was new and that the excessive rainfall that season caused the streams to flood the plains and the cattle to stampede at every clap of thunder.

McCoy experienced financial troubles the second season. The railroad insisted on canceling the contract and making a new one on the ground that such large shipments had not been anticipated. McCoy finally agreed to cancellation and settled for a sum "not equal to one-third of the expenditures" he had incurred in establishing the market.

At the close of 1869 he invested every dollar he could get hold of in a herd of 900 cattle, intending to winter-feed them. He planned to use the $5,000 due him from the railroad company to pay the feed bills. When it was time for a settlement on the year's business, the railroad refused to pay the sum it owed him. As soon as his creditors learned this, some of them became uneasy and began legal action. Other creditors were frightened and made a rush on him. In the spring he surrendered all his assets to his creditors, even mortgaging his home. "With only a single ten dollar note he withdrew from business" and suffered a nervous collapse. He sued the railroad for the amount due him, and collected two years later.

Meantime, he followed the cattle trade to Newton and superintended the construction of the stockyards. A year later he went to Wichita in a similar position and made that city his home for several years. In 1881, with Wichita as his headquarters, he served as agent for the Cherokee Nation in collecting their land revenues. He lived for a time in Oklahoma and ran for Congress on the Democratic ticket in 1890, but was defeated. Later he moved to Kansas City, where he died in 1915.

Abilene continued to be the leading Texas cattle market for two years after McCoy withdrew. M. B. George, a cattleman located at Kansas City, took over the hotel, and others ran the stockyards.

The Illinoisan's dream had come true. A new era had dawned for the cattlemen and for the Kaw country. Kansas became the annex of the cattle kingdom, and the Kaw the lane down which the stock went to world markets. A million-dollar industry was started, a million-dollar industry whose glamour and romance have never been duplicated elsewhere.

7

The Texas-Kansas Cattle Trails

At the time Joseph McCoy selected Abilene as the shipping point for Texas cattle there were no well-defined trails between Texas and Kansas. The cattlemen who drove to Abilene the first season went north from the Red River, where they struck the trail blazed by Jesse Chisholm in 1865 and 1866 from his ranch near the present site of Wichita, Kansas, to the Wichita Indian agency in the Indian Territory, a distance of 220 miles. They followed his trail to the Arkansas River and went by a circuitous route from there to Abilene. The following spring, in order to straighten the trail and bring the cattle direct to Abilene, McCoy employed a force of engineers and laborers under the direction of Tim Hersey to survey and mark the trail from Abilene to the Arkansas River. At the streams they cut down some trees and blazed others, and on the prairie they threw up mounds of dirt, as signals.

The Eastern, or Chisholm, Trail, as finally established, ran north from Red River Station across the Indian Territory, entered Kansas near Caldwell, crossed the Arkansas at Wichita, and continued north past Newton to Abilene. On the way the trail crossed rolling prairies, passed a few stretches of timber, and went through miles of prairie-dog towns. McCoy says it was more direct and had more prairie and less timber, more small streams and less large ones, and better grass and fewer flies than the other trails then in use.

To the east of the Chisholm Trail was the "Old Shawnee Trail" which left the Red River near Snivel's Bend and led to Baxter Springs. Between the two main trails was the West Shawnee Trail which left its namesake near the Canadian River and ended at Junction City. A new trail known as Cox's Trail, or Ellsworth Cattle Trail, was surveyed to Ellsworth in the spring of 1873. The party making the survey consisted of William M. Cox and four Texas cattlemen. The new route left the Chisholm Trail near Pond Creek Ranche, Indian Territory, and ran by way of Kingman and Ellinwood to Ellsworth. In 1875 the drovers returned from the northern drive and said that Dodge City in southwestern Kansas was the coming cattle market. Early in 1876 the cattlemen met at San Antonio and sent Jim Netherlan to blaze a trail from Texas to Dodge City. This route, called the Western Trail, crossed the Red River at the place where Doan's store was established later and ran in a northwesterly direction past the sites of Altus, Elk City, and Woodward, through Dodge City, and crossed western Kansas into Nebraska. Trails were established to other points in Kansas, and many herds were driven to Nebraska and other northern and western states and territories.

In time enterprising merchants opened stores along the trails for the sale of supplies to the drovers. One of the best known of these stations was the Pond Creek Ranche and Store located at the point where the Chisholm Trail crossed Pond Creek in the Indian Territory. Sewell, a government post trader formerly of Council Grove, owned this store. The Ninnescah River Station south of Wichita was one of the chief halting places in Kansas. At this point the roads to the grazing grounds in the Arkansas valley branched off from the main trail. Two stores—John Dunscomb's and the Ward McKee Company's—were located at this station. There were roadhouses along the trail south of Abilene. Old-timers say that a man and wife ran one of these joints. While she was serving liquor to the cowmen and encouraging them to have another glass, her husband would drive off some of the cattle to a hiding place in that vicinity.

On the Ellsworth Trail there were two stores which made a specialty of drovers' supplies—C. H. Stone's Ranche and Store, at the Bluff Creek crossing, and E. C. Manning's store, near the place where the trail crossed Hunter's Creek.

Probably the best known supply house on the old cattle trails was the store established by J. Doan in the spring of 1878 on the south, or Texas, side of the Red River where the Western Trail crossed the river. Doan made a specialty of cowboy supplies and general outfitting for cattlemen. During the summer of 1878 C. F. Doan, a brother of J. Doan, became a partner in the business. The brothers enlarged their store and increased their stock. Doan's Store was known up and down the trail and throughout the West. The crossing of the Red River was called Doan's Crossing.

In the early years of trail-driving a thousand head of cattle was considered a large herd, but in the seventies and eighties a larger number was sometimes driven at one time. The size of the crew depended on the size of the herd. The trail hands were selected with the greatest care. Besides the herders, the outfit consisted of a trail boss, a cook, men to care for the extra horses, a chuck wagon, tents, and a supply of firearms, saddles, lariats, bedding, and clothing and other personal belongings of the riders.

As soon as the drovers received all the cattle for the northern drive they put them into a large corral or enclosure and began the job of road-branding. With plenty of help this was soon completed. Then the drovers secured and recorded the bill of sale from each ranchman from whom they had purchased the stock. The ranch brands and all the earmarks were noted in the bill of sale. McCoy says the appearance of a bill of sale was much like Egyptian hieroglyphics; the more a northern man looked at it the less he knew about it. But it was necessary, for the drover might have to produce it as evidence of ownership almost any time.

When everything was ready the drovers started the herd up the trail. A herd of a thousand cattle would string out a mile or so in length. Certain animals took the lead, and others followed. Each day the same animals were usually at their posts. Two of the more experienced men, riding one on each side, pointed the herd. Other cowboys rode along the flanks and brought up the drags in the rear. When the cattle became excited or restless, a cowboy rode ahead and sang a low lullaby, like a mother to her child, to quiet them.

Hard driving the first few days was the custom. The first three or four days many drovers traveled at the rate of twenty-five or thirty miles a day. There were at least three reasons for doing this. First, the drovers could control the animals more easily after they got them off their accustomed range; second, hard driving would tire them out so that they would lie down to rest at night; third, it was advisable to break them in as soon as possible. The drive was decreased to twelve to fifteen miles a day as soon as it was safe to do so.

At daybreak the cook had breakfast ready and

called the herders. After breakfast the cowboys saddled their horses and commenced the day's work. The cook mounted the camp wagon and pushed on ahead to a suitable resting place for the night. The herd grazed until about eight o'clock and then was driven slowly up the trail, being permitted to rest and graze as it went.

The herders reached the camping place about five o'clock in the afternoon. The cattle grazed until dusk, when the trail hands rounded them up for the night; that is, they circled slowly around the great army of beasts, driving them in closer and closer together and singing as they rode. Two or more of the men stayed with the cattle in regular relays until morning. In some outfits, one-third of the drivers did guard duty at one time, being relieved at intervals of three or four hours by other hands who had, in the interim, snatched a few hours of sleep. A well-behaved herd generally slept until eleven or twelve o'clock, then got up, stretched, and lay down on the other side and rested until morning.

The cattle rested better when they knew that someone was near them. The night herder usually sang to the animals, especially when he was riding on the outside of the herd. If his horse stumbled the cattle would know where the noise came from and would be less likely to stampede.

About the cow camp and on the drive Captain Eugene Millett, a pioneer trail driver, once said "everything is good humor, with singing, whistling and lullaby. These conditions are most conducive to the easy handling of the herd. Ask any old cowman."

So the author asked Colonel Jack Potter, another veteran of the saddle, who agreed that singing was a necessary part of the cowboy's duties and told a story:

I landed in San Antonio once badly in need of a job. I made contact with Ab Blocker, noted trail boss who was starting to the Red Cloud Agency with an Indian contract herd. I asked him for a job. He said, "I'm shorthanded but I've got to know whether you are eligible or not. Can you ride a pitching bronc? Can you rope a horse out of the remuda without throwing the loop around your own head? Are you good-natured? In case of a stampede at night, would you drift along in front or circle the cattle to a mill?"

I said I certainly knew enough to mill them providing my night horse was fast enough to outrun the cattle.

"Well," he said, "that is fine. Just one more question: can you sing?"

I said, "Yes" when I knew that I couldn't even call hogs, but I was sure needing a job.

Things moved along pretty well for about twenty days. It seemed every time I went on guard the cattle would get up and low and mill around the bed ground. I was afraid the boss would find out the trouble sooner or later. One night I hadn't been out ten minutes when I commenced singing to them and most of them got up and commenced milling. I was doing my best singing when all at once the boss slipped up behind me. He was in a bad humor and said:

"Kid, you are fired. I thought you were causing this trouble. I thought you told me you could sing. It's a hell of a note that cattle can't stand your singing.

"You go back to camp and I'll finish your guard." Old Trail Boss Ab was a good singer and in a few minutes the cattle commenced laying down.

Trail-driving usually required more patience and perseverance than labor. But it was a tiresome job. The men were out in the blistering hot sun all day long for weeks, sometimes months. After putting in twelve hours on the trail they were on guard at least three hours at night. They had to do their own laundering and often had to eat the poorest kind of chuck. They didn't have milk, butter, or eggs, and they never had ice water. The cook drove into the creek or river and filled the fifty-gallon barrel. This constituted their supply of drinking water until they reached the next stream. At times they lacked plates, knives, and forks and had to eat out of the camp kettle with pocket knives. Captain Millett and his men were in the saddle six to eight months on drives to Dakota or Nevada and had to live on hardtack for days. Sometimes they ran out of salt and became so hungry for it that they used the sweat under the saddles. The longer the men were out on the trail the harder it was for them to endure the food.

The cowboys dreaded the stampede most of all. Some trifling thing often started a stampede. The meeting of a wagon on the trail might excite the cattle. The shaking of a saddle, the cry of a wild animal, some chance noise when everything was still at night would start one of the longhorns to his feet, and in an instant the whole herd would be running madly over the prairie. On one occasion a blade of grass, blown by the wind, struck a steer's eye. The eye began to smart and the steer got wild. In a few minutes the whole herd was up and running across country at a twenty-mile-an-hour gait. A thunderstorm at night often caused a stampede. In rainy seasons, like 1867, the cattle were running a good share of the time. Colonel Jack Potter was driving a herd to Ogallala in 1884. Thunderstorms caused the cattle to stampede several times. One night they ran past the chuck wagon, and he jumped on his horse and started after them. He says, "I went out in the lead and about three hundred yards off my horse stepped in a prairie-dog hole, fell and broke his neck. My leg caught under him. The cattle split around us. One of the boys happened to see the fall and came back and pulled me out."

When the cowboys saw the cattle disappearing over a hill or toward a canyon, they put their skill and daring to a severe test. They tried to keep the herd together and get the cattle to milling. With this object in view they pressed their mustangs against the column of flying cattle and gradually forced them to run in a circle. When this was done, the first step toward controlling them had been accomplished. Sometimes the longhorns would run for miles. The cowboys rode this mad race at the risk of their lives. If a horse slipped and fell, there would be a mass of flesh and blood and leather somewhere on the trail of the stampeding herd.

Next to a stampede, the boys dreaded the taking of a herd across a stream when it was swollen by heavy rains. They usually took the cattle across in groups of twenty-five or thirty. The cowboys swam their horses along with the cattle. Sometimes they took the entire herd across without any trouble. At other times a group of cattle would be brought almost to the opposite shore when some moving object would scarce a steer, and he would turn back. In a moment the entire group would be swimming wildly round and round in the middle of the stream. Sometimes hours of work were required to break up the mill and get the cattle started for the shore again. The cowboys often had to leave their horses and swim among the cattle. The cattle sometimes drifted downstream for miles before the mill could be broken.

In the early days of trail-driving, Jesse Day and his sons James and William started with a herd over the trail to Missouri. When they reached the Brazos River it was at flood stage. They had piloted the herd across when Day's horse became panic-stricken and threw him into the raging current. He was drowned despite the heroic effort William made to save him. In 1866 Captain Millett tried to take a herd across the Red River near Denison when it was swollen by heavy rains. The cattle would not take to the water. While he was working with them, another herd arrived and started across. Millett's cattle followed. The men had a time crossing the turbulent stream. One horse was drowned, and it was midnight before the last of them reached the opposite bank. A near tragedy occurred at the ford of the Arkansas at Wichita in 1872. A drover was getting a herd across when the river was high. A crowd of spectators lined the north bank. A herder's horse went under with him, and as they arose the horse kicked its rider who was struggling with the current. The man sank, came up, and went down a second time when a stranger on the bank took off his coat, vest and hat, and while the crowd stood in silence he plunged into the stream, swam out to the drowning man, grasped him, and after a desperate effort succeeded in getting him into shallow water, then to the shore. It took some time to resuscitate the cowboy.

The drovers knew that trouble could be expected north of the Red River with Indians or outlaws. They prepared for it by taking along a supply of firearms and ammunition and by hiring cowboys who could fight. The crews usually contained hard characters. Some of the drovers employed professional gunmen.

In the early days the Indians gave no end of trouble, frequently killing or driving off cattle or committing some other form of devilry. A band of redskins would come to a drover and demand a certain number of cattle on the threat that they would stampede the herd. Sometimes the whites put up a fight and drove the Indians off or compromised by giving them a steer or two. Some of the tribes levied a tax on all cattle driven through their domain. Drovers who refused to pay this tribute usually had trouble on their hands. The vigorous defense of the cattlemen caused the redskins to cease their raids on the herds. In the late seventies and eighties, Indians were seldom seen along the trails.

There was little wonder, says a contemporary writer, that after weeks of weary, restless riding by day and sleepless anxiety and watching under the stars by night, of wild rides after stampeding cattle and perhaps a battle with Indians or cattle rustlers, when the lights of Abilene or Dodge showed across the prairie, the cowboy kicked his feet out of his stirrups, drove the blood out of the pony's sides and came into town with both guns going at once, and yelling as though the pent-up speech of the past weeks of loneliness was striving for utterance.

When the herd arrived in the vicinity of the Kansas cattle market, the trail boss selected a suitable place for a permanent camp, or a man employed by the cattle interests of the town located the herd on eligible grounds. There the cattle grazed and recuperated a month or two before they were marketed. Since the whole country around the cow town was soon filled with longhorns, the drovers found it advisable to arrive as early as possible in the season. Herds were started north in March and April. A large part of the cattle reached the Kansas cow town by July. Most of the shipping was done late in the summer and fall.

The drive from the Red River to the Kansas cow town was usually made in thirty or forty days. The losses sustained by the drives were from 5 to 10 per cent, and they were caused by death, lameness, thievery, and stampeding. The estimated cost of driving was from $1 to $3 per head. The cowboys were paid on an average $30 a month. The trail boss received $50 per month.

Trail-driving to Kansas lasted for about two decades. Definite figures on the total number driven are

not available, and estimates do not agree. According to Joseph Nimmo, the government statistician, between five and six million cattle were driven up the trail. Other writers put the number as high as twelve or fifteen millions. The hoofs of these marching animals tramped out the vegetation and pulverized the soil, and wagon wheels made deep tracks. The wind blew the loose dirt away, and the water washed it down, making a trough. The trails in many places were as bare as a city street and were marked by the bleaching bones of animals and broken-down wagons, with here and there a mound which bore mute testimony that some cowboy had lost his life.

Farmers moved in, broke the sod, and closed the trails. They found the ground on the trails packed as hard as cement. Even today their plows turn up hard chunks in places. South of Wichita the route of the Chisholm Trail can be followed down through the fields by the size of the grain. There the wheat and corn are shorter and thinner, and in dry weather this strip of grain is the first to wither. In some of the pastures and at some of the river crossings the troughs made by the marching hoofs and the wagons are still visible. South of Dodge City the route of the Western Trail is quite distinct in some of the pastures, especially on the hillsides where troughs several feet wide and six to eight inches deep were worn. Once in a while an old bridle bit or other piece of rusty metal is found on or near the old trail.

8

The Kansas Cow Towns

Abilene

As soon as McCoy started building his depot at Abilene, the dead little village awakened and teemed with activity. One force of men was building the shipping yards and putting the scale in place. Another group was erecting the hotel. An outfitting store went up near the hotel, and two Jews extemporized a place of business out of an empty corncrib in which they sold ready-made clothing to the cattlemen at a huge profit almost as fast as the garments could be taken from the boxes.

In the months that followed, other business houses were erected and the town took on an air of prosperity. In 1870 there were four hotels, ten boardinghouses, five dry goods and clothing stores, nine or ten saloons, and other establishments. The majority of the buildings were one-story frame structures, though some were two or even three stories high. The first buildings constructed of other than wood were the jail and courthouse erected in 1870. The sidewalks were of wood, irregular in width, and uneven in height. They trembled and clattered as the cowmen, wearing high top boots and spurs, walked on them.

The railroad divided the quiet and moral part of town from that half which was wild and romantic. In the one were the churches, the courthouse, and the newspaper. The other portion was a museum of wonders, a great panorama of real action.

The Lone Star district began on First Street (Texas Street) near Mulberry, about two blocks east of Mud Creek, ran east on First Street to Cedar, north on Cedar to A Street (Railroad Street), then east on A Street. H. H. Hazlett's Drover's Outfitting Store was on the southwest corner of Mulberry and First streets. In the block east: Planter's Hotel; Bull's Head, Applejack, and Old Fruit saloons; and Jacquis (Jake) Karatofsky's Great Western Store on the corner of Cedar.

Around the corner on Cedar, and facing west, was the Alamo Saloon, Wild Bill Hickok's headquarters when he was city marshal. The name sent a thrill through the breast of every Texan. To him the name symbolized Texan independence. A chapter of wild life centers about this saloon. The entrance consisted of three sets of double doors which extended across the front of the building. Crowds swarmed within and about its doors in the cattle season. At night the place was brilliantly illuminated. There were tables covered with the "green cloth"; on them were piled the checks of ivory, the gold and silver. About the bar costly mirrors, pyramids of sparkling glasses, and vases of the choicest flowers gave the place an air of elegance. The harmonious strains of piano and violin and the intense excitement of the games gave the room a sort of weird enchantment. Here, unlike the Alamo of history, the Texan didn't fight the "Greaser"; instead, the Texan and the "Greaser" joined forces and fought the "Tiger."

On A Street, facing the railroad, were four saloons in a row; east of them the Novelty Theatre opened in

July, 1871, under the management of George Burt of Leavenworth, one of the theatrical pioneers of Kansas. He presented "upon the boards" the ridiculous eccentricities of the dusky sons of Africa, the amusing and popular farces, interspersed with gems of vocal and instrumental music; and the talented Eva Brent, a noted operatic star. Beyond the theater was the Gulf House, a two-story hotel. This building still stands. Another story has been added and the name changed to National Hotel. Up the street was the Drovers Cottage under the management of J. W. and Louisa Gore. This hotel was three stories high, painted a delicate wood color, had green Venetian blinds at the windows, hardwood finish, and handsome accommodations for eighty guests. Back of the hotel was a vast livery stable for the drovers' horses. The hotel and stable were both enlarged later to handle the increasing volume of business.

In 1868 the northern drive exceeded 75,000 head, most of which were marketed in Abilene. The number increased to 150,000 in 1869, and to at least 200,000 in 1870. The cattle trade brought thousands of drovers, cattle buyers, commission men, and speculators to Abilene. During the shipping season of 1870 as many as five hundred drovers were in town at one time, and the arrivals for the season totaled about fifteen thousand. Some of the toughest characters in the country came there to prey on the cattlemen. The local paper stated that at one time in 1871 there was a "larger number of cut-throats and desperadoes in Abilene than in any other town of its size on the continent. Most of them were from Kansas City, St. Louis, New Orleans, Chicago, and from the mountains."

During the first two seasons there was no municipal government, no jail, and no effective police system.

The town was wide open, and little attempt was made to control the disorder and curb the lawlessness.

In September, 1869, the town was incorporated as a third-class city. The court appointed a board of trustees consisting of five members: James B. Shane and Theodore C. Henry, partners in real estate business; Thomas Sheran, a grocer and former sheriff of the county; Tim Hersey, one of the founders of Abilene; and Joseph G. McCoy. The board chose Henry as chairman which, in effect, made him mayor of the city. Since it was almost time for the shipping season to close, little was done that fall toward curbing the violence. The following spring the board was reorganized. C. H. Lebold, a young real estate man, and Dr. C. H. Brown took the places of Messrs. Hersey and McCoy. Washburne Fancher, a young schoolteacher, was appointed secretary.

The new board passed ordinances licensing the saloons, regulating the houses of ill-fame, punishing the more flagrant crimes, and forbidding anyone to carry firearms in town. They printed and posted copies of this ordinance. The cowboys shot the copies to pieces.

The new government decided to employ a city marshal. Several local men applied. The board employed one after another of these men, but each failed to stop the lawlessness. Finally, the mayor asked the chief of police of St. Louis to send two competent men. He sent two highly recommended soldiers. The cowmen "shot up the town" the day these soldiers arrived. Both men went home on the midnight train.

Then the city fathers decided to employ Thomas J. Smith, one of the first applicants for the position, who had come down from Kit Carson, Colorado, when he learned that a marshal was wanted.

Tom Smith was born of Irish parents in New York in 1830. He received a fair education and was reared in the Catholic faith. As a young man he served on the New York City police force, and in 1857 was in the Far West.

He was a handsome, broad-shouldered, athletic man, five feet eleven inches tall, weighed about 170 pounds, stood erect, had grayish-blue eyes, auburn hair, light-colored mustache, and was a stranger to fear.

Smith had been employed in various capacities in the construction of the Union Pacific Railroad when it was building across Nebraska in 1867. In November of the following year he was working for a large contracting firm whose headquarters were at Bear River City, Wyoming, and took part in the bloody Bear River riot. He received severe wounds in this fight, and by the time he recovered the construction gang had abandoned Bear River City and moved on. His conduct had been such in the riot that the railroad appointed him marshal of each town as one "hell on wheels" was abandoned and another located along the right of way.

The trustees of Abilene met late in the afternoon of June 4th for the purpose of "reorganizing the police force." They passed a motion employing Tom Smith as chief of police for one month at a salary of $150, and requesting the "old police" to resign. Another motion provided that "Mr. Smith select a man to assist him." At the next meeting the board voted to employ a man named Robbins as policeman. The municipal records fail to show how long Robbins served or how many other men were on the police force that season. Late in the summer or in the fall, James H. McDonald was on the force. He was a native of Canada, twenty-one years old, tall, of medium weight for his height, and had a fair complexion.

Tom Smith immediately launched his campaign against lawlessness. First of all he decided to enforce the ordinance against gun-toting. He enlisted the help of the businessmen and asked the proprietors of the hotels to use their safes as depositories for the pistols of drovers and other guests. Then he posted copies of the ordinance.

Smith rode on horseback while on duty and used his fists to enforce the law, whereas his predecessors had walked and depended on firearms. As he rode Silver Heels, his favorite gray, down the middle of Texas Street, the roughs made bets that they could run him out of town.

The first to test his metal was Big Hank who boasted that no officer could disarm him. On Saturday night he came to town wearing his six-shooter conspicuously. Approaching the marshal, he said:

"Are you the man who proposes to run this town?"

"I am employed as marshal and shall try to maintain order and enforce the law."

"What are you going to do about that gun ordinance?"

"See that it is obeyed; I must trouble you to hand me yours."

With an oath the man refused to surrender his arms. In a calm voice Smith repeated the demand. This was greeted with more profanity. Smith sprang forward and struck Big Hank's jaw a terrific blow. Then he took the ruffian's pistol from him and ordered him to leave town. Big Hank at once sought a "healthier climate."

The news of this encounter spread like wildfire, and in a few hours was the leading topic of conversation in the cow camps around Abilene. In a camp northeast of town Wyoming Frank, a husky cowpuncher,

made a wager that he could go to Abilene and put that
upstart peace officer in his place. Early next morning
Frank rode to town. When Smith came down the street
Frank went out to meet him. As he approached the
marshal, he began talking insolently with the idea of
involving him in a quarrel as an excuse for not sur-
rendering his gun. Knowing the man's purpose, the
officer quietly asked him to hand over his pistol. Frank
refused and began backing as Smith advanced asking for
the gun. He continued to back and tried to draw his
gun, but the marshal's close reach prevented that. The
cowman backed into a saloon, followed by the marshal,
and stopped in the center of the room. Again Smith
asked for the gun. An insulting oath was the reply. The
officer vaulted and with a double blow sent Frank to
the floor and stood over him.

"I give you five minutes to get out of this town,
and don't ever let me set eyes on you again."

The witnesses stood speechless. The proprietor was
the first to break the silence. He stepped from behind
the bar and said:

"That was the nerviest act I ever saw. You did
your duty, and that coward got what he deserved. Here
is my gun. I reckon I'll not need it so long as you are
marshal of this town."

Every man in the room came forward and offered
to hand over his gun. Smith thanked them and said:

"Hand your guns to the bartender to keep until
you want to go out to camp."

No more tests were made. Thereafter most of the
visitors obeyed the deadly-weapon ordinance. On
August 9th the trustees expressed their appreciation of
Smith's work by increasing his salary to $225 per month
to date from July 4th.

At this time a Scotchman named Andrew McConnell and his friend Moses Miles, a native of Massachusetts, were living in a dugout near Chapman Creek, ten or twelve miles northeast of Abilene. Rumor said that McConnell and Miles· had lived in Colorado and had left a shady record there. Consequently, the neighbors regarded the bachelors as suspicious characters and kept away from them.

One Sunday afternoon, late in October, McConnell was out hunting deer and on returning met Shea, an Irish neighbor, driving cattle across his land. The cattle had been in his cornfield. Words passed between the two men. The Irishman drew his pistol and snapped it twice at the Scotchman. As he was cocking it for a third attempt, McConnell shot him through the heart. Then he went for a doctor and afterward surrendered to the authorities. Miles testified that the act was done in self-defense and secured his release.

Some of the neighbors told the officers that Shea had not been the aggressor, and one of them swore out a warrant for the arrest of McConnell. The sheriff, or one of his deputies, tried to serve the warrant but was driven off the place and returned to Abilene for help. Tom Smith, who was deputy United States marshal as well as chief of police, volunteered to make the arrest. Smith and Officer McDonald rode out to Chapman Creek to make the arrest. Upon reaching the dugout, they found McConnell and Miles there. Smith told McConnell that he had a warrant for his arrest, whereupon the Scotchman shot the officer through the right lung. Smith also fired, wounding the Scotchman. The two men, being close together, grappled. Meantime McDonald and Miles exchanged shots. Miles drove the policeman off the place and then turned on Smith, who was bringing McConnell out of the dugout. Miles struck the marshal on the head with his gun, knocking him senseless; then killed him with an ax. Thereupon, the two men mounted their horses and fled. They reached Junction City that evening, then started up the Republican River valley toward Clay Center.

McDonald witnessed the death of his chief. Leaving his horse where it was tied, he ran to the nearest claim, a half mile or more west, mounted a pony, and rode back to Abilene for assistance. In a few minutes a posse repaired to the scene of the murder.

C. C. Kuney, police magistrate, and James Gainsford, a butcher by trade, who were with the posse, started in pursuit and continued on the trail, traveling almost day and night until they captured the men early Saturday morning at a farmhouse fifteen miles northwest of Clay Center. Both men surrendered without offering resistance.

The officers brought their prisoners to Abilene on the Sunday morning train. The prisoners were tried at the March term. Both men were found guilty and sentenced to prison.

The year 1871 was outstanding in Abilene's history as a cow town. It is estimated that 600,000 Texas cattle arrived in Kansas during the season. Approximately one-third of these were driven to Abilene. The drive started from Texas in March. On April 6th the Abilene *Chronicle* estimated that not less than 90,000 longhorns were on their way. The herds began to arrive in May. For miles north, south, and west of town one was scarcely out of sight of a herd. As the season advanced, a person standing on top of a commanding hill could often see from 30,000 to 50,000 head at one view. There were not only "cattle on a thousand hills" but a thousand cattle on each and every hill, and in the valleys too.

Abilene was a lively place that summer. The municipal authorities prepared to fend off trouble by appointing J. B. ("Wild Bill") Hickok as city marshal. Wild Bill was the best antidote for badmen on the frontier. After winning his spurs in the Border and Civil wars he became a guide, scout, and Indian fighter; then added to his fame by cleaning up Hays, one of the toughest towns in the West.

Wild Bill was called the "handsomest man west of the Mississippi." He was six feet tall and had a well-formed body. His eyes were blue, but seemed to turn to a steel-gray when he was angry. His hair and mustache were golden brown in color. He was immaculate in person and dress and fond of fine clothes. A contemporary says, "I have seen him in a Prince Albert coat, checkered trousers, a silk waist coat embroidered with colored flowers, and over his shoulder, a cape with a flowered silk lining. He took as much pride in his boots, as in his wealth of blond hair."

The old-timers enjoy reminiscing about Wild Bill. Those who gambled say that Bill often sat in on card games but that he was never known to cheat. One time in Ellsworth he fired ten shots at a post in a demonstration of markmanship. A bystander said:

"Why, Bill, you hit the post only once."

"Cut into the post with your knife and see," answered Hickok.

The man did so and found ten balls lodged on top of each other in the hole.

One of Hickok's outstanding traits was his liking for children. He sought out the youngsters and bestowed much attention upon them. A Hays woman recalls with pleasure and pride the times he bought candy for her and her playmates when he was town marshal.

The rough element came in larger numbers than usual that season. Among the badmen were Ben and Billy Thompson and Phil Coe.

Ben Thompson came up from Austin that spring to spend the season and win some money at cards. His brother Billy was in town off and on. They were two of the best known gunmen in the old West. Bat Masterson once said that the "very name of Ben Thompson was enough to cause the general run of 'man killers,' even those who had never seen him, to seek safety in flight." Ben was an excellent general under trying circumstances, possessed above the average intelligence in handling a gun, had the steadiest nerves, and shot at a man with the same coolness and precision he shot at a rabbit or a target.

Ben was twenty-seven years old. Born in Nova Scotia of English parents, he had spent his boyhood days in Austin, Texas, where he learned the printer's trade on the *Southern Intelligencer*. He was five feet nine inches tall, of rather swarthy complexion, and had blue eyes; he stood erect and was fastidious about his clothing and personal appearance. He was a likeable fellow and made friends wherever he went.

He took his first human life when he and a Frenchman fought over a girl in New Orleans. Friends helped him escape. When the Civil War began, he enlisted in the Confederate Army and was the badman of his regiment. After the war he served a two-year term in prison for shooting a man. He was released in 1870, and the next spring came to Abilene. He arrived without much money, but sat in on a card game and won $2,600.

Billy Thompson was four years younger than Ben. He resembled his brother in complexion, erect form, attractive appearance, and friendly manner, but was taller and more slender, and had brown hair and gray eyes. Bill was in one scrape after another, and Ben was usually on hand to help him out.

About the time Ben Thompson won the huge stakes at cards his old friend Phil Coe arrived in town. Coe was a man of huge proportions, being over six feet four inches tall, and had a brown full beard and mustache. He had served for a time in the Confederate Army. After the war he drifted from one frontier town to another, eventually coming to Abilene and bringing some thousands of dollars with him.

Coe and Thompson combined their resources and opened the Bull's Head Saloon. They purchased expensive equipment; their faro bank was the best that money could buy. Ben's biographer says that "a gold mine could not have been more profitable." However, they were in business only a few weeks. At a meeting in July, the city council permitted the transfer of Phil Coe's license to Tom Sheran. About this time Ben went to Kansas City and Coe devoted his efforts to gambling.

Before Ben left town hard feelings had developed between Wild Bill and Coe. The cause of this friction isn't known. Some of the Texans said Wild Bill permitted crooks to fleece innocent cowboys and shared in the spoils; and that Bill and Phil Coe came to blows in the Gulf House over Jessie Hazel, a beautiful woman of loose morals. Wild Bill's friends say Coe became angry when Bill reprimanded him for cheating at cards and threatened to kill the marshal.

Trouble broke in the evening of October 5th when a group of Texans, who planned to start home next morning, were on a farewell spree. Phil Coe seldom wore a gun, but that evening he put on a six-shooter and joined the boys. The merrymaking began about sunset. The revelers seized Jake Karatofsky and carried him on their shoulders to the Applejack Saloon where they forced him to treat the crowd. Then the boys compelled others to stand treats. They caught some of the citizens, tore off their clothes, and carrying them into a clothing store, fitted them out with a better suit. It was a rough kind of fun, but everyone was in a jovial frame of mind. Then the merrymakers sought Will Bill and found him in a restaurant. He invited them to drink at his expense at the bar of the Novelty Theatre and admonished them to keep within the bounds of order or he would stop their celebration.

At nine o'clock the revelers, numbering about fifty, went west on First Street to Cedar, where a dog tried to bite Coe. He pulled out his pistol and shot the animal. Then the crowd turned north and stopped at the Alamo Saloon, the doors of which were wide open.

Hearing the shot, Wild Bill ran up the alley and entered the saloon through the rear door. Coming to the front he inquired roughly:

"Who fired that shot?"

Coe stood with his revolver in his hand, as did others in the crowd, but no one answered. In response to the marshal's second inquiry, Phil said:

"I fired the shot; I shot at a dog."

Bill drew two revolvers on the Texan. The two men were not over eight feet apart, and both fired simultaneously. Bill shot Coe in the abdomen, exclaiming:

"I've shot too low!"

Coe was a poor marksman. His first shot went through Bill's coat, grazing his side. He fired another which passed between the marshal's legs. Mike Williams, a policeman stationed at the Novelty Theatre, hearing the firing, came running around the corner and down the dark sidewalk for the purpose of assisting Bill. The latter, surrounded by the crowd and standing in the light, did not recognize the policeman and shot him twice, killing him instantly.

Then Wild Bill declared an end to the celebration, ordered the cowboys from the streets, and dispersed the crowds of excited people.

Coe was taken to his cottage in the southwest part of town, where an effort was made to save his life. He lived in great agony for three days. His body was taken to Texas for burial.

The cattle season soon closed, and Wild Bill's services were no longer needed. Under a resolution of the city council, his official connection with the city terminated on December 13th.

Farmers had settled on most of the land around Abilene, and considerable opposition to the cattle trade had developed. Early in 1872 a group of farmers and hostile citizens in town asked the cattlemen not to return. After that they drove their herds to Ellsworth and other markets. The rough element and a considerable number of business men followed the trade.

Ellsworth

The resident population of Ellsworth in cow-town days was about a thousand. The chief business was the trafficking in cattle and trade with the cattlemen. The main street ran along both sides of the railroad, making two streets called North Main and South Main. The business section was approximately three blocks long. The store buildings, mostly one- and two-story frame structures with wooden awnings on the front, lined the outer side of the street and faced the railroad. Here and there structures made of brick had been erected. Board sidewalks were generally in use, though in the spring of 1873 Arthur Larkin constructed a stretch of sidewalk twelve feet wide, made of magnesium limestone, in front of the Grand Central Hotel. It was said that no other town, not even Kansas City, had a sidewalk equal to it.

The location of the leading business houses (commencing at the west end of South Main) was as follows: Drovers Cottage, a three-story hotel equipped with eighty-four nicely furnished rooms, and operated by J. W. and Louisa Gore and M. B. George, who moved part of the building from Abilene in 1872. Beyond: two drovers' supply stores; D. W. Powers's bank; Minnick and Hounson's brick drugstore; and John Bell's Great Western Hardware Emporium, on the corner of Douglas. East of Douglas: Jake New's saloon; John Kelly's American House; Nick Lentz's saloon; Jerome Beebe's big general store; Joseph Brennan's saloon east of Beebe's; and Whitney and Kendall's furniture store a half block east of Lincoln. Whitney was sheriff and was a silent partner in the firm. The railroad station was almost directly in front of Beebe's store.

The courthouse and jail were located on the north side of the railroad two blocks east of Douglas. Near by was the Ellsworth lumberyard. The Grand Central Hotel was on the corner of Lincoln. This building was constructed of a good quality red brick and was said to be the finest and costliest hotel west of the Missouri, excepting in Topeka. The building still stands—the only landmark of longhorn days—and is now called the White House Hotel. In the block west: Larkin's dry goods and clothing store, J. C. Veatch's hotel and restaurant, Bill Nagle's livery barn, a gambling place, the post office; and Seitz's drugstore on the corner of Douglas, advertised as the "oldest established drugstore in western Kansas." George Seitz, the proprietor, was a native of Germany, and for many years was a member of the Ellsworth city council.

The stockyards were located in the west part of town and covered several acres of ground. The yards had seven chutes from which two hundred cars of cattle per day could be loaded. According to the Ellsworth *Reporter,* these yards were the largest in the state in 1872. Colonel R. D. Hunter, favorably known among Texas men, was superintendent of the stockyards in 1872 and 1873.

The first Texas cattle were marketed at Ellsworth in 1869 or 1870. However, figures on the number sold at this point prior to 1871 are not available. In 1871 a total of 35,000 head were shipped, and more than 40,000 were wintered in the county. Ellsworth became the leading market on the Kansas Pacific in 1872. The first three droves of longhorns that season arrived early in June. Two weeks later a total of twenty-eight herds had arrived, and more were on the way. By midsummer more than 100,000 longhorns were grazing around Ellsworth, and cow camps dotted the country side.

The townfolks looked forward to an increase in the cattle trade in 1873. D. W. Powers and Company of Leavenworth opened their bank that spring to care for the financial needs of the cattlemen. The American House was enlarged, remodeled, and refurnished so that the proprietors might better accommodate with "luxury and ease all those fatigued with the toils and labors of the day and especially the Texas drovers upon their arrival at the city after a long and weary journey." J. C. Veatch enlarged and improved his hotel and restaurant. Other merchants painted and polished their establishments. C. H. Freeman and W. B. McClelland opened a theater. Thirteen businessmen secured licenses to sell strong drinks. On March 6th the *Reporter* ventured this prediction:

"Ellsworth will be the liveliest town in Kansas this year."

To which the Leavenworth *Commercial* retorted: "Yes, in flea time."

In April, twenty-eight herds of cattle were on the trail leading to Ellsworth. On May 29th, the local paper announced that 100,000 longhorns had arrived; on June 5th the number was placed at 125,000, and by July the press reported that a total of 177,000 had arrived, and thousands were on the way.

"The great droves cover the hills and knolls, and the valleys are dark with them for miles around," said one writer. Seventy-six cattlemen owned these herds. The roster of drovers included such cattle barons as Colonel O. W. Wheeler, Colonel J. J. Myers, J. M. Day, L. B. Harris, J. L. Driskill, Colonel J. V. Ellison, Alonzo Millett, and Major Seth Mabry, whose names spelled thousands of longhorns, mammoth outfits, and barrels of money in the bank.

The hotels were filled with drovers and their wives, and with buyers from Colorado, Nebraska, Dakota, Wyoming, Missouri, and Iowa. Thousands of cowboys were in and around town.

Noted gamblers and women of flexible morals were there to get their share of the cowmen's money and were ready to start a gun fight if the occasion demanded. Ben Thompson arrived in town about June 1st. A few days later Billy came up the trail with some cattlemen. The brothers put up at the Grand Central Hotel. Ben intended going in the saloon business but found this overdone. By pawning jewelry and borrowing money he got together enough cash to set up gambling tables in Joe Brennan's saloon. The place was known as "gamblers' roost."

Cad Pierce and Neil Cain drove herds up the trail

from Austin and arrived in Ellsworth about the time Ben and Billy got there. Cad was a handsome, well-dressed man about six feet tall, of light complexion, and weighed about 175 pounds. He made a favorable impression on Ellsworth folks. Cain resembled Pierce in physical appearance, but had dark eyes and hair. Cain often dealt monte at Ben's tables, and Cad bucked the board.

John Sterling, James Goodwyn, and other gamblers frequented the gamblers' roost and sat in on the games. Sterling was an erratic fellow who had considerable money and usually won whether the bet was a good one or not. Goodwyn lived at Ellsworth several years and is remembered as a pleasant man who sent and received a lot of registered mail. Something about the man and the big pistol he always carried made the postal clerk tremble every time he saw him coming.

Jennie Field and Mollie Brennan came to Ellsworth in 1872 and were there in 1873. Jennie "fell" for Ben Thompson and Mollie for brother Billy. After Ellsworth lost its glamour Jennie went to Topeka, and Mollie drifted to Texas where she was killed by a bullet intended for Bat Masterson, famous frontier marshal. Alice Chambers, another member of the sisterhood, would be among the host of "forgotten" women had it not been for two incidents: first, she witnessed a murder in Ellsworth's tough district in the fall of 1873, and her testimony has been preserved; second, her body was the last buried on Dodge City's Boot Hill.

The municipal government prepared for trouble. "Judge" James Miller, who had been probate judge, clerk of the district court, and salesman of railroad lands, was mayor. Vincent B. Osborne was police judge. The city council consisted of five businessmen: George Seitz, J. W. Gore, H. D. Stebbins, Andrew Schmidt, and John Kelly; the last-named was elected in June to fill the vacancy created by the resignation of Nick Lentz, saloonkeeper.

Chauncey B. Whitney, a Civil War veteran and an Indian fighter, was county sheriff. Ed O. Hogue, a fearless little Frenchman, who had served a year on Ellsworth's police force, was serving the second year as deputy sheriff. John W. ("Brocky Jack") Norton, one of Wild Bill Hickok's deputies in Abilene in 1871, was city marshal. John ("Happy Jack") Morco, John De Long, John S. Brauham, and Deputy Sheriff Hogue made up the regular police. Happy Jack Morco, an illiterate fellow with a surly disposition, had come from California in the spring of 1873 and claimed to have been an Indian fighter and to have killed twelve white men on the Pacific Coast. John De Long had served with distinction on the Topeka police force. Little is known of Brauham's previous record beyond the fact that he was an experienced gunman.

The police maintained good order considering the number of roughs and transients in town. The most common crimes were violations of the drunk and deadly-weapon ordinances. Judge Osborne tried more than sixty cases in two months.

Most of the lawbreakers were ordinary folks, so the judge must have trembled a little and perhaps turned pale when Ben and Billy Thompson appeared in his court, and in less than three weeks Billy was before him a second time. On the evening of June 10th Ben and Billy and some friends gambled and fought the tiger too hard. Brocky Jack Norton, expecting trouble, occupied quarters in the dance house. Late in the night the Texans tried to gain admittance, and the marshal prevented it. Then they plugged a few wooden clocks, shot signs full of holes, fired a few shots around town, causing unnecessary alarm, and then turned in to sleep. The police arrested Billy and four or five others and brought them before Judge Osborne. Billy was fined $25 and costs. The following day Ben appeared in court, entered a complaint against himself, and paid a $10 fine. Billy got drunk and disturbed the peace again on June 30th. He was arrested by Happy Jack and was fined $10 and costs amounting to $15—a total of $25.

No gun battles or other serious disturbances having occurred, the city fathers decided that a smaller police force could maintain order. Accordingly, they discharged Brauham on July 19th and De Long on August 12th. Then three days later a tragedy occurred which gave Ellsworth the name of being a wild cow town.

Trouble broke on Friday, August 15th. That day a group of noted gamblers were playing cards in Joe Brennan's saloon. The stakes were unusually high. Ben Thompson was present but was not playing. The evidence leads one to conclude that Billy Thompson did not sit in on the game either; but he undoubtedly witnessed it, and he was drinking heavily. Neil Cain was dealing monte, and Cad Pierce was betting. Cad had considerable money and wanted to bet larger stakes than Neil was willing to take. Pierce called to Ben and said:

"Send me a man who will take my overbets on Neil's game." Ben saw John Sterling near by and knew that he bet high and usually won. He called to Sterling:

"Cad wants to bet more than Neil is willing to pull for. If you want the 'extra' you can take it."

Sterling replied:

"Ben, I'll take him for all Neil don't want, but say, Ben, if I win, consider yourself one-half in."

Sterling had been drinking when he started to play. As the game progressed, he continued to drink until he lost control of his better senses. After he had won over a thousand dollars of Cad's money, he put it in his pocket and started off.

About three o'clock in the afternoon Ben accosted Sterling in Nick Lentz's saloon, and in the presence of Happy Jack Morco, the policeman, asked for a settlement on the money won in the card game. This made Sterling angry, and knowing that Ben was unarmed, he struck him in the face. Thompson started for Sterling when Happy Jack stepped up and drew his six-shooter on him. Ben told Jack not to interfere but to mind his own business and take that drunken man away. Happy Jack and Sterling went out on the sidewalk and up the street west toward Jake New's saloon. Thompson went to Brennan's saloon where Cad Pierce and other Texans were loitering. A few minutes later Ben was in conversation with Cad in the back part of the saloon; Sterling and Happy Jack came to the front door, the former armed with a shotgun and the latter with one or more pistols. One of them called out in a loud tone, "Get your guns, you damned Texans, and fight." Then they went up the street and remained somewhere between the saloon and New's corner. This challenge created considerable excitement in the saloon. Ben asked several of the men for a pistol or arms but could not get any, whereupon he ran out the rear door and up the back way to Jake New's saloon, seized his pistol and sixteen-shooting Winchester rifle in the back room, and ran out in front intending to go out on the railroad, where bystanders would not get hit, and fight it out.

At the same time Billy also rushed to New's saloon and grabbed Ben's double-barreled breech-loading shotgun. This gun was a present from Cad Pierce and was worth about $150. The brothers met in front of the saloon. Billy had both barrels of his gun cocked and was handling it rather carelessly. Just then one barrel went off, the charge striking the lower part of the sidewalk near the feet of Major Seth Mabry and Captain Eugene Millett, who were standing in front of the saloon. Ben took the gun from Billy and started to remove the shells when someone said to him:

"Look out, Ben, those fellows are after you!"

Ben handed the gun back and ran to the railroad, followed closely by Billy carrying the shotgun.

Meantime, a crowd had gathered around the door of Lentz's saloon curious to learn the cause of the trouble. John Sterling, Happy Jack Morco, and Brocky Jack Norton were in the saloon. Everyone was excited. Someone hallooed so loud that John Montgomery, Sheriff Whitney's brother-in-law, who was at work in the *Reporter* office across the tracks in the next block, heard him. There was good reason for the excitement. John Sterling had slapped Ben Thompson's face, and he was on the warpath.

When the Thompson brothers reached the railroad near the west end of the depot they stopped. Ben shouted:

"You murdering Texans, get your guns; if you want to fight, here we are."

At this point Sheriff Whitney, who was in front of Veatch's restaurant, tried to quiet the disturbance. He was unarmed and in his shirt sleeves at the time. He walked out to the Thompsons and said:

"Boys, let's not have any fuss or any difficulty."

"We don't want any trouble but will defend ourselves if they want to fight," replied Ben.

"Put up your guns and I will see that you are protected," Whitney promised.

"I am satisfied that you will. We will go to the

saloon and take a drink and get Billy to put his gun away," said Ben.

The three went toward Brennan's saloon, the sheriff walking between the brothers, and engaged in a friendly conversation as they crossed the street. When they reached the saloon Billy went in, followed by Whitney. Ben was in the rear and just as he stepped into the doorway W. A. Langford, a Texas farmer and cowman, who was standing in front of the saloon, shouted:

"Look out, Ben! Here they come with guns!"

Ben whirled around and saw Happy Jack coming on the run down the street toward Brennan's armed with one or two six-shooters. Ben started toward Beebe's store with his Winchester in readiness. The cry of warning created considerable commotion in the saloon. The sheriff rushed out and went toward Beebe's a few steps behind Ben, stopping on the inside of the walk near the mouth of the alley between the saloon and the store, and called out:

"What does all this mean?"

When Jack got along by Beebe's, Ben brought his rifle down on him. Jack yelled, "What the hell are you doing?" and ran into the store. Ben fired at him, hitting the door casing, which probably saved the policeman's life.

Ben had stepped forward until he was about a foot from the east gallery post of Beebe's store, and on the opposite side of the walk and a little in advance of the sheriff. At the moment Ben fired at Jack, Billy came to the door of the saloon, and possibly stepped out on the walk, and fired his gun, hitting Whitney, who was about ten or twelve feet from him. The gun was loaded with buckshot and the charge entered Whitney's right arm, shoulder, and breast. The Thompsons and their friends claimed that the gun went off accidentally; that all three men were looking in the direction of the threatened danger. The local paper and many of the Ellsworth people said that Billy pointed the gun at the sheriff, who made two attempts to get out of the way and said, "Don't shoot; it's Whitney."

As the gun went off Whitney leaned over and screamed:

"Oh! I'm shot."

Then he stood up straight, and the next moment he reeled as though he were fainting, and cried,

"Send for my wife, I have received a bad shot." At the same time Ben yelled to Billy:

"Look, Billy! My God, you shot our best friend!"

The shot attracted quite a crowd. Langford was the first to reach the wounded man. John Montgomery and a score of others rushed up a few moments later. Friends carried the sheriff to his home two blocks north of Brennan's saloon. Everything possible was done to save his life. Two local doctors, Fox and Gregg, attended him, and Dr. William Finlay of Junction City, the post surgeon at Fort Riley, was sent for, but he could not help him. His lung had been pierced, producing an internal hemorrhage. Blood poisoning set in and could not be checked. He lingered three days, dying on Monday morning, the 18th, and was given a Masonic burial. The county coroner, Dr. W. M. Duck, held the inquest the forenoon of his death, at which six witnesses testified.

After the shooting, Ben went across the street to the Grand Central Hotel. Billy went back into Brennan's saloon, out through the rear door, and mounted a horse. The common story is that he appropriated some fellow's cow pony. Montgomery says the horse belonged to Billy and that it was in Sam John's livery stable back of the Grand Central. Neil Cain went after Billy's horse and held it while Billy mounted. He rode to the Grand

Central. Ben met him out in front; Billy remained on his horse, Ben stood on the stone pavement. They exchanged guns. The shotgun was a gift. Ben prized it for that reason, and he preferred it to the rifle, which was a cheap weapon, in case of further trouble on the street that day. Someone handed Billy a pistol. Cad Pierce or Neil Cain thrust a roll of bills, amounting to $100, into his pocket, remarking, "Billy, you'll need this."

Ben urged his brother to go to one of the cattle camps for a few days and await the outcome of the sheriff's wounds. Billy did not seem to sense the seriousness of his situation. Ben is quoted:

"For God's sake, leave town or you will be murdered in cold blood. You have shot Whitney, our best friend."

Billy's reply was, "I do not give a damn; I would have shot if it had been Jesus Christ."

According to the local paper, Billy "then rode slowly out of town cursing and inviting a fight." The court records show, however, that when he rode away from the hotel he did not leave town. Word soon reached Ben that his brother was still in Ellsworth, and he sent Watson Good to urge him to go to one of the cow camps. Billy took time to ride down to Nauchville, the tough district a half mile east of town, to see Mollie Brennan, before he finally left town.

Ben reloaded the shotgun immediately after Billy left and remained at the Grand Central Hotel, retaining his arms for at least an hour. The local press stated that the street was "full of armed men" ready to defend him. The older residents agree that this is an exaggerated statement, though a number of Texans were prepared for battle.

Mayor Miller was at his home during the shooting. He was notified and came down to investigate. Impatient at the delay of the police in making arrests, Miller discharged the entire force, leaving no one but Deputy Sheriff Hogue to make arrests. Then Ben Thompson bargained with the mayor. He agreed to surrender on condition that the mayor would disarm Happy Jack, John Sterling, and others. Miller agreed to these terms and relieved the men of their arms. Hogue received Ben's arms, and thereupon hostilities ceased.

Thompson appeared before the mayor to answer any charges that might be preferred against him. He was released on bond; no one appeared against him, and the case was dismissed.

Some of the citizens formed a vigilance organization for the purpose of ridding Ellsworth of undesirable Texans. The vigilantes adopted a system of warnings called "white affidavits." These were served on the Lone Star men by some member of the clan or by a policeman. Ben Thompson learned about the formation of the committee and went to Kansas City.

A week after the shooting of Sheriff Whitney, Governor Thomas Osborn issued a proclamation describing Billy Thompson and offering a reward of $500 for his arrest and conviction.

Billy went down the cattle trail to Texas and was a fugitive from justice for over three years. For several weeks in the fall of 1876 he was staying at the home of Neil Cain, northeast of Austin, where he was arrested by Captain J. C. Sparks of the Texas Rangers. After an almost endless battle of law and wits, Billy was placed on board a train and started for Kansas in November.

Sheriff Samuel Hamilton of Ellsworth met the party at Salina. Billy was lodged in jail, most of the time at Leavenworth, until he was brought to trial the next September. Robert Gill, a brother-in-law, was in Ellsworth several weeks in the interests of the defense and made many friends. Billy was a friendly fellow and was on his best behavior. The good ladies of Ellsworth became so interested in him that they forgot he was a noted badman and showered him with bouquets of choice flowers and fed him the delicacies of the season. He was acquitted on the ground that the shooting was accidental.

Wichita was a strong competitor for cattle trade in 1873 and received the lion's share of the drive in 1874. Then Ellsworth ceased to be a market. The landmarks of trail days went one by one. The stockyards were removed, fire destroyed some of the buildings, others were torn down. Today only the Grand Central Hotel is standing, but this building has been altered and the name changed.

9

The Kansas Cow Towns

(*Continued*)

Newton

THE Atchison, Topeka and Santa Fe Railroad, building southwest across Kansas, reached the townsite of Newton in July, 1871, and erected stockyards that summer. The town was the "end of the railroad" for several months, and an important market place for Texas longhorns for one season. In those few months the place acquired the reputation of being the bloodiest town in the state.

The main street ran north and south through the center of town. The railroad ran in a southwesterly direction through the townsite, crossing Main Street near Fourth.

The first building on the townsite was moved there in March, 1870, and was used as a blacksmith shop. In April, 1871, the first stack of lumber was unloaded for S. J. Bentley, who arrived early in May and built the Newton House, the first hotel in town. Business houses and homes went up at a rapid rate. The sound of saw and hammer could be heard at all hours of the day and night, including Sundays. By the middle of August two hundred residences had been built or were in process of construction, and a row of frame business buildings lined each side of Main Street in the three blocks north of the railroad. The railroad depot and the post office were the respective termini of the town, and between them about every second building was a saloon or gambling joint. The regular population was about a thousand.

The tough district, known as "Hide Park," was south of the railroad and some distance from the main portion of town. The buildings consisted of five roughly constructed houses, two of which were dance halls. One dance house was kept by Perry Tuttle; the other, the Alamo, was kept by E. P. Krum. They were thirty yards apart, and around them were the other houses. The bar in each dance house was patronized by the dancers upon the conclusion of each dance. The bar realized $2 from each dance, and drinks cost 25 cents each. In one corner of each hall was a gaming table. A half dozen girls were on duty in each dance house.

The stockyards were located about a mile and a half west of town. Early in the spring the railroad company made arrangements with a cattleman living near Topeka to erect and run the stockyards. He employed Joseph G. McCoy to design and build the yards.

There was no village or city organization that summer. Consequently, the citizens had to rely on the township for their government. The two justices of the peace and two constables lived there. One of the constables and the deputy sheriff served as policemen.

The chief business of Newton was trafficking with Texas cattle. McCoy stopped the incoming herds on the prairies near town. By the middle of August two thousand head had been shipped, and it was estimated that before the season closed the shipments would amount to forty thousand. Not less than two thousand

drovers and buyers were in town and in the neighborhood. Cowpunchers were everywhere—on the streets, in
the gambling houses and saloons, and in the establishments in Hide Park.

Roughs, gamblers, homebreakers, murderers, and
courtesans flocked to Newton in large numbers to be
free from the restraints of organized society. That class
outnumbered respectable folks five to two. There were
at least eighty professional gamblers in town, and they
were held in high esteem.

In fact, the liquor and gambling interests ran the
town. There were twenty-seven places where liquor was

sold and eight gambling institutions. The Gold Rooms, operated by Doc Thayer and Bill Pierce, was the most famous and influential of these establishments. Thayer looked more like a preacher than a saloonkeeper. He wore faultless linen, always kept his coat on, and wore his trouser legs outside of his boots. He was decidedly the swell of the town. Pierce was a popular fellow who had been a miner and had owned a large cattle ranch. He had the reputation of getting more business than any other saloonkeeper in the Southwest. Associated with them were six noted gamblers who dealt monte.

This saloon was in a roughly constructed building on the west side of Main Street midway between Fifth and Sixth. Its influence was greater than that of any other house, and sometime or other during the day it came in contact with almost every male inhabitant of Newton.

There was a mania for gambling. With eighty professionals in town and hundreds of cowmen ready to take a chance with their money, gambling establishments did a flourishing business. Some houses operated only one table, others two or three, and so on until the climax was reached in the Gold Rooms with six tables, a mammoth bar, music, and side shows. Every device invented for gambling could be found in these gambling shops—faro, chuck-luck, poker, old sledge, the tobacco box game, and a thousand other devices made to obtain money dishonestly.

The policemen received their pay for police services from a fund raised by the gamblers. This was the only tribute the gamblers had to pay for their privileges. The keeper of a saloon obtained his license from the county for $150.

There was neither a church nor a religious organization in town, so the Gold Rooms opened its doors occasionally for preaching services. In July the Reverend R. M. Overstreet of Emporia was to preach in the Gold Rooms. A horse race and a badger fight were scheduled to take place immediately after the services. A heavy rain prevented all three events.

At an early hour one Sunday evening in September a stranger entered the Gold Rooms, approached the bar and asked for the proprietor, stating that he was a clergyman and would like to have permission to conduct divine services on the premises.

The games were going full blast, crowds stood around the tables, and the voices rose on the night air in discordant and babelic harshness. The fiddlers were squeaking their loudest, the melodeon was growling out its deepest bass, the song-and-dance man was executing one of his most brilliant pirouettes, the waitresses with huge trays loaded with glasses were dodging here and there among the crowd, the two rival dogs of the town were being rubbed and pulled for their third and great fight of the day, and the badger and coons were washing their faces preparatory to starting in when time was called for them.

Divine services amid all this! thought the proprietor, and coughed and expectorated.

"I don't exactly understand; will you repeat the question?"

"I would like your permission to hold divine services here this evening."

The proprietor, seeing an opening for business, answered quickly:

"By all means, sir, we would be most happy to have you preach. When would you like to open up?"

"At eight o'clock, if you please," was the answer. Then the gentleman withdrew.

Here was great news. It traveled down the streets

and into peoples' homes until the whole town knew there was to be preaching in the Gold Rooms. A great crowd had gathered by the time the preacher came.

He had to pass by the bar.

"Say, old chap, let's have a drink," greeted him on all sides. The preacher had a red nose. He disregarded the invitations, but his nose blushed deeper, and he sniffed spasmodically. Someone saw it and was crude enough to call out:

"Don't go back on your spiritual friends, old fellow."

Services began with a prayer. Somebody was playing faro in hard luck. The queen had beaten him three times. He lost again just as the prayer was drawing to a close.

"Damn the luck," broke from the gambler's lips just as Amen followed from the platform. The whole house roared. Someone let the dogs loose, and a dog fight, aided by the barking of the coons, was added to the scene. Nevertheless, the services went on, and hymns and a sermon followed.

The preacher took up a collection, had a drink, and left. A few days later it was learned that he was no preacher at all; merely a hard-up sharper in want of a week's board money.

The first gun battle occurred on June 16th between two cowboys, Snyder and Welch, in front of the liquor house operated by Gregory and Means; Welch was killed. A few days later a man named Irvin, about whom little is known, was accidentally killed in the Parlor Saloon by a pistol shot. About the first of August a young man by the name of Lee was shot and killed in one of the dance halls in Hide Park—accidentally, it was claimed. Another man was killed by being thrown violently from a wagon while drunk.

The big gun fight of the season, known as the "general massacre," in which nine men were shot, took place in August. The trouble began on Friday, August 11th. An election was held on that day in order that the citizens might vote on the proposition of subscribing $200,-000 in county bonds to the Newton and Southwestern Railroad. William Wilson, alias William Bailey, a Texas gambler, who was reputed to have killed two or three men in drunken brawls, served as special policeman at the polls. He was of medium height, had dark-brown hair, and like most gamblers, was well dressed. While on duty at the election he used abusive language. In some way he won the enmity of Mike McCluskie, who was in the employ of the Santa Fe Railroad and for a time had been night marshal of Newton.

About eight o'clock that evening McCluskie met Bailey in the Red Front Saloon, which was located on the east side of Main Street between Fifth and Sixth. Bailey was drunk and asked McCluskie to set up the drinks. The latter refused, whereupon Bailey, with an oath, assaulted him. They exchanged blows. The Texan ran across the street and stood in a crouching position in front of the Blue Front store. At that moment, McCluskie reached the sidewalk in front of the Red Front Saloon and fired two shots. The first bullet missed Bailey and lodged in the door of the Blue Front. The second shot hit the gambler in the right side; the ball plowed through his body and lodged below his heart. He was carried to the Santa Fe Hotel nearby and placed on a bed upstairs. His "lady of the night," having heard of the tragedy, rushed up and followed the men upstairs, crying:

"Oh, my baby! Oh, my baby!"

Bailey died the next morning and was buried on Boot Hill. The townsmen tried to procure a man to offer a prayer at the grave, but no one was accustomed to the business.

McCluskie fled, and no effort was made to find him, for the citizens felt that the shooting was justified.

Bailey was popular among his fellows. A small group headed by Hugh Anderson of Salado, Texas, and consisting of Jim Wilkerson, of Kentucky, and William Garrett, Henry Kearnes, and other Texans, swore to avenge Bailey's death and declared "war" on McCluskie should he ever return to town. Two of these men lived in Anderson's home town. They formulated their plans, and molded the bullets with which they intended to shoot McCluskie.

McCluskie returned to Newton and was there on Saturday night, August 19th. Hearing that he had returned, Anderson came to town with his henchmen and selected Tuttle's dance house as the seat of hostilities. McCluskie was warned that his life was in peril, but thinking himself proof against powder and ball, scorned the warning and went across the railroad tracks to the dance hall.

At this time a tall, young Texan by the name of Jim Martin was boarding at the Santa Fe Hotel. His home was at Refugio, Texas, down near the Gulf Coast. He was a favorite with all the boys. They called him "Good-natured Martin." The night of McCluskie's return he ordered a big helping of eggs and a cup of strong coffee for his supper, wholly unaware of the fact that this would be his last meal. After supper, he went down to Tuttle's. Being Saturday night, there would be a big crowd at the hall, and he would see many of his friends.

It was past midnight. The Alamo was closed. The lights still burned in Perry Tuttle's place, and the sound of music and dancing could be heard, the wicked festivities being still in full swing.

The dance in Tuttle's was prolonged until nearly two o'clock when, the crowd thinning out, the proprietor gave the signal for closing. Then the tragedy began. Mike McCluskie was seated at a gambling table in the corner. One of Hugh Anderson's men sat talking to him evidently for the purpose of distracting his attention in order to allow one of the group to strike the death blow. Other assistants stood back watching and waiting for their leader to enter, their eyes roving alternately from McCluskie to the door. Anderson entered, strode across the room and confronted his victim. His weapon was in his hand, and he began talking. His words came hot and hissing, beginning low and rising with his passion until they were shrieked out:

"You are a cowardly —— — ——; I will blow the top of your head off."

At the same time he fired, the bullet passing through McCluskie's neck. The man rose partially to his feet, and pointing his six-shooter straight at Anderson's breast, pressed the trigger. The cap hung fire, and McCluskie, bleeding profusely and discharging his weapon, fell to the floor. Anderson fired again, stooped, and sent a ball through the back of the prostrate man.

When the shooting began, Jim Martin rushed forward and tried to effect a reconciliation between the parties.

Suddenly Jim Riley, a friend of McCluskie's, entered the hall. He was a quiet fellow about eighteen years of age, and was suffering from a bad case of tuberculosis. For an instant he remained motionless, as if studying the situation. Then a sheet of flame poured from his weapons. Jim Martin was hit in the neck and staggered from the room; he fell dead at the door of

the Alamo. Another and another shot followed until
Anderson and four of his followers were wounded, some
seriously: Hugh Anderson, thigh and leg; Billy Garrett,
arm and internal injury; Henry Kearnes, right breast;
Jim Wilkerson, nose; and another whose name is not
known, wounded in the leg. In the melee, two bystanders were shot. The two lookers-on were railroad men
and were hit by bullets intended for others. One was a
foreman on the track named Hickey. He received a
flesh wound in the leg. The other was Patrick Lee, a
brakeman on the freight train, who was seriously
wounded through the abdomen.

Someone summoned Dr. Gaston Boyd. By the time
he arrived they had taken Martin into the Alamo and
carried McCluskie upstairs in Tuttle's dance hall. Both
dance houses were turned into hospitals, and the girls
nursed the dying and wounded.

McCluskie had received three wounds, any one of
which would probably have proved fatal. He died at
eight o'clock Sunday morning. A telegram was sent to
his mother in St. Louis. Cy Bowman, a well-known pioneer lawyer of Newton, held an inquest over the bodies
of Martin and McCluskie that morning for the county
coroner, Dr. E. B. Allen of Wichita. The jury returned
a verdict that Martin came to his death "at the hands of
some person unknown" and that McCluskie came to his
death "at 8 o'clock A.M., this 20th day of August, by a
shot from a pistol in the hands of Hugh Anderson, and
that the shooting was done feloniously and with intent
to kill McCluskie." As the result of the verdict, a warrant was issued for the arrest of Hugh Anderson, who,
with Garrett, Hickey, and Wilkerson, had been moved
to a room in the rear of Hoff's provision store located
near the Lehman hardware store.

On Tuesday Patrick Lee passed away and was buried in Topeka. That day or the next Garrett died.

Intense excitement prevailed. The city marshal, Harry Nevill, had the warrant for the arrest of Anderson, but didn't serve it because of the condition of the wounded man. The magistrate declared his intention of suppressing the dance halls. The city built a calaboose, and added five men to the police force; one of these was Tom Carson, a nephew of Kit Carson, who had served for a time as first deputy to Wild Bill Hickok, marshal of Abilene. The law-abiding citizens held a meeting and took steps to bring a semblance of order and decency to the town. They nominated Tom Carson and Captain C. B. King "sheriffs." The Gold Rooms opposed the ticket, while the railroad interests supported it. The men rode to victory on the wave of reaction caused by the bloody gun battle.

The police planned to arrest Hugh Anderson as soon as he was able to be moved. Anderson's father was in Newton, and with the aid of friendly citizens, placed the wounded man aboard the train early Monday morning and took him to Kansas City. There he received medical treatment until he was able to travel, when he returned to Texas. He was badly crippled and died a few years later.

The power of the Gold Rooms and the gambling interests was shattered. Early in 1872 James H. ("Pop") Anderson and others decided to clean up the town. They formed a law and order committee at a meeting on Main Street and gave every outlaw twelve hours time to get out of town. One fellow was sick in bed at the National Hotel and was carried on a cot to the train.

In February Newton was organized as a third-class city, and in April the first election of city officers was held. William Brooks, a buffalo hunter, was appointed to the office of city marshal, and Charles Baumann, a native of Germany, was made assistant marshal. These men and their successors cleaned up the town.

The Newton and Southwestern Railroad, a branch of the Santa Fe, was completed to Wichita in 1872 and opened a cattle market closer and more convenient than that at Newton. Wichita became the leading cow town on the Santa Fe and the chief competitor of Ellsworth on the Kansas Pacific.

Wichita

Wichita looked much like the other cow towns, only larger and noisier. In 1874 it was reputed to be the noisiest town on the American continent. The leading business street was Douglas Avenue, which extended from the toll bridge across the Arkansas River east to the Santa Fe Railroad. North Main Street was built up for about two and a half blocks, and there were a few business houses on South Main. Most of the business houses were built of wood, and wooden sidewalks were still used.

The intersection of Douglas and Main was the most important spot in town. Keno Hall—so called because it specialized in the game of keno—was situated on the northwest corner of this intersection. Across the street east was the New York store to which the cowmen came to get fitted out when they arrived in town from the long drive.

There were two well-known hotels in the second block west of Keno Hall—the Douglas Avenue House, where the Pennsylvania now stands, and the Texas House, diagonally across Douglas west of Water Street. The corner east of the Texas House was known as

"Horsethief Corner," and in cow-town days it was a weed patch.

The police court and jail were in the basement of the old courthouse at the corner of Main and First Streets. A huge triangle of iron bars was hanging outside and on this an alarm was sounded when a shooting scrape or other serious trouble occurred.

During the season of 1871 cattlemen drove thousands of head of longhorns to Wichita and kept them on the fine range along the Ninnescah, the Cowskin, and other streams near by in the hope that better prices might be obtained that winter. By June of 1872 the stockyards were completed. The first season the shipments amounted to 4,000 cars, containing upward of 80,000 head of cattle. The traffic in longhorns in 1873 almost equaled that of the previous year. In 1874 Ellsworth dropped out of the picture, and Wichita became the leading northern market. The first herd that year arrived in April and was located on the north fork of the Ninnescah. By midsummer at least 100,000 head were grazing on the fine range to the south and west of town.

A tough district, known as "Delano," was at the west end of the Douglas Avenue bridge and was the seat of much of the wild night life and several of the gun battles. There were two dance halls and a few shacks out there. The dance houses stood side by side. One was run by Joseph ("Rowdy Joe") Lowe and his wife Kate; and the other by John ("Red") Beard.

Rowdy Joe was a short, heavy-set man who had seen plenty of the rough life on the frontier and had engaged in more than one gun fight. Kate was a small handsome woman and had the reputation of being "straight." Joe and Kate were particular about their personal appearance and wore fine clothes.

Red Beard was the opposite type of individual. He was well educated, had been reared in a respectable home in Illinois, and had come to the frontier, evidently, to get away from culture and refinement. He was a large, redheaded fellow, careless in personal appearance, and slow in his walk.

The outstanding gun battle in Delano took place in Rowdy Joe's on a Monday night late in October, 1873. On that night Red Beard and a party of friends were indulging in a drunken frolic in his dance hall. Then they went next door and entered Joe's place, where a dance was in progress. Red's greeting to his neighbor was a shot from his pistol into the crowd, wounding Annie Franklin, a dance girl, who was sick at the time. The firing became general, revolvers and shotguns being used. Rowdy Joe was shot in the back of the neck with a pistol ball, but the wound was not serious. Red was wounded in the arm and hip by buckshot. William Anderson was shot in the head, the ball passing just back of his eyes, blinding him.

Rowdy Joe gave himself up to the police and was released on $2,000 bail. No other arrests were made. Red died a few days later from the effects of his wound. Joe was not prosecuted and continued to run his dance hall.

During the cattle season of 1874 Wichita was a noisy, lawless place. A man named Saunders secured a license to open a variety theater. Professor S. Gessley, the armless wonder, put on daily performances, while near by the child wonder and the freak pig were displayed. A hand organ ground all day long to attract a crowd. Across the street a brass band played from early morning until late at night. An eyewitness describes a night scene:

As the evening approaches the business of the day draws to a close, and the business of another class begins. In one place we find a Negro mounted on a high elevation, picking on his guitar and singing plantation melodies to attract a crowd to an auction room. Saloons are lighted up, the billiard tables are uncovered. Back rooms, though not secreted, are filled with others, who seek a more solid amusement at cards, poker, monte, and faro. In another place we hear a man in a hall on the second floor, calling out loudly the numbers in the game of keno, and going round we find a large hall containing from one hundred to one hundred and fifty players. Large amounts of money, though in small sums, are lost. At about nine o'clock in the evening, the band from the beer garden strikes up, and going round we found a crowd of men and women dancing to the music as it screeches out on the still night air. There is still another class of houses, numbering perhaps twenty or thirty, filled with females. But while these nightly revels are going on, the churches are lighted up, and ministers are preaching within the sound of the keno man's voice."

At least three hundred women and about two thousand transient men, who made easy money, were on hand. William ("Hurricane Bill") Martin and his followers, known as the "Texas gang," spent much of their time in Wichita that spring and summer. Hurricane Bill was known to trail drivers as a cattle rustler and a dangerous badman.

For several weeks Bill and his men terrorized the town. They would ride down the streets shooting and yelling like demons. The citizens were scared to death, and the city marshal, Bill Smith, and his assistants seemed unable to stop the lawlessness.

The night of May 25th, a Texan named Ramsey and a colored hod carrier by the name of Charlie Saunders quarreled, and both were arrested. Ramsey was indignant, and he and his friends planned revenge on the colored fellow. About two o'clock the afternoon of the 27th, while Saunders was attending the masons at work on the Miller building on Main Street, Ramsey walked up and shot him twice, the first shot hitting him in the ear, the second in the breast. The gang was on hand to aid Ramsey. Simultaneously with the shooting, the Texans pulled a dozen revolvers. Marshal Smith was standing near, but being threatened by the drawn weapons, was powerless. While the Lone Star men held off the police and citizens, Ramsey mounted a horse and fled down Main Street, out Douglas Avenue, and across the bridge followed by two or three hundred citizens, who grabbed the nearest weapon that they could get hold of and ran shouting after the fleeing horseman.

Saunders died two days later. This crime aroused the town. The better element organized a vigilance committee or citizens' police, consisting of upward of a hundred men. In this force were Civil War veterans and others who knew how to use firearms.

Late Monday afternoon, July 6th, Sam Botts, a policeman, arrested a Texan for disorderly conduct and carrying concealed weapons and was about to take him to jail when a dozen or fourteen men drew their revolvers on him. The police alarm sounded, and in less time than it takes to tell it, forty or fifty vigilantes, armed with shotguns and Henry rifles rushed to the aid of the officer. Had it not been at the supper hour, a far larger number would have appeared on the scene.

When the tocsin sounded S. M. Tucker was sitting in his law office talking with William P. Campbell, judge of the district court. Tucker kept a shotgun and a rifle in his office ready for action. He grabbed the shotgun and ran out into the street followed by Campbell with the rifle.

The Texans went west on Douglas Avenue and stopped on Horsethief Corner, some of them going into the Texas House. The vigilantes gathered on the opposite side of the street.

Bill Smith tried to persuade the citizens to disperse, telling them that if any arrests were made some of the townsmen would be killed. Tucker came up about this time and overheard the marshal's remarks. He said:

"This is the third time I've been out on this kind of call, and we have never made an arrest. I don't care for trouble; I am used to it. Point out the man you want arrested, and I'll arrest him, kill or get killed."

"All right, arrest Hurricane Bill," replied Smith.

A complete silence came over the opposing groups. As Tucker cocked one barrel of his gun, the sound could be heard distinctly by everyone. He stepped into the street, and leveling his gun at Hurricane Bill, said quietly:

"William, I want you; you are under arrest."

The Texan started to raise his revolvers. The lawyer shouted:

"Lay down those guns!"

"You can have me," was Bill's reply, as he dropped his two revolvers; one cocked, the other of the self-action type. He remarked later that the barrels of the shotgun leveled at him looked as big as stovepipes.

"Walk over to the police station," commanded Tucker.

The badman obeyed. When the Texans saw their leader surrender they became panicky, and many of them dropped their guns. For a week after this episode searchers found revolvers in the weed patch on Horsethief Corner. Before the gang could recover from the shock and get ready for action, the citizens lined up fifteen or twenty and marched them over to the police station where Judge Jewett fined the group and sentenced Hurricane Bill to jail.

The roughs acted peaceably during the remainder of the cow-town period. There was drunkenness and disorderly conduct, but no gross defiance of the law.

By 1876 settlers had homesteaded or purchased most of the land in south central Kansas, and the legislature changed the boundaries of the quarantine line so that Sedgwick, Sumner, and other counties in that section were included in the prohibited area. The Texas cowmen drove their herds to Dodge City, the newly opened market in southwestern Kansas that season.

Dodge City

For ten years Dodge City was the leading Texas cattle market of the plains. During that decade Dodge gained the reputation of being the wickedest town in the country. While this rating is unjust, a combination of circumstances gave Dodge this name. It began as a rail town in the buffalo country and had the longest cow-town history of any Kansas market. Furthermore, a publicity man advertised Dodge's tough features, her bad men and worse women, her good whisky and swell gambling joints. Then, too, magazine writers and representatives of eastern dailies broadcasted the town's wickedness.

Dodge City had a resident population of about 1,200 when it became a cow town. Main Street ran along the railroad. Most of the buildings were on the north side, though a few were south of the tracks. There were six or seven general stores, the largest of which, Charles Rath and Company, did a quarter of a million dollar retail trade a year; four or five hotels; nineteen saloons; and the usual number of drugstores, bakeries, and butchers found in a frontier town of that size.

An editor, who visited Dodge in the early years of the cattle trade, left a description of the town:

The buildings were of such varying and irrelevant patterns, and so lacking in neighborliness of size and altitude, that one was justified in wondering if they had not been bought at auction. Few of them boasted any underpinning, and many of them sat dizzily perched upon awkward cornerprops, as if fearing a flood. There were no fences, and hence no dooryards; no trees and no awnings, and therefore an unchecked excess of sunlight. Above the town, a spray of sandy loam blew northward in frequent and rapid whirlwinds, and settled with a sort of resentful disdain about the overlooking cupola at the center of the public square ("the park," by courtesy), which proved to be the ambitious top of a structure designed to serve in time the purpose of a courthouse, but contenting itself for the present with the humbler, though more popular, uses of a shooting gallery. Here and there, too, tents were pitched, with blankets spread upon the guy-ropes; and opposite our hotel, a railroad freight-car, shorn of its wheels and squatting in the dust, abjectly besought patronage with a placard announcing "Meals at all hours."

Of the four or five hotels, the Dodge House run by Deacon Cox was the favorite with the cattlemen. The buyers and the stockmen stopped at this hotel where, according to one guest, "a man can, in fifteen minutes, hear more about 'cutting out,' 'rounding up,' etc., than he can in such small towns as Chicago or St. Louis in a lifetime." A newspaperman who registered at this hotel one morning remembered the scene:

Just as we saw him last summer, just as handsome, just as happy, sits Uncle Mitch. A stranger sometimes addresses him as J. L. Mitchener Esq., but strangers to Uncle Mitch are getting very scarce. Here, too, is Ike Johnson, and Oburn and Captain Littlefield, and the famous Jim Reed, all listening to the cattle gospel as expounded by Uncle Mitch in this his forty-second year as a "buyer."

We now learn that everybody not at the Dodge House is at the "Alamo." The Alamo is presided over by a reformed Quaker from New York, and it is hinted that the manner in which he concocts a toddy (every genuine cattleman drinks toddy) increases the value of a Texas steer about $2.75.

J. L. Mitchener was the senior partner in the firm of Mitchener and Son, commission men at Kansas City. He was a native of Pennsylvania, the son of a livestock man, and schooled in the business from early boyhood.

Some of the most noted peace officers on the frontier served Dodge City in its cow-town days. Charles E. Bassett and W. B. ("Bat") Masterson were county sheriffs, and Ed Masterson, Luke Short, William ("Bill") Tilghman, Wyatt Earp, and others made up the town's police. The exploits of these men have been told and retold until their names are almost household words throughout America.

Early in 1876 the railroad company erected stockyards which were described as the largest west of St. Louis. "The railroad denoted the boundary of the town proper on the south," wrote a visiting journalist, "and thence spread a succession of yellow pine-board pens filled with cattle—antlered, uneasy, alien-looking cattle—out over the level bottom-land pen after pen, until the boards became shadows, and all that was left was a queer, sinister perplexity of uplifted and tossing horns." In the early eighties the railroad built new yards over two miles in length and put in five switches on the south and four on the north side of the track to handle the livestock.

When the yards were first erected the railroad company employed A. H. Johnson, well known among Texas men, as general stock agent, and J. Herbert Phillips as local railroad agent. One writer said of Phillips, "Everywhere you go you meet Phillips. Phillips is the A. T. & S. F. Agent. He loads, brands and ships all the cattle, gives everybody a pass that wants one (or talks him into not wanting one), knows everybody, is personally acquainted with every beef, bull, steer or cow between this place and the Rio Grande, can take a drink and is never busy." Considerable credit is due these two men for the success of the market at Dodge City.

Early in 1876 some Texas cattlemen blazed a trail to Dodge City. In April the first herds, driven by Dewees and Ellison, Millett brothers, Jerry and Noah Ellis, Bishop and Head, and others, started up the trail. That year 30,000 head were shipped east over the Santa Fe. Thousands were sold locally, were driven out, or were put in winter quarters.

The following spring, the town got ready for a busy season. In April the local paper announced that "places of refreshment are being gorgeously arrayed in new coats of paint and other ornaments to beguile the festive cowboy." Messrs. Hutchinson, Bassett, and Campbell went down the trail to direct the leading herds to Dodge. The first herd arrived early in May. On the 26th the press reported that forty herds were on this side of the Washita and would reach Dodge early in June. A month later there were upward of 100,000 head of cattle in the immediate vicinity of the town. As far as the eye could reach, for miles up the river, longhorns dotted the velvety green carpet.

Nearly a hundred purchasers made their headquarters in the town. On one June day, 25,000 head changed hands. One writer said, "everybody is buying and selling. Everything you hear is about beeves and steers and cows and toddies and cocktails." The Kansas City *Times* called Dodge City the "greatest bovine market in the world."

For the next seven or eight years Dodge continued to be the longhorn metropolis of America, and each year received a lion's share of the northern drive, which ranged from 250,000 to 400,000 annually.

In the cattle season daily life in Dodge ran about as follows: The town awoke late in the morning and remained surprisingly quiet all the forenoon, and with but few interruptions the general lethargy continued well on into the afternoon. Then the scene changed and the excitement began. One visitor says that Dodge "wakes from her slumber about 11 A.M.; takes her sugar and lemon at 12, a square meal at 1 P.M., commences biz at 2 o'clock, gets lively at 4 and at 10 P.M. it is hip-hip-hurrah 'till 5 o'clock in the morning." An editor who visited the place noted the quietness during the day but with the first approach to darkness the town "rubbed its eyes" and "leaped to its feet," and in a twinkling Main Street was a "carnival of light, and motion, and music. The broad board sidewalks were crowded with promenaders; milling groups passed in and out of the drinking-saloons and gambling-places; in every quarter glasses clinked and dice rattled (is there another sound in the world like that of shaken dice?); violins, flutes and cornets sent out eager, inviting strains of waltz and polka from a score or more establishments, and a brass band was playing patriotic airs in front of the theater, where, oddly enough, the crude morality of 'Ten Nights in a Bar-Room' was about to be presented, 'with the full strength of the company in the cast.' Everywhere the cowboys made themselves manifest, clad now in the soiled and dingy jeans of the trail, then a suit of many-buttoned corduroy, and again in affluence of broad-cloth, silk hat, gloves, cane, and sometimes a clerical white neck-tie. . . . But as the night sped on, the festivities deepened, and the jovial aspect of the picture began to be touched and tainted with a subtle, rebuking something which gradually disclosed the passion, the crime, the depravity, that really vivified and swayed it all, and made it infernal. The saloons became clamorous with profanity and ribald songs and laughter. . . ."

Men quarreled over cards or more often over women and settled their dispute on the spot with fists or guns, or they waited until the next day to settle it. A quarrel of the latter type took place in November, 1877. Bob Shaw had lost $40 and was sure that Texas Dick had taken it. The two met in the Lone Star Dancehall. Shaw accused Dick of stealing the money and trouble began. Someone went for Assistant Marshal Ed Masterson, who hurried to the scene. When Masterson arrived, Shaw was standing by the bar with a pistol in his hand ready to shoot Texas Dick. Not wishing to hurt Shaw, Masterson ordered him to put away his gun. Shaw refused, and the officer tapped him on the head. Shaw then turned his gun on the officer and shot him, the ball striking a rib and passing around under the shoulder blade paralyzing his right arm. Masterson fell, but grasping the pistol in his left hand, fired at Shaw, hitting him in the left arm and leg. During the melee, Texas Dick was shot in the right groin, making a painful wound, and Frank Buskirk, a curious onlooker, standing in the doorway, received a ball in the left arm. Fortunately no one was killed.

In the following April, Ed Masterson, who had been promoted to the office of marshal, engaged in a gun battle with Texas men and lost his life. A party of six cowboys came to town and enjoyed themselves with dancing and drinking at the Lady Gay Dancehall on the south side. Jack Wagner, consuming more liquor than was good for him, became noisy. Marshal Masterson noticed he carried a six-shooter and disarmed him, turning the pistol over to Wagner's boss, A. N. Walker.

The dance progressed peacefully for a time when the marshal stepped out on the sidewalk. He met Wagner and found him again in possession of the pistol. He attempted to take it. There was a general rush of men to the sidewalk. Policeman Nat Haywood tried to come forward to assist the marshal, but two cowmen drew their pistols and held him.

At that moment Wagner placed his pistol against the side of the city marshal's abdomen and fired, tearing a large hole in his body and setting his clothes on fire. Five other shots followed in quick succession. Wagner and A. N. Walker were seriously wounded. Men ran from the scene, and all was over.

Marshal Masterson walked across the street, and entering Hoover's Saloon, said to George Hinckle, "George, I'm shot," and sank to the floor. He was carried to his brother Bat's room, where in a half hour he died.

Jack Wagner ran into Peacock's Saloon and fell on the floor; friends carried him away. He died the next day.

Walker ran through Peacock's place and fell some distance in the rear of the building. He was carried to a room over Wright, Beverly and Company's store where he lay between life and death for several days, but eventually recovered.

Most of the noted gun fighters of the old West visited Dodge at some time or other. Clay Allison, the fighting cowman of the Washita, was the most spectacular. Clay killed only badmen, so he said, who needed killing for the good of society. It is not known how many men he killed. The estimates range from less than twelve to eighteen.

He is described as a "fine-looking man" six feet two inches tall who weighed about 175 pounds and had black hair and a mustache and beard of the same color. He had dancing blue eyes which seemed to look through one. He seldom laughed, but smiled pleasantly when he was not wrought up over something. He was shot but once; that time he shot himself accidentally in the right instep. This caused him to walk with a limp.

Allison was born and reared in Wayne County, Tennessee. He served in the Confederate Army as a member of Company F, 9th Regiment of Tennessee Cavalry. The last two years of the war he was a scout for Generals McCulloch and Forrest.

He was captured, tried, condemned as a spy, and sentenced to be shot. He had a small hand. The night before he was to be executed the smallness of his hand enabled him to slip off the handcuffs. He killed the guard and escaped.

After the war he removed to Texas and located on a ranch in Hemphill County, and later lived in Colfax County, New Mexico.

One time Allison drove a herd of steers to Cheyenne and sold them at a good profit. He was suffering from toothache, so went to a dentist. The dentist thought he was a green cowboy with a lot of cash. Instead of relieving the pain in the aching tooth, he drilled

a hole in a sound tooth, and worse than that, broke half of the tooth off. Clay left the office and went to another dentist, who repaired the damage for $25. He was boiling with rage by this time. Rushing back to the quack's office, he seized a pair of forceps, threw the man on the floor and drew one of his best molars. Not content, he grabbed for another and caught one of the front teeth and a piece of the man's upper lip; he was tugging at it when the man's shrieks attracted a crowd, and the matter ended.

While Allison was still living on the Washita, he came to Dodge for supplies and wore his guns on the streets in violation of the city ordinance.

"Check in your pistols," ordered the city marshal.

"It'll be as much as my life is worth to lay them off for one hour," protested Clay.

The officers decided that he must obey the law. When they reported their decision, he said:

"Gentlemen, when these pistols go off they will go off smoking."

They decided not to press the matter.

Allison was killed in the summer of 1887 when he fell from a loaded wagon. He fell between the wheels, and the rear wheel ran over his neck, breaking it.

The Kansas legislature passed a new "tick law" in 1883, which moved the "dead line" westward and included Dodge City in the quarantine district, and two years later prohibited the driving of Texas cattle into the state. Then Dodge City ceased to be a cattle market; but to the old trail drivers the town will always be the "Capital of Cow Land," and when they hold their annual powwow they never tire of telling stories of that famous place during its glamorous days.

The Trail That Runs Around
the World

WHEN Lead Steer arrived at Abilene at the
head of his herd, he might well have said to the drover:
"You have reached the end of your trail. You can
put up in comfortable quarters in Drovers Cottage and
take life easy for several weeks before you return home.
My trail leads to the end of the world. In a few weeks
I will be prodded into a cattle car with seventeen or
eighteen other longhorns. Then we will be transported
down the Kaw and run through a packing plant, and
eventually our flesh will strengthen the bodies of English peasants or will give the Bashi Bazouk fresh courage
for chopping up Christians and carrying out the dic-
tates of his Koran." Maybe Lead Steer did say this in
cow language. If so, this narrative will reveal how
wisely he spoke.

Joseph McCoy shipped the first trainload of Texas
cattle, consisting of twenty cars, from Abilene in September, 1867. He invited guests from Illinois, Missouri,
and Kansas—beef packers, cattle dealers, railroad officials, and their wives and daughters—to see the shipment. They arrived in the evening of the appointed day
on a special train. Several large tents, including one for
dining purposes, were ready for the guests. They saw

a train full of cattle weighed and loaded, and then in the great tent they celebrated the event with a feast. The tables were loaded with the best food that could be provided, and it was cooked to perfection by Mrs. Tim Hersey and other women of Abilene. The best chefs couldn't improve on their cooking. As "Boss" of the dining room at the stage station, Mrs. Hersey had got meals for more than one bigwig. She cooked a "square meal" for Bayard Taylor when he was in the West and is reputed to have satisfied the hunger of Horace Greeley when he made his journey across the plains. They devoured the food with a relish peculiar to outdoor life, after which wine was served and speeches were made until a late hour. The speakers outdid themselves in their praise of Abilene and its future as a cattle market. An elderly gentlemen named W. F. Tomkins made an impromptu and witty speech that evening, and as a result received the sobriquet of "Almighty Dollar." Joseph McCoy afterward employed him to locate the Texas herds on eligible grazing grounds as fast as they arrived at Abilene.

McCoy, describing this event, says:

Before the sun had mounted high in the heavens on the following day, the iron horse was darting down the Kaw Valley with the first train load of cattle that ever passed over the Kansas Pacific Railroad, the precursor to many thousands destined to follow. This train of cattle was sold in Chicago to a speculator at a small profit to the shipper.

McCoy made the second shipment, consisting of nearly 900 head, a few days later. He didn't find a buyer at Chicago, so he forwarded the shipment to Albany; there he sold the cattle, which cost about $17,500 for $300 less than the freight bill.

A number of things were against the success of the market at Abilene. There was a strong prejudice in the East against Texas cattle. The beef wasn't considered eatable and was as unsalable in the eastern markets as the flesh of prairie wolves would have been. Most of the drovers were careless about the kind of cattle they brought to market. They drove everything that was gathered and included old, thin animals. Since there had been no market for Texas cattle for so many years, the ranchers owned a lot of old stock. If horns, legs, and age had been removed there wouldn't have been much left of some of these critters. The season of 1867 was one of excessive rainstorms. The rains caused an immense growth of grass that was too coarse and washy to be good food. Because of the storms the cattle stampeded easily and ran off the little tallow on their ribs. As a result, most of the arrivals at Abilene were unfit for marketing purposes. Furthermore, a corn crop failure in Ohio, Indiana, and Illinois forced thousands of head of northern cattle on the market and caused it to sag. The market continued to decline until midwinter.

Despite these impediments, almost a thousand carloads, or twenty thousand head, were shipped down the Kaw. All except seventeen cars were sent by way of Leavenworth, over the Hannibal and St. Joseph Railroad, to Chicago where they were packed largely on the owners' account.

During the winter of 1867-68 McCoy put on an intensive advertising campaign, expending $5,000 to tell Texans about Abilene. The Texas newspapers published his circular letter, and every office, business house, and hamlet in the state was the recipient of one or more of his letters.

By spring the cattle market had recovered, and there were prospects for a good year. Thirty days before the first herds reached Abilene, quite a delegation of buyers were at the Drovers Cottage. Illinois grazers purchased about twenty thousand head and shipped them down the Kaw to pastures during the month of June, and buyers from the territories took several thousand head. Then an outbreak of Texas fever caused excitement throughout the North, and the bottom fell out of the market.

A firm in Chicago had gone to Texas and contracted with large drovers to deliver about forty thousand head of cattle on the Mississippi River at the mouth of the Red River. Upon delivery the cattle were crowded on the hot, unventilated decks of large steamboats and sent up the river to Cairo, Illinois, where they were shipped by rail to Tolono, Illinois. There they were unloaded and turned on the prairies with the domestic animals. Many of the longhorns were sold to feeders, and some went into Indiana. In less than thirty days the domestic cattle began to die. Nearly every cow around Tolono died. Grazers became alarmed and sold their cattle. Domestic beeves which had been exposed were shipped east and spread the disease. A panic throughout the northern cattle market and a feeling of hostility toward southwestern cattle resulted.

The governor of Illinois called a convention in Springfield. Delegates came from most of the northern states, and two or more from Canada. Texas was not represented. Most of the delegates were prejudiced and wanted to deal a deathblow to the Texas cattle trade. The convention recommended the enactment of prohibitory legislation. This recommendation formed the basis of legislation enacted by several of the northern states the following winter.

The market broke in July. Those drovers at Abilene who had not sold began to talk of driving to other points. The owners of mixed, or stock, cattle, for which there was little or no demand, were especially uneasy. The cattle interests decided to hold semi-monthly public sales of stock cattle at the stockyards. A supply of handbills, dodgers, etc., announcing the sale, were issued and young men went by train over western Missouri and Iowa, eastern Nebraska, and Kansas to distribute them. Regarding the first auction the Junction City *Union* said:

At the stock sale of Abilene, a few days ago, five hundred head were disposed of. The large sized work cattle averaged thirty dollars per head, and cows twelve dollars per head, 2-year-olds ten dollars per head. A large number of bidders were present from four States. The sales will hereafter occur semi-monthly, E. H. Gaylard, salesman. The next one comes off on the 5th of August.

The auctioneer at this sale was the "irrepressible" Ed Gaylard who, each spring for a succession of years, opened at Abilene a cattleman's livery barn containing a hundred or more stalls and known as the "Twin Barn." Rarely was an applicant turned away unaccommodated. No matter what he thought he wanted Gaylard had it or convinced the customer that the available accommodations were what he really wanted. If the applicant was overparticular, the liveryman would manage sooner or later to get him on the back of a "gentle" Spanish pony which was noted for ability to throw its rider. When the man landed on the ground, the irrepressible Ed would swear he had bought the pony from a preacher who recommended the animal as being gentle enough for any woman or child to ride.

Before the fifth of August, the date set for the second sale, every herd of stock cattle was sold, but there were twenty-five or thirty thousand head of grown beeves for which there were no buyers. The cattle dealers conceived the plan of sending east a carload of wild buffalo, covering the side of the car with advertisements of the cattle.

They strengthened the frame of a stockcar by bolting thick planks to the sides. Then they put the camp outfit and supplies in one car and a half dozen well-trained cow ponies in another. The party, consisting of four Texas cowboys, M. A. Withers, Jake Carroll, Tom Johnson, and Billy Campbell, and two California Spaniards, all experts with the lasso, went to Fossil Creek siding near the present site of Russell where the cars were put on a side track, the horses unloaded, and camp pitched. After dinner the men saddled their ponies and started out in search of buffalo. They soon came upon a large old bull, and circling around started him in the direction of the railroad. When he was within a few hundred yards of it, the Spaniards made a dash for the animal and threw their lariats around his neck. The animal was furious and charged first at one and then the other of the men who, by means of strategy, got him close to the stockcar. Then the men threw a third lasso around his hind legs, and in a moment he was lying helpless upon the ground. When he ceased to struggle they tied his legs together securely, and took the lassos off. Next they adjusted the inclined plane and got a block and tackle ready, one end being attached to the animal's head and the other to the top of the opposite door. In a few minutes the bison was aboard the car. The men bound his head to a post of the car frame, and removed the ropes from his feet. He lay and sulked for hours. In two days ten full-grown bull buffaloes were captured, but four of them died of heat and anger. Three became sullen and lay down some distance from the car, so but three were got aboard in good condition.

Those in charge hung a large-sized canvas, upon which was painted an advertisement, in striking colors, of the cattle near Abilene, upon each side of the car; then sent it down the Kaw to Chicago by way of St. Louis. The car attracted considerable attention and caused much newspaper comment. When the car arrived at Chicago, the buffalo were taken to the Fair Grounds where Withers, Campbell, and the Spaniards roped them again to show the people how it was done. These animals were presented to Professor John Gamgee, an English veterinary surgeon, who sent their mounted hides to London.

This advertising feat was followed by an excursion of Illinois cattlemen to the Kaw. The party went out to Sheridan, "the end of the railroad," and upon returning to Abilene was shown the herds of cattle. Some of the excursionists decided to invest, and before long the market became active. When the season closed two-thirds of the year's drive had journeyed down the Kaw in cattle cars, and most of the balance was disposed of in some other way. In McCoy's words, "Texas cattle became suddenly very popular and those of suitable size and quality outsold the shorthorns of the same weight. It was held that a fat Texan was better for packing purposes than a native, that their meat was 'marbled,' that is, the fat distributed in alternate layers with the lean fiber and when cut presents the appearance of variegated marble."

The legislature of Illinois met that winter and narrowly missed dealing the deathblow to the Texas cattle trade. The senator from the Danville District, which had been hardest hit by Texas fever, was elected and especially deputed to secure the passage of an act totally prohibiting the introduction of Texas cattle into the state. He introduced a bill prohibiting southern cattle at all times of the year and under all circumstances from passing through Illinois on foot or by rail. Since all railroads to eastern markets ran through the state, the passage of this bill would have meant the end of the Texas trade. Joseph McCoy worked vigorously to defeat the bill. Finding that it couldn't be defeated, the opponents secured the adoption of an amendment which took the teeth out of the measure. The amendment permitted wintered southern cattle to come into the state at any time. The evidence that the cattle had been wintered should be the certificate of any officer "bearing seal."

This prolonged battle of the solons served to advertise Abilene and longhorns, and aided rather than hindered the Texas trade. More buyers than ever appeared in Abilene in the spring of 1869 and began buying herds of good beeves at from $25 to $35 per head. Eastern buyers were afraid to invest at first because of the Illinois law but soon found that practically every cow around Abilene four or five years old had been "wintered" north of Texas. A notary public, with an empty pocketbook and an easy conscience, who was on hand to issue the necessary certificates for a small consideration, was responsible for the large number of certified beeves.

By 1870 the Texas cattle trade was an established industry in the Kaw country. Abilene was still the leading shipping point though markets had been opened at Solomon, Salina, Brookville, and Ellsworth.

Two major disasters occurred in the years 1871 to 1873. Fully six hundred thousand head of cattle arrived in western Kansas in 1871. Since the animals were poor in flesh and there were few buyers, half the season's drive were put in winter quarters, most of them having been driven west into the buffalo-grass region.

Scarcely had the herds arrived in the short-grass country when a severe rainstorm set in, followed by a cold wind which froze ice two and three inches thick. A furious gale blew for three days and nights. Many men and horses froze to death, and thousands of cattle perished. The winter was a severe one. It is estimated that several hundred cow ponies and a quarter of a million head of cattle died before spring. Wealthy cattlemen were bankrupted by losses which mounted into millions of dollars.

The cattlemen recovered some of these losses the following year and entered 1873 with rosy prospects. A season could scarcely have opened with a brighter outlook and closed with deeper gloom for everyone connected with the cattle industry. In the first place, buyers didn't appear in large numbers because of a short corn crop. Then the financial crash came upon the country.

About the middle of September the livestock men held a mass meeting at Kansas City for the purpose of bringing northern and southern cattlemen together; if possible, to do something about the drooping market; and to form an association. The meeting opened with a banquet and nearly two thousand cattlemen were seated at the table when an amusing incident occurred.

An unshaven, long-haired, roughly dressed cowboy from New Mexico had obtained a seat at the banquet table. He had heard of the exhilarating effect of pure wine but had never tasted the stuff. As soon as he was seated he grabbed a quart bottle of champagne.

"What's this hur trick—I guess I'll try the critter." Popping the cork he poured half the contents down his throat without stopping. Then he hesitated for a moment.

"This hur stuff is too damned thin, it won't make

nobody drunk; I could drink the Gulf of Mexico if it was like this and not be drunk neither."

Then guzzling the balance of the quart, he reached for a second bottle which he was uncorking when the effect of the first bottle seemed to reach his brain. With eyes sparkling he arose to his feet; then jumped about two feet in the air, brought his huge fist down on the table, and screamed in tones not unlike the war whoop of a Comanche:

"I'm a cow puncher from New Mexico, by God. I'm just off the Chisholm Trail—wild and woolly—and I don't care a damn. I can whip any shorthorn — — — — in America, by God." All the while he jumped up and down; his long uncombed hair hung in a profused mass over his face, and his eyes shot forth piercing glances. Fortunately he was unarmed.

After quiet had been restored, the banquet went on, followed by addresses by the governor of Missouri and other men prominent in the West and Southwest. At the meeting the following evening an organization was formed under the name "The Live Stock Men's National Association," and officers elected, but because of the panic efforts to extend the organization were suspended.

The financial crash reached the West in October and paralyzed every form of business. The cattlemen, most of them already in debt, were unable to borrow money and consequently were forced to put large numbers of cattle on a marekt that was already drooping. Most of the drovers, traders, and shippers lost heavily, and scores were bankrupted. The owners put at least forty per cent of their cattle in winter quarters in western Kansas or drove them into Colorado. They killed thousands of head and made them into tallow.

Despite the reverses, there were bright spots. A decrease in the northern drive and a slight decline in the carloadings followed each disaster. In the eight seasons closing with 1874, the Kansas Pacific transported approximately nine hundred thousand head of cattle. Furthermore, the Santa Fe reached central Kansas in 1871, and in 1873 and 1874 carried nearly a hundred thousand longhorns annually to the banks of the Kaw where two-thirds or more were delivered to the Kansas Pacific for transportation to Kansas City.

By this time native cattle, hogs, and sheep had become a factor in the flow of livestock to the mouth of the Kaw. In most of the towns the stockyards handled both local and Texas stock, and the records do not always distinguish longhorns from shorthorns.

The first native cattle came to the Kaw on foot behind the wagons of the settlers. Here they reached a cows' paradise. They grew fat on the nutritious grasses that carpeted the country. From time immemorial these grasses had sustained immense herds of buffalo. In the words of an early report of the Kansas Board of Agriculture:

Our plains are the native land of the bovine race, and they will continue to sustain it. We only make a slight change when we substitute domestic cattle for the buffalo. The latter, under the persecution of Indians, hunters and sportsmen, will in a few years be extinct. The former will multiply indefinitely. The railway is fatal to the buffalo, but fosters the domestic herd.

When the advance guard of longhorns marched from the Red River to the Kaw there were approximately two hundred thousand head of native cattle in Kansas. In the early years of the trade the ratio in the receipts at Kansas City was four Texan to one native.

The number of cattle on Kansas farms and ranches increased to nearly a million head in the next decade, and to three millions in recent years, placing Kansas third among the states for number and value of cattle within its boundaries. The percentage of native beeves on the Kansas City market gradually became larger, and after 1880 they began to figure conspicuously in the offerings. In the middle eighties the drives from the Red River ceased, and the Texas stock on the Kaw soon lost their southern characteristics.

Other farm animals made even greater increases in numbers, and at an early date bleating sheep and squealing pigs joined the bawling cows in the ever-growing procession that traveled down the Kaw. The receipts at Kansas City between 1871 and 1881 increased as follows: cattle, from 120,827 to 285,863; hogs, from 41,096 to 1,014,384; sheep from 4,527 to 79,924; horses and mules, from 809 to 12,592.

Kansas City was not equipped to feed or market any large number of livestock when the first contingent of longhorns was transported over the Kaw route. At that time the Missouri Pacific had yards large enough to accommodate only ten cars of stock. With the exception of seventeen cars, the cattle shipped from Abilene in 1867 went by way of Leavenworth to Chicago. Since Leavenworth manifested little desire to retain the trade, the Texas cattle shipments went to Kansas City the following year. The Hannibal and St. Joe Railroad built small yards in 1870. The moving spirit in this enterprise was Colonel L. V. Morse, at that time superintendent of the railroad. He mapped off and fenced in five acres of ground, divided it up into eleven pens, and put in a small pair of Fairbanks scales. These two yards were inadequate to handle the growing business.

Consequently, in the spring of 1871 a joint-stock

company was formed for the purpose of erecting and operating feed and transfer yards. The company secured a suitable tract of land on the east bank of the Kaw, erected yards covering 26 acres, and built a small Exchange Building. The yards provided ample room for 7,000 head of cattle and 6,000 head of hogs at one time, and in case of emergency 50 per cent more could have been taken care of. The stock drank water fresh from the Kaw conducted through underground pipes to troughs in each pen.

In 1876 the company enlarged the yards, erected a fine barn and sheds for horses and mules; built a race track with covered amphitheater; put in four 60,000-pound scales; and constructed a new Exchange Building, a three-story structure fitted up with commission men's offices, a restaurant, and two bank rooms. The yards covered a hundred acres.

For the better protection of native cattle, those in charge erected quarantine yards for "through" Texas cattle in 1886 on the west bank of the Kaw and built a bridge across the stream.

In order to take care of the growth through the years, the company has erected new buildings, walled the Kaw River to reclaim wasteland, and enlarged the yards. Today the area of the stockyards property is 238 acres. The nine-story Exchange Building provides quarters for commission firms, telegraph companies, railroad companies, a national bank, the livestock exchange, and other enterprises allied with the livestock industry.

The industry has had its ups and downs in the past fifty years. The prices of cattle and hogs were high in the early eighties and then dropped, reaching a low mark in the latter part of the decade.

The farmers and ranchers blamed the packers for

the declining prices. The politicians took up the cry, and a Congressional committee investigated the matter. The packers maintained that overproduction of livestock was the cause of the low prices; that men ignorant of the cattle industry had stocked large ranches and put big herds on the range; then they had gone broke and flooded the market with cattle.

The financial crash in the nineties hit the livestock industry hard and bankrupted many substantial cattlemen. For instance, a successful cowman who owned a 50,000-acre ranch in Kansas and 100,000 acres in Texas, had lent large sums to friends who were unable to repay the loans. He was forced to mortgage his property and eventually lost both ranches.

The recent depression and drought has slowed down the movements of livestock in the central West and Southwest. The receipts at Kansas City dropped each year from 112,977 cars in 1929 to 65,897 in 1938, with the exception of 1934 when thousands of government cattle were moved.

Nevertheless, the stream of livestock has continued to flow down the Kaw, and the trade has run into unbelievable figures, making Kansas City not only the gateway of the Southwest but also one of the world's leading livestock markets. A total of almost six million cars of livestock were received at Kansas City between 1884 and 1934. These ranged from 55,000 cars hauling two and a half million head in 1884 to 161,000 cars carrying more than eight million animals in 1918, the high point of the trade. If these cars were placed end to end they would reach more than twice around the world. Railroads and truck lines radiate from Kansas City like spokes from a hub. Farm animals have been brought in from every direction, but more than half have come by the Kaw route.

The flow of livestock early attracted the notice of meat manufacturers. According to the historian of the livestock trade, Edward W. Patterson and Company were the pioneer packers in Kansas City, coming in 1868. The head of the firm was a Kentuckian by birth who, in early childhood, had removed to Indiana. As a young man he drove livestock to Cincinnati, and then forming a partnership with William Epperson, he engaged in the packing business at Indianapolis for several years. He and his partner came to Kansas in the fall of 1867, formed a company at Junction City, put up a packing house, and slaughtered five thousand Texas cattle. The following year they decided to locate in Kansas City. Taking J. W. Slavens, a Kansas City cattleman, into the firm they erected a small stone building near the mouth of the Kaw, known as the "Stone House," first killing cattle, then hogs. The daily capacity was 250 cattle and 1,000 hogs.

The same year Thomas J. Bigger came from New York, rented a building on St. Louis Avenue, and packed hogs for the Irish market. He was a native of Belfast, Ireland, and came to New York City for the purpose of preparing meats adapted to the taste of the Irish people. After engaging in business there for five years, he decided to come west, and located at Kansas City in the fall of 1868. In a short time the inhabitants of the Emerald Isle were putting their teeth into choice Kaw hams and bacon and telling their friends how good they were. The following year he bought ground near the mouth of the Kaw and built a house of his own.

The decades of the seventies and eighties saw new plants erected on the banks of the Kaw and old plants enlarged to take care of the growing demand for Kaw meat.

The first packing plant in Kansas City slaughtered

4,209 cattle and 1,300 hogs the first year. Twenty years later the plants were killing 160,290 cattle and 1,889,054 hogs annually. The packing plants have grown with the increased demand for their products until today they slaughter annually upward of three million animals. In addition to the Kansas City plants, packing houses have been established at Topeka, Wichita, and other Kansas towns. Kansas now ranks fourth among the states of the Union in the meat-packing industry.

The Irish were enjoying Kaw pork as early as 1868. Kingan and Company, who established a branch plant at Kansas City in 1887, gave special attention to English cuts and carried on an extensive business with Great Britain, Ireland, France, and Germany. Some of their products were well known in India, Australia, and the Sandwich Islands. In the early nineties Kaw meats were attracting attention throughout America and had won an enviable name abroad, finding eager buyers both in Great Britain and on the Continent, two of the largest packing houses exporting fully half their products.

At an early date much of the livestock transported over the Kaw route was destined for some distant place. The story is told that in the fall of 1874 some Texas steers arrived in New York one evening and were being driven through the lower part of the city when they became infuriated by the noise and lights. Eight broke from the drivers and rushed in various directions. Before they were captured nearly fifty people had been injured, some seriously. About thirty-five per cent of the livestock received at Kansas City during the past half century has been shipped or driven to other points, some of them far from home.

Kaw meat on the hoof, or as a packed product, is known in the far corners of the earth. The trail blazed from the Red River to the Kaw seventy years ago by that herd of two thousand longhorns now runs around the world. Over it millions of Kaw animals have passed, and millions more will pass—an endless procession, the clatter of which will be heard by generations to come.

The Invasion of Cow Land

"THE grass is remarkably fine, the water plenty, drinks two for a quarter, and no grangers. These facts make Dodge City *the* cattle point." These are the words used by an early-day booster in pointing out the merits of Dodge City as a longhorn metropolis. Every Texas man understood his language, especially his reference to "grangers." The drovers and farmers mixed no better than oil and water. One Texan said he preferred Indians to grangers any day.

At the close of the Civil War most of the inhabitants lived in the east third of Kansas. Junction City was called the "west edge of civilization." It was correctly named. To the west and southwest of Junction were small settlements here and there, mostly along the streams and trails, and a vast expanse of prairie on which Indians and buffalo roamed. When the Chisholm Trail was blazed in 1867, it ran through an open country most of the way to Abilene.

At this time emigrants began to push westward into the unsettled area where they could obtain cheap farms. This real estate came chiefly from two sources: public land under the homestead acts; land sold by railroad companies.

Young people, wanting a start in life, and older folks, dissatisfied with things in the East, loaded a few possessions into covered wagons and started for the Kaw where they took up claims or bought railroad land.

Those who settled near the beef trails soon clashed with the Texas drovers. The homesteaders were afraid the longhorns would spread Texas fever among the native stock. The cattle got into their fields and destroyed the crops. The cowboys sometimes tore down their fences to let the thirsty cattle have water.

Each act made the settlers more resentful, and they emphasized their indignation with sawed-off shotguns which they turned on offending cowmen.

An old fellow, who was spoiling for a fight, lived on a claim along the trail north of Dodge City. He had whipped several trail bosses before he tackled Jack Potter, a strapping-big Texas cowpuncher. Potter tells the story of his encounter with this fighting granger:

There was a fog on, and I let the herd graze across the furrow and they were munching on that fine fresh gramma. After a bit the fog raised, and I found that we were grazing our herd around a dugout. After a while an old grizzly-looking nester came out of his hole, and motioned for me to come to him.

As I rode up to his dugout, he said, "You great big Texas rawhide, cigarette-smoking, important-looking son of a gun, get them longhorns off my premises."

I kind of swelled up and said to him, "Ain't you a little bit personal in your remarks?"

"No," he answered, "I meant just what I said."

I asked him if he had any sons or hired help around, and said I thought that I was insulted and wanted to fight.

He answered that if fighting was what I wanted, he could whip twenty like me. I crawled off my horse and went walking up to him with both hands reaching out. I was going to pull his old chin whiskers and make him apologize.

First thing I knew he hit me twice, just like a mule kicking me. One of his licks hit me on the left cheekbone.

When I got up I was sure mad. I took in after him, and he was running in a circle. Finally he ducked, and I stumbled

over him, and as I went over he grabbed the big bandanna handkerchief around my neck and commenced twisting it. Finally he had me choked down, and I was wheezing like a four-year-old bronc. And then he said, "When you get enough say so and I'll loosen up." I hollered, " 'Nough, 'nough." But this old porcupine was hard of hearing and had not slackened up. Finally I wrote "NUFF" in the sand with my finger, and he slackened his twist and turned me loose.

"Now," he said, "get on that cayuse, and I'll just give you five minutes to get them cattle back across the furrow."

I mounted, answering, "Old man, there is no use wasting time—I believe I can do it in one minute and a half."

The next day Colonel Potter learned that the granger had been a training partner for John L. Sullivan, and on one occasion had given John L. a sound thrashing. When the colonel heard this, he said:

"Well, I'm glad to learn that my fighting reputation is not so bad after all."

The events in the cattleman-homesteader war fall under two heads: First, the clashes between individual farmers, or groups of farmers, and the cattlemen. These battles were unrelated and ineffective. Possibly they discouraged some drovers, but mostly they intensified the ill-feeling already in evidence. Many of the acts of both parties were illegal, others of doubtful legality. Second, the quarantine laws of the state Legislature for the purpose of preventing the spread of Texas fever.

Scarcely had the northern drives begun when friction arose between the cattlemen and the farmers. The war continued throughout the trail-driving period. As the settlements moved westward, the cattlemen found it advisable to lay out new trails, skirting the settled region, but in the end the settlers drove them out of the state.

The farmers residing near Abilene became greatly excited when they learned that a market for longhorns was to be established in their midst. They organized a company for the purpose of stampeding every drove of cattle that came into the country. They elected one of their number as captain and bound themselves to keep up their organization until the proposed introduction of Texas cattle was abandoned.

Joseph McCoy and others sought to conciliate the hostile element. They sent word to the captain to call as many of his group as possible to a meeting at his cabin on a designated evening. On that evening several Texas drovers accompanied McCoy to the meeting place where a few settlers had gathered. McCoy addressed the farmers, pointing out the advantages of the cattle trade to them and their community. While he was talking, the drovers went among the farmers bartering for such produce as they could use, paying as high as double the price asked by the settlers.

At the conclusion of the meeting the captain said to his farmer friends:

"I've got a sight of the cattle trade that is new and convincing to me. And, gentlemen, if I can make any money out of this cattle trade I am not afraid of Spanish fever; but if I can't make any money out of this cattle trade, then I am damned afraid of Spanish fever."

Some of the captain's neighbors accused him of selling out to the cattle interests. Several other homesteaders were also "convinced," and the hostile organization dissolved.

The bulk of the trade on the Kansas Pacific shifted to Ellsworth in 1872. The farmers of that county had suffered losses from disease and damaged crops in 1871. Before the 1872 season opened they took steps to protect their property. In March they met at the Thompson Creek schoolhouse southeast of Ellsworth for the purpose of formulating plans for preventing the spread of disease among the domestic cattle and of stopping the driving of cattle promiscuously over the farms. They formed the Ellsworth County Farmers Protective Society.

When Wichita became a cow market, the chief opposition came from the farmers in the western part of Sedgwick County. In June, 1872, the citizens of that section of the county held a mass meeting at which they adopted resolutions hostile to the cattle trade. Those present, feeling that either the "driving of Texas cattle must be stopped; or the citizens must leave their claims and homes," declared they were in favor of notifying the drovers that they couldn't and wouldn't allow the driving of Texas cattle through the county, that they would resist to their "utmost capacity," and that they would prevent it peaceably if possible, forcibly if necessary.

In 1874 the cattlemen laid out a new trail which crossed the Arkansas three miles below town for the purpose of avoiding trouble with the cattle in town and the farmers on the west side.

The cattlemen had a peck of trouble with the settlers over water for the herds. The first homesteaders usually took up claims along the streams. When the cowman reached the water hole he found a nester squatting on the bank, with a sawed-off shotgun ready for use and a pack of ugly dogs at his call. If the cattle were thirsty and the granger was unreasonable, trouble was sure to break.

The story is told that when the Negro colony came to Nicodemus in Graham County they settled along the Solomon River and shut the cattlemen off from water. A dispute followed. The cowboys ran off some of the cattle belonging to the settlement. The colored men retaliated by capturing one of the cowboys and holding him as a hostage until the cattle were returned.

On one trip up the trail a drover wanted to water his cattle. He learned that a certain section through which a creek of good water flowed belonged to the railroad, and not to the old man who lived on it and had plowed the furrow designating ownership. The drover started his cattle in the direction of the water. The man lived in a dugout on the hillside where he could see everything. When the cattle crossed the furrow he came out with a shotgun, rolled up his sleeves, waved his arms and shouted:

"Take those cattle off my my land or I will have every damn one of you arrested."

The trail boss, being in the lead, reached the man first and said:

"Old man, there must be a mistake; we have some fat cattle and the agent of the railroad said he had no stock cars and for us to throw the cattle on Section 115."

Then the old man turned loose on the railroad agent and the country in general, stating that the drought had come and he was saving that little grass for winter. The boss compromised by promising to water on half the land and to give him a stray calf in the herd. The old man agreed to this arrangement.

The winter of 1871-72 was a severe one. Thousands of head of cattle wintering on the range in western Kansas froze to death. That fall more than forty thousand head were put on the prairies of Ellsworth County. Then the owners went to their homes in Texas and let the cattle take care of themselves. Large numbers froze to death and were skinned by the settlers for their hides. The streams froze over, and numerous other cattle died from lack of water. Scores of the beasts came to the settlements and drank out of the water holes with the domestic animals. Some settlers drove them away, knowing that they would die without water. One man made it a practice to drive the longhorns onto the ice on the Smoky Hill, and there the frightened animals would fall and break their legs. The hide hunters made a good living that season, and when spring came not one of the forty thousand longhorns was alive.

Out in Sherman County the cattlemen had been in possession of the range so long that they had ceased to employ herders to stay with the cattle. The animals were rounded up once a year and branded. The rest of the year they roamed at will over the prairie and destroyed the crops of the settlers.

The settlers didn't consider it a crime to kill a beef once in a while. Finally the owners decided to put a stop to the killing. In the winter of 1886-87 they sent cowboys out to protect the herds and punish the culprits. They also offered $500 for sufficient evidence to convict the guilty parties. The people who bought the beef were as liable as the man who killed it, and most of the settlers had eaten range beef that winter.

Some of them became alarmed and formed a protective association. There was one man in the neighborhood who was under suspicion; they believed he planned to betray a neighbor who had sold beef, so they decided to give him a good scare.

Accordingly, they invited him to attend a meeting of the association. It was held in a dugout. They took him through many oaths and finally administered the last and most solemn of them all:

"I do solemnly swear not to tell anything that may in any way lead owners of cattle which are running at large contrary to law and destroying the settlers' crops to discover who has killed or crippled or in any way injured these same cattle, when driving them away from the crops or at any other time. If I do, then I shall expect this society to use me thus—"

Here a straw man with a rope around his neck was suspended before the astonished candidate, who said "I do" so quickly that he bit his tongue.

He never told anything for money after that. Other members were taken in, and soon the whole county was organized, thirteen lodges in all. The association bought a case of Winchester rifles and held meetings all winter.

The Kansas legislature in 1867 passed the first of a series of acts for the protection of native stock from Spanish fever, commonly called tick, or quarantine, laws. This act established the quarantine line on the sixth principal meridian, a line running north from the southern boundary of Kansas through Wellington, Wichita, and Newton, to an east and west line between townships eighteen and nineteen. The law prohibited the driving of "through" Texas cattle east and north of the quarantine line each year, between March 1st and December 1st; imposed a fine of not less than $100 nor more than $1,000 and from thirty days' to six months' imprisonment for the first offense; and doubled the penalty for a subsequent offense. The drovers were liable for all damage done by cattle imparting disease to the native stock. Another law made the cattlemen liable for damage to the crops of farmers without regard to fences.

The tick law became effective March 11th, six months before the cattle market was in operation at Abilene. The town was inside the quarantine line, but the authorities didn't enforce the law against the drovers who brought their herds into the county. The governor gave a letter commending the selection of Abilene as a shipping point. The founder of the cattle market says the governor's action brought down on his head the "maledictions of certain pothouse politicians" who were back of the tick law.

Only a few farmers lived south and west of Abilene the first year of the northern drive. In the next two or three years the population of the county trebled, and homesteads in increasing numbers dotted the prairie between the Texas herds and the railway. The cattlemen made arrangements to pay the settlers satisfactory amounts for the privilege of driving over their lands. When Texas fever broke out in the East in 1868, a few domestic cattle at Abilene died of the disease. The drovers and the owners of the shipping yards paid claims for losses amounting to $4,500. A board of arbitration took care of the unsettled claims. Cattle were to be restricted to the trail and herded in certain parts of the county, the expense of herding to be paid for out of a fund raised by citizens of Abilene.

At the same time settlers poured into the area between Abilene and the south line of Kansas and took claims on or near the trail. With the building of the Santa Fe Railroad into central Kansas in 1871, settlers rushed to Harvey and adjoining counties, and homesteaded land or bought farms from the railroad.

The newcomers didn't have on or near their claims the materials out of which to construct fences and lacked the funds to buy fencing, so many of them plowed furrows around the edge of their land to designate ownership. The drovers found it increasingly difficult to keep on the right side of the numerous furrows and to find suitable grazing grounds and watering places.

The farmer element brought pressure on the legislature of 1872 to move the quarantine line westward. Accordingly, that body established a new line which became effective in March. The dead line followed the Arkansas River from Wichita west and then north to the northwest corner of Rice County, taking in Harvey, McPherson, Rice, and Saline. This act cut Newton off from the trade and placed Abilene far inside the dead line.

While this bill was up for consideration in the legislature, enemies of the trade at Abilene published a signed notice telling Texas drovers not to return to that place. Thereupon, friends of the trade petitioned the cattlemen to drive their herds to Abilene, but to no avail. They drove to Ellsworth on the Kansas Pacific and to Wichita and Great Bend on the Santa Fe.

The trail to Great Bend and Ellsworth left the Chisholm Trail at Pond Creek Ranche, Indian Territory, and ran by way of Bluff and Turkey creeks west of the quarantine line.

Most of the drovers observed the law and followed the established trail, avoidiing the settlements. Some, to save time and distance, traveled up the Arkansas through Reno County. In August the commissioners of that county published a notice warning Texas men that they would not be permitted to drive herds up the river through the county and stating that the authorities had "already prosecuted several parties" for violating the law. However, toward the close of the season the juries weakened and failed to convict in a number of cases.

With the close of the season of 1874 Ellsworth ceased to be an important shipping point. Through 1874 and 1875 Wichita was the leading market, though Great Bend received a fair share of the trade. Meantime settlers by the thousands had come into the counties along and west of the Ellsworth Trail. Twelve counties in that area were organized within three years, and for a time in 1875 the entries in the federal land office at Larned averaged 4,000 acres per day.

The legislature met in January, 1876, and through the efforts of the farmer members passed a bill by a huge majority moving the quarantine line westward so it took in Sumner and Sedgwick and counties north and west. The east boundary of Ford County, of which Dodge

City was and is the county seat, became the dead line.
By this act Wichita and Ellsworth were closed as shipping points for "through" Texas cattle. The drovers
turned their herds toward Dodge City where they believed grangers wouldn't annoy them. Here they made
their last stand against the invading agrarians.

Dodge City was located in the heart of the buffalo
country. As one writer put it, "Here civilization ceases,
and the wild romance and freedom of the plains begins."
Only 813 people lived in Ford County in 1875, and the
most of these were residents of Dodge City. "As a farming country," a newspaperman wrote, "the vicinity of
Dodge City is not a success. But as a grazing country I
have never seen its equal in the West. The Arkansas
and its tributaries furnish an abundance of water, and
the bottoms are covered with grass, which both in
quantity and quality, is unexcelled. The business men of
Dodge City don't want the country settled up with
farmers, and they very frankly tell you so. They oppose every move made in that direction on the ground
that it would ruin their trade."

The good farm land was on the north side of the
river, while that on the south was especially suited to
grazing. On this subject the local press said:

"There is an immense section south and southwest,
that will remain open without agricultural improvements for some years to come. The settlements will reach
along the line of the railroad and the counties contiguous
to railroad counties on the north. In Ford County the
general desire is for settlement north of the river. The
advantages open better for settlement on this side of the
river. Yet the south side will be sought for the propagation of the Texas and native cattle."

Mike Dalton, boss herder for Powers, Bulkley and
Company, who drove the first herd up the Western

Trail in 1877, found that the settlers could make a peck of trouble for trail drivers. In Comanche County southeast of Dodge he drove into territory protected by the quarantine law. He says:

"The grangers went for them like a swarm of mad hornets, and heavy fines and damage money had to be yielded up before the stock could proceed."

As the time for the session of the legislature of 1879 approached, the question of a change in the quarantine line was up for discussion. A petition was circulated and extensively signed in Ford County asking the legislature to change the line so as to prevent the driving and herding of Texas cattle north of the river. The local newspaper and Robert W. ("Bob") Wright, representative from Ford County in the legislature, believed the farmers should have this protection.

A bill was introduced in the lower house providing for a change in the boundaries of the quarantine district and was referred to the committee on interstate commerce of which Wright was chairman. The boundary line fixed by the committee and adopted by the legislature gave "general satisfaction."

The line commenced at the northeast corner of Decatur County, on the Nebraska boundary, and ran south through the center of Ford County to a point just east of the stockyards at Dodge, followed the river east to the county line, then went south to the Indian Territory.

This remained the quarantine line for the next four years. Meantime, settlers poured into western Kansas. New counties were organized, and most of the older counties made remarkable growths, some of them doubling their population. In 1883 six counties and parts of three others in southwestern Kansas were taken into the quarantined area, leaving only a narrow strip near the Colorado border open to "through" cattle.

Thus the granger had gradually pushed the drover westward. The cowman had made his last stand at the cowboy capital, and at the end of eight years the agrarian drove him out of that place. His final expulsion from Kansas was effected in 1885 when the legislature passed an act prohibiting the driving of "through" Texas cattle into or through any county in the state between March 1st and December 1st.

12

Breaking the Prairie

WHEN the pioneer settlers invaded cow land, the first thing they did was to build dwellings for their families and shelter for their stock. Then they broke the sod and planted crops.

The type of home depended largely on the taste and pocketbook of the builder. Because of the small amount of timber available, there were few log cabins in central and western Kansas. The homesteader who had means usually built a frame house, while the man whose chief asset was a pair of willing hands made a dugout or erected a sod shanty.

In south central Kansas frame houses were quite common. This is particularly true in Harvey County. It was said of Newton, the county seat, "It burns no coal and builds with wood." Numerous homesteaders in these parts also "built with wood." In fact, few of the first settlers in the county lived in sod shanties or dugouts.

However, many of the pioneer settlers in central Kansas and a large portion of those who homesteaded farther west lived in sod houses or dugouts. The high plains were dotted with homes made of the "natural soil."

Sod houses and dugouts figure in the literature of

the plains. Much sentiment was attached to these crude homes. The first families have fond recollections of the years they lived in a soddy. Eugene Fitch Ware and other Kansas poets have caught the spirit of the times and paid tribute to these humble dwellings in verse. The sod house is the theme of two folk songs. One is entitled "The Little Sod Shanty on the Claim" and is sung to the tune "The Little Old Log Cabin in the Lane." The author is unknown, but he must have been a Kansan; at least he was familiar with life on the sod-house frontier. The other song is "The Lane County Bachelor" and is probably the best known literary product of the period.

Frank Baker composed this song in 1887. At that time he was living on his homestead near the Ness County line. He sang this song to the tune of "Irish Washer-woman" at the meetings of local literary societies and other social gatherings in the community. Many a youngster, with open mouth and wide eyes, listened intently while he fiddled and sang. The grownups also enjoyed his performances. The song became popular in western Kansas and spread to neighboring states. One version is known nationally. The song contains five stanzas and a refrain for each. The first stanza gives a description of his sod shanty. The text printed here is taken from a manuscript copy in Baker's handwriting:

> Frank Baker's my name and a bachelor I am,
> I'm keeping old batch on an elegant plan.
> You'll find me out west in the county of Lane,
> I'm starving to death on a government claim
> My home it is built of the natural soil
> The walls are erected according to Hoyle.
> The roof has no pitch but is level and plain
> And I always get wet when it happens to rain.

Among the pioneers who put up frame dwellings in central Kansas were seven families named Prouty—Amos Prouty and his six sons. These families were typical pioneers in other respects. Amos Prouty, a Civil War veteran, sold his eighty-acre farm in Mercer County, Illinois, in 1871, and with his sons and daughters and others, started for Harvey County, Kansas, on August 3rd.

Their train, consisting of eleven covered wagons and a herd of cows and extra horses, drove on the boat at New Boston, Illinois, about six o'clock in the evening and was ferried across the Mississippi. When they reached the west bank the setting sun reflected a soft golden glow on the town and countryside across the river. Tears dimmed their eyes as they looked for a few moments on this scene. Then a driver yelled "Giddap," then another, and another, whips cracked, wagons moved and fell in line; and they started forward. The train soon entered a timbered area, and the Illinois scene disappeared from view.

The wagon wheels rolled and splashed the mud caused by a heavy rain. They traveled until late that night before they found a suitable camping place.

Nothing unusual occurred until the night of the 18th when they camped near St. Joe, Missouri. H. W. ("Cap") Prouty wrote in his diary:

We corralled our wagons and some of us stood guard all night on account of horse thieves. Frank and I were on guard about midnight when Frank discovered some one behind a tree. He went for him and ran him down into the bushes, then fired at him as he fled.

They arrived at their destination in the afternoon

of August 29th. They were among the first settlers in that locality. They could look for miles across the prairie and see only a few homes. Herds of Texas cattle were grazing in every direction. The long journey was over and they were happy. That evening they joked and told stories.

Four of the boys were members of a dance orchestra —Prouty Band, they called it—which had played for some of the leading dances in Illinois. The musicians got out their instruments and played, and the families danced on the prairie. Between dances Cap Prouty, whose specialty was jig dancing, placed his mother's big bread board on the grass, reverse side up. The musicians struck up a lively tune, and he danced a jig on the board. He put on his act many times before and after that evening. Whenever he did so, the crowd greeted it with resounding applause. No audience was ever more appreciative than this group of relatives that night on the lonely prairie.

They erected a large frame building on one of the claims which served as the headquarters of the colony until they built the modest frame houses on their respective homesteads. They spent the fall and winter erecting their houses and getting settled. They built their homes mostly of lumber shipped from Aledo, Illinois.

The writer's father also built a frame house. He came to central Kansas from Vermont in 1876 and bought a quarter section of Santa Fe Railroad land for $1,200, on which he put a frame structure a story and a half high. The building was constructed of rough lumber and the walls were not plastered. It was the family residence for several years, when a house was built. Then it was used for a granary.

When shelter had been provided for the family

and the livestock, the homesteaders broke the sod. The Proutys soon found that their horses were not strong enough for this work, and they lacked grain to feed them. They sold the horses and bought oxen, which stood the work and lived on the native grass. The writer's father walked forty miles across the prairie to buy two yokes of Texas oxen. They were huge animals with immense long horns. Each horn was tipped with a brass knob to lessen the injury if the horns were used on man or beast.

The first settlers in central Kansas generally used oxen. These work cattle consisted of native animals and Texas longhorns. Some of the Texas drovers brought work cattle up the trail with their herds and found a profitable market for them in Kansas. Thus the Texas cowmen supplied the power for the grangers to turn the sod, thereby hastening the day of their own exit from the Kaw country.

The breaking of the tough sod was mighty hard work. Two or more yoke of oxen were required to pull the heavy breaking plow. The average settler owned but one yoke, so two or more farmers worked together, or someone who owned a big outfit was hired to break the sod. It was quite a job to hold the plow in place. Usually one man guided the animals, while another held the plow, and sometimes a third sat on the beam. Quite often the homesteader's wife or daughters helped him. The writer's father held the plow in place, while Grandfather guided the oxen. Working together, they turned more than a hundred acres of ground. Cap Prouty broke sod with a fourteen-inch John Deere walking plow drawn by four oxen working abreast.

Corn was the favorite sod crop, so the homesteader generally planted corn in the freshly broken prairie.

This is not surprising, since a large percentage of the pioneers came from "corn states."

In the absence of better implements, the early settlers used a hoe or a shovel or even an ax to plant corn. Cap Prouty dropped the seed for his first crops behind the breaking plow. The next year he used a hand planter.

Although corn was the leading crop, the sod breakers planted other grains. Cap Prouty broke ten acres of prairie in 1872 and put it in rye. Some of his brothers planted wheat that year. In 1873 all the Prouty families put in wheat. They planted Red May, a variety of soft winter wheat generally grown by Kaw pioneers. They sowed the seed by hand, known as "broadcasting," and harrowed it in. The first two seasons they cut their grain with a buckeye mower brought from Illinois. The yield was fifteen to twenty bushels per acre. In 1874 the Prouty colony bought a Hodge header. Eight families used this machine to harvest a wheat crop totaling about two hundred acres.

Garden truck made a prolific growth in this new soil. A settler who farmed newly broken sod near Junction City, says:

"Some pumpkins grew to a tremendous size, one measuring about two feet by eighteen inches, and turning the scales at sixty-eight pounds. Melons, squashes, cucumbers, tomatoes, and hosts of other things grew without attention, and in such quantities that we used them to feed the pigs upon."

The first families usually planted shade and fruit trees, and set a row of Osage orange hedge around the homestead. Amos Prouty set out a large orchard of fruit trees and sixteen acres of maple trees. When the maple trees were big enough to make shade he built a dancing pavilion in the grove, and for years this was a favorite place for country dances and picnics. Thirty years ago one could drive up and down central Kansas and see numerous fine orchards and an endless row of Osage hedge on each side of the road. Today both are gone. The orchards have died and have not been replaced, and the hedges have been pulled out by the roots.

The homesteaders began early to stock their farms with cattle and drew heavily on the Texas supply for this purpose. They sold grain and other farm produce to the Texas drovers and were paid in money or stock. When a herd of longhorns was driven across or watered on a farm the owner received a cow or two in payment. The drovers gave the settlers the calves born on the trail and the crippled animals. The farmers also bought Texas cattle. On this subject the Topeka *Daily Commonwealth* in 1869 said:

Never before in the history of our State have so many Texas cattle been purchased by Kansas men, especially farmers, as there has been this fall. Farmers and stock growers have discovered by actual experiment that the common Texas cattle crossed with first class domestic stock produces an excellent grade of cattle and have consequently invested all their means in stock cattle from Texas, for the purpose of stock raising. Especially is this true of Western and Southwestern Kansas. Thousands and tens of thousands of cattle have been purchased with this in view, and it will result in the development of a great source of wealth. Millions of dollars are lost every year in Kansas because the people have not herds "to go to grass." Let the stock herds increase and multiply.

Evidently the Kaw farmers listened to this advice, for in 1885 Joseph Nimmo, the government statistician, estimated that one-half the cattle on the plains were of Texas strain.

The farmers also found the winter feeding of Texas cattle a profitable business. Major J. S. Smith, a cattle buyer from Springfield, Illinois, was one of the first to experiment with winter feeding. In the fall of 1867 he bought a small lot of scrub cattle and put them into winter quarters. The results were astonishing. Soon the farmers around Abilene engaged in winter feeding as a business. In time farmers and ranchers in all parts of the state were wintering longhorns. Andrew Wilson, of Kingston, was Kansas' heaviest feeder. During the winter of 1872-73, he "roughed" five thousand head of Texas cattle through the winter and fattened them on grass the following summer. The next fall he bought seven thousand head at panic prices and put them into winter quarters near Topeka.

Fuel was scarce on the prairie, especially on the tablelands where there was no timber and little brush. In the absence of wood, the first farmers burned buffalo or cow chips. At times the supply of this kind of fuel was low. How much it was prized is illustrated by the story of the young man in southwestern Kansas who was leaving the state and wanted to give his sweetheart a useful present, so he brought her a load of cow chips and a load of pumpkins.

The settlers living along the Texas cattle trails depended on the herds of longhorns for their fuel, and consequently each farmer tried to get the cattlemen to bed their herds on his land. The farmers figured that a thousand cattle would leave enough chips on the ground in one night to provide them with five hundred pounds of fuel in a few days. Sometimes the competition became so keen that a fight resulted. An incident of this sort occurred south of Abilene. The prairie was covered with cattle for miles in every direction. One evening several men and women in buckboards and buggies went to the different herds and begged each boss to bed his cattle on their respective claims. Soon they began quarreling with each other. Each said that a boss named Levi Anderson had promised to bed his cattle on his land. Anderson, not being used to the ways of these people, made the promise because he thought they were joking. He remarked:

"Down in Texas, if you gave a man dry dung he would fight you, but here in Kansas they will fight each other for dry dung."

These pioneers experienced all the hardships and reverses incident to life on the frontier. There were long days of hard work, empty pocketbooks, calico-dress wardrobes, droughts, blizzards, prairie fires, and crop failures.

The year 1874 was the worst of all. The winter of 1873-74 had been an unusually severe one which left the stock in poor condition with a scanty supply of hay and grain. The spring was backward, requiring additional feed for the stock from the depleted supply, with the result that a large amount of stock perished. The spring months were favorable for small grains, but there was a shortage of moisture; the mean rainfall east of the sixth principal meridian for the first six months of the year was twelve inches, west of that line eleven and a third inches for the same period. Through the month of July and the most of August the temperature continued high with little or no rainfall, which injured field crops, gardens, and pastures. The chinch bugs came early in the summer and damaged the small grains, corn, sorghum, and the tame hay. The spring wheat suffered the greatest injury, the average condition having been reduced 14 per cent by July 1st. Then late in July the grasshoppers made their appearance in western Kansas and traveled east and southeast. They went down the Kaw River to its mouth, and before the close of August the ravenous hordes enveloped the whole state. The air was so filled with them that they obscured the sun for hours and they alighted on the houses, the fields, and the fences, covering everything. They were thick on the ground and flew in vast swarms from either side of locomotives like snow before a snowplow.

They began on the green corn and vegetables. They could easily dispose of a quarter section of corn in an hour and a half, taking for dessert whatever watermelons or pumpkins came their way and leaving not even a vestige of rind. After they passed a cornfield, nothing was left but the stubs of stalks two or three feet long. They stripped the trees of their leaves and fruit and gnawed the bark off young trees and hedges. They devoured nearly all the green stuff excepting sorghum and tobacco, but finally ate the sorghum and chewed the tobacco. When they couldn't find anything more palatable they ate clothing and gnawed at shovel handles and fenceposts. After a few days' destruction in each community, the bulk of the army moved on to greener fields.

The invaders left a desolate country behind them. The corn crop was generally damaged and in some localities entirely destroyed. The failure of corn necessitated the feeding of wheat or the sale of livestock. Farmers were forced to sell their hogs at ruinous prices and to sacrifice their cattle. In the western counties, where the new settlers depended mainly on corn and garden vegetables, the calamity fell with greatest force. Twelve thousand people living in counties west of the sixth principal meridian were destitute. Starvation or emigration seemed inevitable unless aid could be furnished. The governor convened the legislature in extra session on September 15th. Two laws were passed providing for the issuance of special "relief bonds." The governor set up a relief committee headed by the lieutenant governor for the purpose of aiding the destitute. The committee received and disbursed among the needy: cash, $73,863.47; supplies, 265 car loads and 11,049 packages.

The first families had a good time along with the drudgery and hardships. There were church socials, camp meetings, parties, family reunions, husking bees, "spelling downs," and dances, not to mention other community and family gatherings. Cap Prouty led the singing school in his community. The Prouty Band played for dances in central Kansas. The Prouty families came together each year on August 29th to celebrate the anniversary of their arrival from Illinois. This became an annual affair, and now the third and fourth generations take part.

Good years followed lean, and the families who stuck it out were amply rewarded for their toil and patience. They made the prairie "blossom as a rose," and they and their children have built a great agricultural empire in which wheat has become king.

13

The Beginnings of an Agricultural Empire

T HE Indians were the first farmers of the Kaw. It is not known when they grew their first grain and vegetables on the banks of the stream, but it probably was long before white men came to these parts. One of the first white men to mention the agricultural pursuits of the Indians was Thomaas Say, chief zoologist of the Major Stephen H. Long Expedition, who visited the Kaw Indian village in 1819. He said their food consisted of bison meat and various preparations of Indian corn or maize and that they also used pumpkins, muskmelons, and watermelons. Daniel Morgan Boone, son of the famous frontiersman, was appointed farmer to the Kaw Indians by the government about 1827 and moved his family to the reservation where he built a log house on the north bank of the river. In the spring of 1835 the government selected about six hundred acres in the Kaw valley in what is now Shawnee County and carried on farming on an extensive scale.

A rhymester once said that

Indians are good to raise hair and good to raise rows,
And good to raise essence of corn—in a horn.

220

But records show that the aboriginal inhabitants of the Kaw also raised some grain. The treaty of August 8, 1831, for the removal of the Shawnee Indians to Kansas provided that the government should build a gristmill containing two pairs of millstones and a bolting cloth. This mill is said to have been the first in the Kaw country. The exact date of its construction is not known, but it was built shortly after the Indians reached their new home. There is evidence to this effect in the diary of the Reverend Jotham Meeker who came as missionary to the Shawnees in 1833. In the fall of 1834 he mentions a trip to the mill to bring home flour and bran.

The erection of this gristmill would imply that the Shawnees began growing corn and wheat soon after their arrival in Kansas.

The Delaware Indians, who lived on the north bank of the Kaw near its mouth, were raising grain as early as 1835. In the summer of that year Samuel Allis and John Dunbar, Presbyterian missionaries, visited them. Allis reported that they owned a "saw and grist mill furnished by the government, raise some wheat, considerable corn and vegetables."

In his annual report dated October, 1839, Richard W. Cummins, Indian agent at Fort Leavenworth, said that the Shawnees "may fairly be considered an agricultural people, they depend almost entirely on their labor for support; they have raised the present year bountiful crops of corn, pumpkins, Irish potatoes, cabbage, beans, some wheat and oats." He said the Delawares and Kickapoos were not far behind the Shawnees in their farming activities, while the Kaws "raised more corn than is good for them." Subsequent reports add further evidence that the Indians engaged quite extensively in agricultural pursuits.

The missionaries were responsible for much of this interest in agriculture. They planted grain and gardens and taught the Indians how to farm. They also built blacksmith shops and put flouring mills in operation. The Indian boys worked in the shops and on the farms part of each day, and the Indian girls were taught housework. One of the earliest crop reports giving figures on farm produce is for the Shawnee Indian Manual Labor School in Johnson County and bears the date September 18, 1840. According to this report, the school raised about 2,000 bushels of wheat, 400 bushels of oats, 3,500 bushels of corn, and 500 bushels of potatoes the first year. Another is for the Delaware Baptist Mission in 1842, which states that the mission farm "last year" produced 750 bushels of corn, 90 bushels of wheat, 120 bushels of potatoes, and an "abundance of culinary vegetables."

The first white families of the Kaw were mostly farmers. The vanguard arrived in the summer and fall of 1854. Since agricultural statistics prior to 1860 are not available, the writer has used other sources for information on the farming activities of the early settlers.

The settlers broke the sod and planted corn in the spring of 1855. There had been little rainfall during the previous fall and winter, but rains came in the spring. The crop was put in late and yielded well.

That fall and the following spring some of the farmers sowed wheat.

In the summer of 1857 the press reported that oats and corn were in good condition and that the wheat crop was uncommonly heavy. In July the *Herald of Freedom*, published at Lawrence, said, "The harvest has been abundant, and the best ever known. Sod wheat, sown early in September and well put in, is estimated to yield 20 to 30 bushels to the acre. Spring wheat which was sown in considerable quantities in this direction, is of the best quality." This paper urged the farmers to put in large crops. "Particularly sow wheat—Sod wheat, if sown early, is considered a very sure crop, and yields from twenty to forty bushels per acre."

There were heavy rains through the growing season of 1858, and Kaw farmers were jubilant over the promising appearance of their crops, their wheat in particular. Before the wheat was ready for harvest much of it was almost six feet tall. In July the press said, "The wheat crop which is now generally harvested, all agree in saying, is such as is rarely witnessed in any country. We hear of quite a number of fields which will produce from twenty-five to thirty bushels to the acre, which have received no attention during the last year, not even that of plowing or seeding, deriving its entire crop from the waste of a former crop." Wheat was $1.50 and corn 40 cents per bushel on the Lawrence market that summer.

The 1860 crop is the first for which there are statistics. The farmers raised a total of 194,173 bushels of wheat, half of which was grown in the Kaw valley, and five million bushels of corn that year.

In the early years most wheatgrowers used crude methods of production. They usually sowed the seed by hand. They harvested the grain by cradling, and three acres was considered a good day's work. They often threshed the wheat by oxen trampling the grain, and cleaned it of chaff by the wind.

In a pioneer community, mills to grind the grain raised by the settlers were a great convenience, if not a necessity. On the Kaw, gristmills were erected soon after the first crop was harvested. One of the first mills in Kansas Territory was built at East Leavenworth, or "Slabtown," as it was called, and was put in operation in January, 1855. Other early mills were: Palermo, 1855 or 1856; Topeka, 1856; Spring Creek, 1856-57; Leavenworth, 1857; and Blue Mound, Douglas County, 1857. The census of 1860 reported thirty-six gristmills in fourteen counties. The total value of the products of these thirty-six mills was $293,841. Douglas County, on the Kaw, led all others in the value of products, the mills in that county, three in number, representing more than a third of the total output.

Most of the first mills were combination affairs, sawmills and gristmills. The majority were operated by water power. Water mills were cheaper to build and cost less to operate than steam mills. Furthermore, with poor wagon roads and no railroads, it was quite a task to transport the heavy engines and huge boilers for steam mills across the prairie. This was found to be true when the first steam sawmill was built in Topeka. The owners could not haul the heavy boiler up the trail, so they took it from Kansas City to Topeka on a sled over the snow-covered ground in wintertime.

The Kaw was a cruel frontier for agricultural pursuits. The early geographers and mapmakers had included much of this region in the Great American Desert. At times it appeared they were right. Agriculture met with one reverse after another. It seemed that man and nature conspired to prevent the building of an agricultural kingdom.

Soon after Kansas Territory was opened to settlers, the contest over slavery took place. While one cannot measure the effect of border wars, bloody raids, claim jumping, and other disturbances on husbandry, there is no doubt that when men were fighting instead of farming agricultural development was retarded.

Peace came in the late fifties, but before its ameliorating influence could be felt the drought of 1860 struck the Kaw country and dealt a serious blow to agriculture. This was probably the most severe dry spell in Kaw history. One writer calls it the "granddaddy of Kansas droughts."

The spring of 1860 opened promisingly, but there was a shortage of moisture in the soil. The usual rains did not come in the spring and summer. In some parts of Kansas there was not a drop of moisture, rain or snow for months. The hot blasts blew out of the south all summer. Each day it became drier and hotter. A contemporary said, "The heavens above seemed brass, the ground iron under our feet, the air around us the very breath of hell." Vegetables and field crops withered, the grass dried up, and the leaves fell from the trees. The country looked as if a giant prairie fire had swept over it. Wells dried up; so did the cows. The Kaw and other large streams were lowered, and the small ones went dry. In the low places some vegetation escaped the drought, but grasshoppers came in clouds and ate most of it.

The distress of Kaw folks was terrible. Butter and eggs were scarce. The ponds dried up, so the wild geese and ducks which ordinarily came in the fall passed on through Kansas. Prairie chickens were so thin and tough they weren't palatable. It was estimated in October that there were not provisions enough in the territory to keep more than half the population from starvation, and it was reported that most of the inhabitants were living on corn bread, hominy, corn-meal mush without butter or milk, hickory nuts, and a little meat, mostly dried buffalo flesh.

The generosity of eastern people saved the distressed settlers from starvation. Provisions came as fast as the steamers and overland freight caravans could bring them. Samuel C. Pomeroy, chairman of the Relief Committee, won the sobriquet "Baked Beans" Pomeroy by soliciting and sending a great many carloads of New Engand beans to the drought-stricken area. It was largely his efforts toward bringing relief to his unfortunate neighbors that elected him United States senator when Kansas was admitted to the Union in 1861.

Thousands of the settlers returned to their former homes in the East, impoverished and discouraged. They told big tales of want and woe in the Kaw country. They said the region was fit only for Indians, buffalo, prairie dogs, rattlesnakes, and horned toads; that it should be given back to the Indians, but they were sure even the redskins would become thin in such a place.

The people who remained in Kansas stayed close to the Kaw and other streams. The drought half convinced them that the blue-backed geographies were right about this being a desert. For some years, the newcomers as a rule located their farms in the valleys and did not venture far from water.

In 1861 Kaw men left their plows and went to war. During the next four years the war drew from the land the labor necessary for its cultivation. An early report of the State Board of Agriculture says that "Kansas furnished more soldiers than it had voters. It supplied 20,097 men, or 3,433 more than its quota. In every one hundred families not less than seventy-five had a representative in the army; and as a rule, only the wife and little ones were found on the farm. It is evident, that of the population gathered by the inspiration which drew men hither, the great mass would neglect the plow for the musket; and that during the war the agricultural industry of the State would shrink rather than increase."

Because of the drought and the Civil War, immigration to Kansas practically ceased between 1860 and 1865; the population made a slight increase, while the cultivated area decreased by several thousand acres. However, the production of wheat in 1862 was more than in 1860, the drought year; but production fell to a lower level in 1865, owing to another drought and a serious grasshopper plague.

The war over, men returned home and began farming. Thousands of veterans in the East found other persons in their jobs. Others believed they could improve their economic status by moving west. So they sold out, if they had anything to sell, and emigrated to the Kaw where homesteads were free and railroad land could be bought at a reasonable price and on easy terms.

From the close of the war until 1872, the general financial conditions of the nation enabled those who so desired to sell their farms in the older states and buy homes in Kansas. Thousands took advantage of the opportunity. The population increased from 140,179 in 1865 to 364,399 in 1870. The area under cultivation jumped from 243,903 acres in 1865 to 2,530,769 acres in 1872. Kaw farmers raised only 191,000 bushels of wheat in 1865, while seven years later they raised three million bushels. The corn crop bounded upwards from six to forty-six million bushels.

Financial reverses followed the flush years. The panic of 1873 prevented thousands, who had planned to move to Kansas, from disposing of their property except at ruinous prices. The following year chinch bugs, drought, and grasshoppers visited the state and damaged the crops, causing many inhabitants to leave, and frightening prospective settlers into staying away. The fluctuations in the corn crop had a retarding influence on the tide of immigration. The early settlers came largely from "corn states" and planned to make corn their main crop in Kansas. They did not foresee the possibilities in wheat. A drop from forty-six million bushels to fifteen millions in two years discouraged immigration.

The reverses in 1874 were not without benefit to the wheat industry. The corn crop was generally damaged and in some localities entirely destroyed and spring wheat and other small grains were injured. The farmers generally turned to winter wheat, in some counties increasing the acreage 300 per cent. With the exception of a group of counties in southeastern Kansas, where the ravages of the chinch bugs had been the worst the previous spring, most counties showed a greater acreage in winter wheat. The actual increase of winter wheat in the state was 83,912 acres.

The state agricultural authorities were convinced that wheat, especially winter wheat, was a safer crop than corn and set out to sell this idea to Kaw farmers. In the annual report for 1875 the State Board of Agriculture called attention to the fluctuations of the corn crop and the steady increase of wheat production; to the zigzagging of the corn line on the chart and the firmness of the wheat line:

If any lines ever said anything in the world, these shout to the farmer, "Don't put all your eggs in the corn basket; put most in the wheat basket, it is safer"; and the exhibit shows another thing, one which the historian would regard as both curious and instructive, that Kansas farmers, each for himself studying his own business and own prospects, are rapidly changing from the old theory that corn was *the* crop to the one already indicated.

Next to the right kind of natural conditions, successful wheat culture depended on certain inventions and legislation of man. Chief among these were labor saving devices—harvesters, headers, threshing machines, windmills, etc.; and the protection of growing crops by fences and by fence and herd laws.

During the decade prior to the Civil War, improved machinery for wheat raising was put on the market. By 1861 the farmers in the Kaw valley were using threshing machines. In the early seventies those in Central Kansas cut their wheat with harvesters and headers and threshed it with threshing machines run by steam engines. As the wheat area grew in size, bigger and better machinery was needed, and the manufacturers provided it.

It is needless to say that fences aided agriculture. The first legislation on the subject of fences was dated February 27, 1860. This law required that when the land of two persons joined it was the duty of each to build one-half of the division fence. Another law that year legalized a wire fence made of three strands of No. 9 fence wire and attached to posts set as specified in the law.

The following year the legislature enacted another law on division fences which provided that the party failing to maintain a lawful fence could not recover damages for injuries done to his crops by stock running at large.

The Kaw country did not contain an adequate quantity of any natural material out of which fences could be built. Therefore, the first families constructed fences out of boards, rails, stone, wire—anything that was available. They planted Osage orange hedge fences soon after they located along the Kaw. In the spring of 1856, the editor of the *Herald of Freedom* looked into the "most certain and sure methods" of raising Osage orange hedge plants "as many of our people are going

into the hedging business," and gave the readers the
results of his findings in an editorial.

In 1871 the United States commissioner of agriculture made a survey of the fence situation in the
country and found styles and kinds too numerous to
mention. He reported:

It is difficult to calculate the comparative prominence of
styles in Kansas. Averaging the returns, the worm-fence
appears to constitute 18 per cent, board 12, and post and rail
9, leaving 61 per cent for a great variety of fences reported
somewhat indefinitely. The Osage-hedge is very prominent,
apparently bidding fair to be the principal fence of the state.

The worm fence, which stood highest in percentage, is defined in the Kansas statutes as a structure
"composed of rails alone laid up in the manner commonly called a worm fence." The Shanghai fence was
also found in some counties. The fence by this name in
Iowa consisted of three to five rails to a panel laid on
the crotches of forked stakes driven into the ground.
Cherokee County reported "fences with names hitherto
unheard of, the eccentricity of whose construction language very feebly conveys."

The settlers who located in central and western
Kansas, where natural fencing materials were particularly scarce and hundreds of thousands of Texas cattle,
in addition to native animals, were roaming on the
range, needed cheap and effective fences to protect their
crops. In 1875 the estimated average cost of fencing
material ranged per rod from 50 cents for hedge to
$2.37 for stone. The cost of maintaining a hedge until
it would turn stock was about 75 cents per rod. The
homesteaders, most of whom had come west with willing
hands and not much cash in them, often found that

$1,000 was required to fence a farm which cost less than $20 in land-office fees.

The use of barbed wire solved the problem. This fence was effective and reasonable in price. The first patents for barbed wire were granted in 1867.

The manufacturers of barbed wire advertised their product in Kansas and began selling it as early as 1875. On July 21st of that year the *Kansas Farmer* ran an advertisement by Kennedy, Barnes and Company of Aurora, Illinois, of Kennedy's patent wire fence which "doubled the effectiveness of the best board fence ever built" and cost "only 30 cents per rod," exclusive of posts. A week later H. B. Scutt and Company of Joliet, Illinois, advertised Scutt and Watkins Spiral Barbed Iron Rod Fence patented on June 1st that year. This fence was on sale in both Atchison and Topeka. The following year the Stover Patent Fence Barb was advertised in the *Kansas Farmer,* and in 1878 the Thorn Wire Hedge Fence Company advertised the Kelly product.

The first barbed wire made in Kansas was manufactured on the banks of the Kaw. In 1878 A. Henley, a mechanic with a capital of $1.50 and a trunkful of tools, came to Lawrence, where he started a factory for making wire armed with four-pointed steel barbs, in an old stone barn near the Kaw River bridge in which a man had been hanged during the turbulent days. He called his establishment Southwestern Iron Fence Company. The business grew, and by 1882 he was operating nine machines with a capacity of 10,000 pounds per day. In March, 1879, A. G. Hulbert and George A. Gould commenced the manufacture of barbed wire in North Topeka. The name of the firm was Western Iron Fence Company, Kansas Branch. Soon five barbing machines were in operation in their factory, and the daily output was 1,000 pounds of barbed wire. There was a large local retail demand, and a whole-sale trade was established at various points on the Union Pacific and Santa Fe railroads.

How the prairies were fenced with barbed wire is an unwritten chapter of Kaw history. In some locali-ties the farmers welcomed the introduction of the new

product. The wire cost 40 to 50 cents a rod and fence-posts $10 to $12 per hundred. They usually put up a fence consisting of three wires around their pastures and corrals. Some of the poorer farmers used one wire at first and later added a second and a third. The writ-er's father stretched two wires in the hedge around the edge of his farm and enclosed the pasture with three wires.

The people in other communities were prejudiced against barbed wire at first, being afraid of injury to the stock. A number of farmers used a smooth wire at the top for fear horses would reach over the fence and cut their throats.

Some of the first wire on the market was poorly made. It was too hard and broke easily. It is said that the Scutt wire gave trouble. It broke easily when it was bent or stretched. When farmers stretched a fence they often fastened the wire to a wagon and started the team. The men, expecting the wire to break, kept out of the way, or ran for their lives when the broken wire came bounding toward them.

The manufacturers soon learned the wire should be pliable and that short barbs close together were better than long ones some distance apart, as the stock could push the long barbs aside and render them ineffective. The Glidden wire was popular with Kaw farmers because the barbs were effective, and it was pliable enough not to be easily broken when bent or stretched.

In 1880 the Kansas Board of Agriculture made a survey of the fence situation. Reports on the cost of barbed wire came in from all but two of the seventy-eight counties which would imply that the sale was quite general in the state. Fourteen counties reported that barbed wire was the prevailing fence, while thirty-one other counties said that "wire" was the leading fence. Barbed wire was legalized by the legislature in 1883.

The families who pushed westward up the Kaw took barbed wire with them and fenced the cattle trails and divided the open range into fields. They pushed the Texas drover out of Kansas and forced the native cattleman to keep his stock within the confines of a fenced tract. Today the country from the mouth to the sources of the Kaw is crisscrossed by a gigantic net-

work of barbed wire enclosing thousands of fields, pastures, and ranches.

As the farm belt moved westward, the windmill
came into use and played a leading role in transforming
the open range into a farming country. Windmills enabled the farmers and cattle ranchers to locate on the
high plains, and have an adequate supply of water for
a large herd of stock. They could also irrigate small
tracts of land or use the mill to grind feed.

Two makes of windmills were advertised in the
Kansas Farmer in 1878. One was the Stover automatic
windmill manufactured by Stover's Wind Engine Company of Freeport, Illinois; the other was the product of
the Eclipse Windmill Company located at Beloit, Wisconsin, which built the "strongest windmills in the
world." Both firms said their mill could be used for
pumping, grinding, or irrigating. That year windmills
were on sale in Topeka and Wichita.

The average farmer usually put down a well when
he built his home. Then he got a barbed wire fence to
protect his crops, and when he was financially able he
put up a windmill. The writer's father and several of
his neighbors put up fences several years before they
bought windmills.

The cost of fencing a farm before barbed wire
came into general use was quite a burden on the
owner. At an early date farmers and farm leaders
voiced their opposition to the fence laws. In 1871 the
federal commissioner of agriculture said in his annual
report that it was "beginning to be seen that our fence
laws are inequitable in a greater degree than is required
by the principle of yielding something of personal right,
when necessary, for the general good." He included an
exhibit of figures which showed that the cost of fences
was nearly equal to the total amount of the national

debt on which interest was paid and about the same as the estimated value of all the farm animals in the United States. At least half this expense, he said, was unnecessary.

The farm leaders and the press in Kansas joined in this protest. They said the Kansas laws were unjust in that the burden of constructing the fence was on the owner of the land, while the owner of the stock was given free range and need not own or improve a single acre. Furthermore, the annual upkeep of fence was ten per cent of the original cost. The money invested in fence was wasted, they said. It did not increase the value of the cattle or of the grain crop. The only increase was on the tax roll. They advocated the enactment of a herd law which would protect the farmer's crops and save him the expense of building fences.

A night herd law was in operation in Johnson County in 1860 and in Saline County in 1867. Residents of the latter county requested the legislature to pass a general herd law applicable to such counties as should adopt it at any general election. In 1870 the solons passed an act applicable to Saline and four other counties which prescribed that the owner of stock was liable for damages if he allowed the animals to trespass on the premises of another person. The state supreme court held this act unconstitutional on the ground that all general laws should have a uniform operation throughout the state.

In 1872 the legislature passed a general herd law which provided that the county commissioners of each county had the power to direct what animals might run at large and gave a lien on the animals for all damages done. This law was amended two years later. The amended act required the county commissioners, on petition of two-thirds of the legal voters of the county, to prohibit stock of all kinds from running at large.

The herd law was a boon to agriculture in the period before barbed wire came into general use. The existence of the herd law in certain sections of the state and its agitation in other parts induced the State Board of Agriculture in 1875 to investigate the question and gather data concerning fences. It was found that nearly 40 per cent of the counties had adopted the herd law. Two-thirds of these were newly settled counties. Reports of the beneficial effects of the law came from several quarters. From Rice County came a typical comment: "Should the law be repealed, it would be impossible to raise crops." A farm leader residing in Reno County wrote an article on the cost of fences, in which he said that before the adoption of the herd law he surveyed the situation in Kansas and found that stock were destroying from 10 to 40 per cent of the crops; that in Reno County where the law was enforced the damage did not exceed 7 per cent.

Many of the newspapers were stanch supporters of the herd law. They made comparisons to show that the counties in which the law was in force were being rapidly settled and were outstripping in growth, settlement, and production those counties which had not adopted the law. The Wichita *Eagle* said enthusiastically, "The herd law is the making of this valley." The Topeka *Commonwealth* sent a reporter up the Kaw in the summer of 1876 to write up the country. It was just before harvest, and the fields were beautiful. He was inspired by the scene and pushed his pen hard and fast to give the readers an adequate word picture of what he saw. He wrote that west of Junction City the land was being settled rapidly and that between Abilene and Ellsworth nearly every section of government land had an actual occupant and the Kansas Pacific was daily disposing of immense quantities of land. "All in consequence of the adoption of the herd law," he said.

The journalist stopped off at Abilene and spent a whole day riding around the "two-thousand acre wheat field" of Theodore C. Henry, at that time the largest wheatgrower in Kansas, whose farming activities were receiving wide notice. He said that Henry "never thought of going into the wheat business until after the adoption of the herd law, about three years ago."

Theodore C. Henry, known for two decades as the "Kansas wheat king," deserves more than passing mention because of his great contribution to the wheat industry. He was reared on a farm in Ontario County, New York, and received a thorough classical education. His father's specialty was winter wheat. From him the son at an early age gained an interest in wheat culture.

In 1865 Henry went to Alabama and tried to raise cotton by the use of northern methods. Impaired health and financial reverses made the experiment a failure. In 1867 the Henry family moved to Abilene, Kansas. Two years later T. C. Henry entered the real estate business in partnership with James B. Shane and was elected to the office of register of deeds of Dickinson County. In the fall of 1869, Abilene was incorporated as a third-class city. The court appointed a board of trustees consisting of Henry, Shane, and three others. The board chose Henry as chairman, which in effect made him the first mayor of Abilene.

Henry had not lost his interest in wheat. He took time off from his arduous duties as mayor of a wild cow town to read the daily reports of the wheat market. He saw that day after day Minnesota winter wheat topped the market in Chicago. He began to wonder if

this wheat could not be successfully grown on the Kansas prairies.

He decided to experiment. He broke a small patch
of river-bottom land in a secluded spot and sowed five
acres in wheat. Like many others, he was afraid to try
raising wheat on the uplands. He didn't tell anyone
about his experiment and cautioned his family to keep
quiet. He didn't like being ridiculed and called crazy.

The experiment was successful. When the grain
was cut the following summer it turned out well. Most
of the farmers in that locality raised spring wheat and
believed that fall wheat would winterkill. When they
heard about Henry's five-acre patch they shook their
heads in doubt. It was an accident, they said. Next year
it would be a failure. Let that "city feller" waste time
and money raising "newfangled" wheat if he wanted
to, they would keep right on growing the same wheat
in the same old way.

Henry was convinced that winter wheat was the
crop for Kansas. In 1873 he was ready to introduce his
system of winter-wheat culture. He selected a tract of
land in the Smoky Hill valley two miles east of Abilene
and next to the Kansas Pacific Railroad. The herd law
made fencing unnecessary. All the work was done by
contract. As he put it, "I farmed in kid gloves, without
horse or hoe." He hired men to break five hundred acres
of sod. This was mostly done with six-yoke teams of
Texas oxen drawing twenty-inch Moline plows, rigged
to self-hold. In August he broadcast Red May seed and
covered it with Scotch harrows drawn by oxteams. The
ground was so dry and hard that when the seeding was
completed the harrow teeth were worn down to mere
stubs.

He purchased two Marsh harvesters and a Weylich
header to harvest the crop. It was necessary to run the

header with team relays night and day to save the grain. At night a man on a white horse, dressed in white and carrying a light, rode ahead of the machine.

He used a steam engine and threshing machine to thresh the grain. The yield was slightly under twenty bushels to the acre, which is noteworthy in view of the fact that 1874 was the year of drought, chinch bugs, and grasshoppers.

In the spring of 1874, Henry broke seven hundred acres adjoining the 500-acre field and planted the whole tract to wheat which yielded an average of twenty-five bushels to the acre of grade No. 1 wheat. He sold the crop to Leavenworth millers and realized a price ranging from $1.05 to $1.21 per bushel.

Henry increased his wheat-farming operations until he reached a maximum of nearly 10,000 acres scattered over the country.

The Red May didn't yield well and was tender to heavy frosts, so he tried Fultz. Next he brought Clawson from New York and finally planted Red Turkey, the variety which has made Kansas famous.

His main field extended from Abilene to a point about eleven miles east. It was quite a sight, especially when the grain was ripening, and it attracted wide attention. The railroad ran through the center of the field. The trainmen called out to the passengers, "We are coming to T. C. Henry's wheatfield—biggest in America." The passengers would turn in their seats, and to get a better view would put their heads out the open windows. Then more than likely some elderly person would exclaim, "Well, I snum. I never seen so much wheat in all my born days." The Fourth Report of the State Board of Agriculture published a picture of Henry's field and cited his methods of production. Newspapermen in Kansas wrote him up. In the early summer of 1876 Colonel Anderson, a staff correspondent of the New York *Herald*, came west to write up the wheat industry. He visited Henry, who relates the incident:

"Just before sunset we drove to an elevation northwest of Abilene, overlooking the valley. The yellow grain, nearly ripe, stretched afield for miles to the east, bordered by the deep verdure of the prairie on either side. . . . My companion caught inspiration from the scene, and exclaimed: 'What a magnificent golden belt!' Such was the origin of the well-known and appropriate term."

Henry became the apostle of winter wheat. He studied winter wheat. He raised winter wheat. He preached winter wheat. In his words: "I spread my winter-wheat propaganda. No evangelist was ever more active. I answered hundreds of letters, sent out thousands of circulars, wrote treatises, and delivered addresses. No townsite boomer in the West ever overlapped me."

He showed a skeptical public that winter wheat could be successfully grown in Kansas on a large scale and in a "fenceless field." He was the first of a long line of "wheat kings" on the Kaw who have startled the world with their exploits. He says his "example became contagious." No doubt many persons witnessed his success and were inoculated with the "mass-production germ." A number of farmers and landlords, in Dickinson County and elsewhere, began to sow large acreages. In 1875 fifteen persons in Dickinson County each planted a hundred or more acres of winter wheat, and several others put in from fifty to eighty acres each. For several years Dickinson County ranked second in the state in the number of acres planted to winter wheat, and eventually Kansas surpassed every state in the Union as a producer of winter wheat.

Wheat and corn were rivals for first place among the crops raised on the Kaw. The homesteaders who located in central Kansas found they could not grow corn twelve feet tall as the farmers did at the mouth of the Kaw. In fact, they could not be certain of a good crop every year. The fluctuation from year to year and the complete failure in 1874 convinced them that wheat was a safer crop on the high prairie. The settlers who pushed up the tributaries of the Kaw into the short-grass region soon learned that the dry weather and blistering sun usually burned the corn before it reached the roasting-ear stage.

They found that the soil, climate, and rainfall were favorable to wheatgrowing. Wheat thrives in a region with a rainfall not exceeding thirty-five inches, a cool, moist fall, a moderately cold winter followed by a moist spring and a hot, dry harvest season. These conditions prevail in Kansas, especially in central and western Kansas.

At the same time two brothers in the wheat family —winter and spring—were contenders for the crown. While the figures are not available, it is believed that the first families planted more spring than winter wheat. In 1870, when the statistics were first separated, the elder brother was slightly in the lead in the number of bushels produced. Then winter wheat forged ahead in acreage and production, while spring wheat fluctuated in the number of acres and yield, and declined in both as the wheat area pushed westward.

Winter wheat won because the Kaw country was better adapted to its culture. The winter wheat was harvested by July. The dry weather and hot winds usually came in July and August. The hot blasts out of the south often caught and damaged the spring wheat. Furthermore, spring wheat was susceptible to injury from insects and damage from rust. The agricultural leaders, aware of its weaknesses, urged the farmers to raise winter wheat. The state board was especially outspoken on this subject in 1875 and concluded with the following statement:

"The fallacy that this, or any other country, is equally adapted to the growing of winter and spring wheat is passing away before the light of experience, and the sooner our farmers get 'tired out' in spring wheat culture the better it will be for them."

Corn did well in eastern Kansas, and the Kaw valley has become famous for its "twelve-foot corn." It is also grown quite extensively in central and western Kansas. However, in that area wheat is usually the farmer's cash crop, while corn is his stock feed. Five million bushels were grown in 1860. The crop has fluctuated greatly between good years and poor years, but production has climbed upward to more than a hundred million bushels some years. A record-breaking crop of 273,000,000 was raised in 1889. From 1879 to 1929 Kansas was among the seven leading corn states in the country. However, with the extension of the wheat area into western Kansas thirty years ago, wheat has gained on corn in acreage and production and has been greater in both quite a number of years.

While soft winter wheat and spring wheat and corn were battling for supremacy, a hardheaded, red complexioned, bearded cousin in the wheat family from Russia, named Red Turkey, seized the crown and established a mighty empire on the Kaw.

14

The Usurper Seizes the Crown

THE early settlers on the Kaw generally raised the soft wheats which they had brought from eastern states. May, Fultz, Mediterranean, Red Sea, Clawson, and Walker were popular varieties. Most of these have beardless heads. The pioneers called them smooth wheats. The scientists call them bald. Soft winter wheats were superior to soft spring wheats and did well in eastern Kansas where the annual rainfall was from 35 to 40 inches and where fairly humid conditions prevailed. The soft varieties were especially adapted to the sandy bottom land of this area, but when moved westward into central Kansas they could not survive the cold winters, the searching winds of spring, and the hot, dry summers.

In cold weather, the wet soil heaved in freezing and thawing until it reached a degree of disintegration which left the roots of the wheat plants without protection and allowed the winds of early spring to dry out, and, in many instances, destroy the crop. When the weather was dry during the winter, the winds blew the soil from the roots and killed the plants. Some of the successful wheatgrowers prevented winterkilling by cultivating the surface only to a depth necessary to kill the weeds. T. C. Henry, the wheat king, plowed but once for two crops, using a harrow between the harvest of the first crop and the seeding of the second. Many farmers, discouraged by repeated failures, abandoned wheat and turned to other crops.

At the time the wheat farmers were searching for satisfactory methods of growing soft wheat in an area not adapted to its culture, the Russian hard, or Red Turkey, winter wheat was brought into central Kansas. The original home of this wheat was in southern Russia just north and east of the Black Sea, and north of the Caucasus Mountains. This area included the Crimea, Taurida, and neighboring provinces. The region has a deep black soil, long and severe winters, hot, dry summers, and is subject to drought. The conditions of soil and climate are quite similar to those of our Kansas prairies, only the drought being more severe in the Russian district.

Red Turkey, having lived in this environment for generations, was hardy and could withstand the extreme cold, heat, and drought which his soft, beardless American cousins could not survive.

It has been generally believed that the Mennonites were the first to bring Turkey wheat to the Kaw, but the Kansas agricultural authorities of thirty years ago reported that before the first party of Mennonites arrived "there was a small colony of French settlers in Marion County who were raising the hard winter wheat, although not to any great extent."

Even if this little French colony did grow the first hard winter wheat, the tradition will persist that the Mennonites introduced the variety into Kansas. The Mennonites deserve credit for being largely instrumental in introducing the Turkey wheat, and in furthering its early development.

The Mennonites, a sect of Protestant Christians, were living in western Prussia in 1783 when the Crimea and provinces adjoining were ceded to Russia by Turkey. At that time these provinces were inhabited by Tartars and other half-wild tribes who dwelt in wretched villages. The Empress Catherine, a German princess by birth, invited the Mennonites to colonize the newly acquired territory. She knew they were excellent farmers and hoped they would intermarry with the natives and improve the race. She exempted these God-fearing people from military service and gave them religious freedom as added inducement. To a sect whose chief religious tenet was peace among nations and the brotherhood of men, these were cherished privileges.

The Mennonites moved to the new land, settling chiefly in the Crimea and in the Molochna (Milk River) district in northern Taurida. There they raised hard winter wheat and employed the natives at harvesttime, but their sons and daughters did not marry into the native families.

In 1871 the czar withdrew the special privileges granted by Catherine. When news of his action reached the Mennonites, there was great excitement throughout the colonies. They talked of emigrating to America where they were assured of religious freedom. In 1873 they sent five delegates who were to look for a location and report their findings on their return.

At that time the Santa Fe Railroad had thousands of acres of land in Kansas for sale. Near the close of the year 1872 the Santa Fe completed its line from Atchison to the Colorado boundary, thereby earning from the government a land grant of 3,000,000 acres consisting of alternate sections in a strip of land across the state on each side of the railroad. The officials put in motion an extensive system of immigration and colonization.

They placed C. B. Schmidt in charge of the foreign immigration department. He got in touch with representatives of the Mennonite colonists. He also went to Russia and traveled through the Mennonite settlements for the purpose of inducing them to emigrate to Kansas. He held two or three meetings a day, but on learning that three of the czar's mounted gendarmes were hot on his trail he traveled rapidly and reached the American consulate at Odessa without being arrested.

After visiting several states and Canada, the Mennonite delegation decided that central Kansas was best adapted to their needs. The soil and climate were more like those of the steppes of Russia than any other section they had visited.

There were additional reasons why the Mennonites chose Kansas. The legislature of 1874 enacted a law exempting citizens from military duty when that service conflicted with their religious beliefs. The Santa Fe Railroad sent literature to Russia and had it distributed among the Mennonites; it contained a copy of the law on military service, described the railroad lands, and extolled the agricultural possibilities of Kansas. As a special inducement the Santa Fe agreed to carry Mennonite passengers on their line free of charge for a period of three months, and to haul, also free of charge, large quantities of household goods and building materials for the colonists.

Bernard Warkentin, a young Mennonite from the Crimea who had been in America for some time, was stationed at New York to meet his countrymen and direct them to Kansas. The first party, consisting of six hundred persons, left Russia on June 20th and arrived at Topeka on September 8th. Two weeks later a colony of eleven hundred people reached that city.

For four weeks, pending the selection of their lands,

the colonists were quartered in the King bridge shops, an immense brick enclosure purchased by the Santa Fe for use as carshops.

The arrival of so many foreigners was quite an event in Topeka. The press had announced their coming and had given the readers information on their history, religion, and means of livelihood. Large crowds gathered at the King bridge shops to see these strangers, and people on the streets gazed at them as they went about the city. Their dress was the subject of comment. One writer said:

The men appear to have conscientious scruples against wearing any clothes that fit them, the idea appearing to be to buy all the clothes you can for the money. The men's vests, therefore, descend toward the knees, and their pants possess an alarming amount of "slack." Their favorite head gear is a flat cloth cap, which they pull off in saluting any person. This habit they will soon drop, now that they have arrived in Kansas where "nobody respects nothing." The females are not fashionably attired. It is evident that the "tie backs" had not struck Russia when they left. The favorite dress goods are a dark green figure on a black ground. The children all have handkerchiefs tied over their heads, which give them a peculiarly round-headed appearance.

The colonists brought more than two million dollars in gold with them. While in Topeka, they purchased many articles necessary for opening their new homes. Farmers living miles from the city, who had no feed for their stock owing to the drought and grasshoppers, brought in farm animals and sold them to the newcomers at ridiculously low prices.

From the Santa Fe Railroad they bought 60,000 acres of land in the counties of Marion, Harvey, Mc-

Pherson, and Reno. They were admirable judges of good land and selected some of the best sections along the line. The first colonists settled in villages as in Russia. The well-to-do among them erected frame houses, while the poor families put up dwellings with walls of earth covered by roofs thatched with prairie grass in which they lived until they could afford better residences.

These people migrated to America to engage in farming, especially wheatgrowing. Before they left Russia they selected the best Turkey seed wheat they had in their granaries, picking it out one grain at a time, and brought it to Kansas with them. Some writers state that the first party didn't bring more than twenty or thirty bushels of seed wheat. However, Mark Carleton, the "wheat dreamer" who learned many things from them about wheat culture in Russia and America, says that "Each family brought over a bushel or more of Crimean wheat for seed, and from this was grown the first crop of Kansas hard winter wheat." Four hundred families arrived at Topeka in September, 1874. If each family brought "over a bushel," that would make a total of more than four hundred bushels of seed wheat.

The Mennonites, having come from a semiarid region, had learned from long experience how to endure drought, how to fight and vanquish grasshoppers, and how to raise wheat on dry land. In southern Russia an important feature of cultivation was the black fallow, called black because of the dark color of the turned over soil. It was a summer tillage and there were four cultivations: first, a deep plowing and then three lighter operations at intervals of a month, made by small gang plows or cultivators. Consequently, they were acquainted with the method of early deep plowing and thorough surface cultivation—practices which were widely advocated among farmers a quarter of a century later in connection with dry farming.

The newcomers were a hard-working, thrifty lot. They erected houses and sowed wheat the first year. In 1875 the colonists in Harvey County had fields of winter wheat ranging from five to thirty acres to each family. A writer, who spent a day in the settlement in Marion County that year, told about the stacks of wheat and immense piles of straw located at the back doors of the homes he visited. The straw was intended for fuel in their "Russian ovens," or oven-fireplaces. The oven was built of brick of their own make and was generally seven feet high, seven feet long, two feet wide, and was situated about equally in each of three rooms. The door of the oven was in the kitchen, as was a door through which to allow the smoke to escape to the chimney. Both doors were opened and closed at will; otherwise the oven was perfectly airtight. The blaze from the straw passed from the front to the rear and then back again to the front of the oven, the smoke passing out through another smaller door near the top and into the chimney. Strange as it may seen, a whole house could be well heated and the cooking done for twenty-four hours during the coldest season of the year from the burning of four good-sized armfuls of straw or an equal amount of a mixture of manure and straw.

The families brought with them many of their clumsy farm implements but soon discarded these for American machinery. The colony in Marion County had a hundred "Russian threshing machines" made but never used one of them. This machine was a cylindrical stone about three feet long by one and a half feet in diameter. The surface was divided into deep cogs, a rod was run through the center of the roller and to this shafts were attached. The farmer scattered the grain on the floor.

Then he hitched a horse to the machine, and the roller went round and round like the elephant in the circus when the band began to play.

A newspaperman visited the colony in Marion County in 1880 and found that the Mennonites had made remarkable progress in five years. They owned good farms ranging from sixty to three hundred acres each; good houses and barns; the best farm machinery of all sorts; and almost without exception they were "entirely free from indebtedness. . . . The staple product of their farms is wheat; they raised also corn, rye, and millet, but the greater portion of their land is devoted to wheat, and every barnyard contains from two or three to twelve or fifteen large stacks of this grain. The first two seasons after they arrived were good, with plenty of rain, and they concluded that this must be an essential for success in wheat-raising. When the next years came and proved to be somewhat dry, they were fearful of the result; but they found their crops to be good and sound, although the yield per acre was not quite so great, and now they say they will risk the wheat crop there in any season in preference to any other cereal. . . .

"There is a painful contrast between the farms of these Mennonite settlers and those of their American neighbors. The latter can be known at a glance by a general air of bareness and neglect, which shows at once a lack of energy and industry, or of interest in what they are doing. The former always have neat, comfortable houses, good roomy barns and granaries, orchards and cornfields as clean of weeds as if they could not grow there, close-trimmed hedges, groves and avenues of forest trees, the neatest of gardens and walks."

The flow of Mennonite immigration into Kansas continued through 1874 and 1875. By the summer of

1876 it was estimated that more than 6,000 members of this faith had settled in the state. By 1883 about 15,000 had located on lands purchased from the Santa Fe Railroad.

Bernard Warkentin was instrumental in introducing hard wheat into Kansas and in selling the seed to American farmers. Associated with him were two other men—Christian Krehbiel, who was first a farmer, but in 1886 erected a mill in Moundridge, and C. B. Schmidt, the immigration agent of the Santa Fe who induced thousands of Mennonites to emigrate to Kansas and was called the "Moses of the Mennonites."

In 1871 Warkentin was traveling through the West seeking a milling location and decided to locate in central Kansas because he believed the soil and climatic conditions were similar to those of his home in southern Russia. He decided that the Turkey wheat could be successfully grown here, so he purchased the site at Halstead and built his mill.

He induced the early Mennonite colonists to bring with them their native wheat for seeding. They planted the wheat, and it proved well adapted to growth in this area, so Warkentin determined to make Kansas a hardwheat country. He commissioned a nephew in Russia to buy and ship several thousand bushels of Turkey wheat direct to Newton. This was to be distributed among the farmers. Before long American farmers were growing this foreign grain, were discussing it with their neighbors over the division fences, and were telling their bankers about it in town on Saturday afternoon.

The section in which the Mennonites settled soon stood at the top in wheat production in Kansas and was known as the "winter wheat belt." Ten counties, each having 40,000 acres or more in winter wheat, made up this belt in 1878. With one exception, these counties were located in central Kansas. In 1872 the acreage of these ten counties was only 9 per cent of the winter wheat acreage of the state; in 1878, 49 per cent. During the next six years the counties in this section led in acreage, average production, and aggregate yields. By 1884 the wheat belt embraced sixteen counties in central Kansas. McPherson County, located in the heart of the belt, had ranked first in the state each year for seven successive years. In that period the winter wheat acreage in the county had risen from 58,000 to 157,000 acres.

This doesn't mean that every farmer in the wheat belt was growing the Russian variety. Not at all. No information is available until 1882, when twenty-seven counties, including most of those in the wheat belt, reported Turkey wheat among the "varieties most successfully grown." Practically all of the twenty-seven counties were also growing the soft wheats.

The Turkey wheat made headway slowly. Nearly a quarter of a century passed before the good qualities of this variety were fully appreciated. For many years after its introduction a considerable portion of the population was prejudiced against it. The farmers said soft wheat had a stiffer, stronger straw than hard wheat and was less likely to lodge in the wet seasons. Under favorable weather conditions the yield of soft wheat was equal to or greater than that of hard wheat. It was possible to sow and harvest the soft wheat earlier, and owing to the rank growth of the plant in the fall, excellent pasturage was assured. The less virile farmers, especially the hired hands, objected to the hard wheat because the stiff beards scratched them. But most important of all, the pioneer growers of Turkey wheat couldn't find a market for their crop or were forced to accept a lower price than was paid for the softer wheats.

This discrimination was due in part to the inadequate equipment for milling hard wheats, but chiefly to the disfavor with which the American public received the flour and bread made from the hard wheat.

The pioneer mills were equipped with stone burrs to grind the soft wheats. The stones were set close together for the purpose of reducing the wheat to flour with one operation—"low grinding," the millers called it. When they tried to grind the Turkey wheat they experienced considerable difficulty, for the flinty character of the wheat made it difficult to mill by the low grinding process, and the flour was inferior in quality.

Here and there a miller gave serious thought to the problem of making satisfactory flour from Turkey wheat. Some of the millers softened the grain by steaming and moistening before grinding—processes later in general use and considered indispensable in flouring hard wheats. Others used the "gradual reduction" method commonly known as "high grinding." They lessened the grinding action of the stones. They didn't reduce the berry to flour the first passage between the stones as in low grinding. Instead, they merely crushed and liberated it from the covering of bran the first time and then ran it through a second and usually a third time before it was reduced to flour. They decreased the speed of the stones from 200 or 300 revolutions per minute to about 100 per minute, and reduced the size of the stones to allow the material to escape as soon as it was granulated in order to keep the reduction to flour the first run at a low point. This process improved the quality of the flour.

Fortunately, two improvements in the flour milling process came about this time. One was the use of the middlings purifier invented by Edmund N. La Croix in 1870. The purifier was a machine for separating dust and fluffy particles of bran from the middlings. It enabled the millers to obtain a greater quantity of flour of a better quality from a barrel of wheat than had previously been possible. The purifier was beneficial also in mills grinding the soft wheats. This machine was first installed in a mill in Kansas in 1873. After 1875 Kansas millers generally adopted this equipment.

The other improvement was the use of rollers in the place of stone burrs. The rolls were made of smooth iron or porcelain. The wheat was reduced to flour by successive passages through the rolls. The first time the berry was split. The process was repeated until the flour was completely separated from the bran. The use of the rollers improved the quality and increased the quantity of flour from a bushel of wheat. The large mills added this equipment in the early eighties. Since the installation of rolls practically involved the building of a new mill, the country millers, in many instances, found the cost prohibitive. In 1885 Kansas mills were equipped as follows: 59 per cent with rolls and 41 per cent with burrs. From that time the small mill declined in importance.

With the advent of the roll and the purifier, the millers could handle hard winter wheat and produce a satisfactory flour. The wheat milled well. The flour-making portion separated readily from the bran coat and the germ. The percentage of flour obtained from a bushel of grain usually ran higher in hard wheat than in soft, while the price of the former wheat on the market was less than that paid for the latter variety—two items not usually overlooked by the miller. Time changes all things. The millers who had called Turkey wheat names in the early days were lauding its good qualities a decade or so later.

From the baker's point of view the hard wheat flour

was better for making bread, because a barrel of good flour would make several pound loaves more than an equal weight of soft wheat flour. This was due chiefly to the larger percentage of gluten in the hard wheat.

The miller and the baker both realized the commercial possibilities of the hard wheat flour. The next thing was to find a market for this product. This was not an easy matter. The housewives were accustomed to the velvety white flour and chalk-white bread made from soft wheat and rebelled against the hard wheat products. Strange as it may seem, in some communities the families of American farmers who grew hard wheat refused to use flour made from it.

When the housewife went to the store to buy flour the exchange of words between her and the grocer ran something like this:

"What will you have today, Mrs. Lambert?" asked the grocer as the woman approached the counter.

"A fifty-pound sack of flour."

"Hard or soft?"

"Soft, of course, Mr. Arnold. I don't like that Russian flour."

"Why? It's good flour and makes good bread. Women like it when they learn how to handle it."

"I don't like the feel of it. It's more like sand than flour; besides, it's yellow and so's the bread. It takes more kneading than I have time for when I have to do all my housework and get four young'uns off to school. We don't like the different taste either."

"There's nothing wrong with the flour. It's gluten that makes it hard and gritty. The 'sand' you feel is the flinty particles of gluten. Even the best mills can't crush these completely, they are so hard—"

"What's gluten?" asked the woman, interrupting the grocer's sales talk.

"Gluten is the substance that makes the hard-wheat berry dark and hard. You know the soft wheat is lighter colored. Well, it's richer in starch. The starch makes the soft wheat flour seem smooth and velvety. Gluten absorbs a lot of water which increases the weight of the flour and causes it to swell. The dough stretches and holds the air you knead into it. That makes it lighter, so you can make more loaves from a sack of flour than you can from the same amount of the other.

"Then, too, Mrs. Lambert, the bread stays fresh longer than loaves from the May or Fultz flour. I think it has a delicious flavor. That good taste comes from the large amount of gluten and oil in the flour. These give the loaf that nutty character.

"We have a special price today. Better try a sack. It's dandy flour."

"I'm sorry, Mr. Arnold, but I won't have the stuff in the house. Put a sack of May flour in my order."

The prejudice against the hard wheat flours nearly ruined the millers who blazed the way. In the words of one writer:

The pathway of the millers who first ground the Kansas hard wheat into flour was not carpeted with roses alone, as thorns predominated. The patrons had been accustomed to the flour from soft wheat, and no one who has not been a miller can appreciate the difficulty to be overcome when he tries to convince women, against their will, that anything new or different is as good as the old product with which they have been familiar.

One illustration will show what the early millers of hard wheat faced. In 1882 a company built a mill in Topeka and installed machinery for grinding hard wheat. Several cars of flour shipped to points in Kansas,

Missouri, and Iowa were condemned, and payment was refused because the housewives wouldn't buy it. Fortunately the price of wheat advanced, so the grocers were induced to retain and work off the flour.

The millers used ingenious methods of disposing of the flour and of teaching the public to appreciate it. They began by mixing a small percentage of the hard with the soft wheat, gradually increasing the amount each year. Kansas hard wheat was nameless in the world market for years after it was first grown. The millers used it to mix with hard spring wheat and sold it as such. They sold the flour under the label of other states.

Eventually the American public learned to like and began to demand hard wheat products. The peculiar qualities of Kansas hard wheat became so well known in grain- and flour-importing countries of Europe that the millers and bakers measured the value of their home-grown wheat by the percentage of Kansas hard wheat admixture required to produce a good breadmaking flour.

The turn of the century found Red Turkey secure in his Central Kansas Empire and ruling over a contented lot of subjects. The most rebellious of these, the housewives, long since had surrendered and accepted the new order of things. The farmers had decided that it was more profitable to grow hard wheat and be certain of a reliable yield one year after another, even though they were compelled to accept several cents per bushel less than the buyers and millers were paying for soft wheat. The millers, paying less for the grain and getting more flour per barrel than they obtained from milling soft wheat, naturally were strong for Red Turkey. The bakers, able to make more loaves of bread from a barrel of hard wheat flour than they made from an equal quantity of soft wheat flour, of course, were satisfied with their lot. The children consumed huge slices of the delicious nut-brown loaves spread thick with butter and jelly, and grew tall and healthy. They were indeed a big happy family and were proud of their King.

15

The Westward Extension of
the Empire

AT THE opening of the present century, the American people fully appreciated the good qualities of Turkey wheat. It was grown by most of the wheat farmers in the winter wheat belt, which at that time extended to the Nebraska line on the north, to the 100th meridian on the west, and comprised thirty counties. With the exception of two counties, this belt was a compact territory and produced 79 per cent of the Kansas wheat crop in 1901. These counties were in the "million bushel" class; none produced less than 1,000,-000 bushels, while Sumner County, the "buckle" of the belt, grew 6,800,000 bushels in 1901.

West of the 100th meridian was the high plains country where agriculture had made little headway. This was a region of extreme temperatures and low rainfall, the average annual precipitation being about twenty inches. Many people considered this area unfit for agriculture. Back of their belief was some truth and a lot of tradition. The early geographers and writers had included this territory in the Great American Desert and pronounced it unsuited to profitable farming.

In the early days thousands of range cattle fed on the buffalo grass that carpeted the ground. Then, in the seventies and eighties, settlers, lured by the promise of free homesteads and cheap railroad lands, moved in and fenced the range. By means of barbed wire and tick laws they drove the range cattlemen out of the state. The scientists warned the homesteaders of dry years and crop failures. They laughed and said, "You fellers talk like cattlemen." They went on turning the sod and sowing soft wheats.

Then came a dry spell and a succession of crop failures. Thousands of farmers left the drought-stricken area.

Meantime, men with money had taken over the farms of unfortunate settlers in payment of taxes or loans of money, or had purchased cheap grasslands, on which they established cattle ranches. The use of windmills made it possible to fence the uplands. Ranches of all sizes dotted the plains. Some were large spreads, consisting of several square miles of land, on which thousands of head of cattle grazed.

In the nineties there was another migration of farmers to the short-grass country. The new settlers brought the Turkey wheat with them. After that, homesteaders continued to move in. The wheat acreage of this section more than doubled between 1890 and 1900. Three-fourths of the 1900 crop was the Turkey strain.

While this transformation was taking place, there arose in the wheat industry a colorful figure who made an outstanding contribution to the extension of the wheat area west of the 100th meridian. His name was Mark Alfred Carleton. His official position was cerealist in the United States Department of Agriculture, though he probably would have held the portfolio of Prime

Minister of the Wheat Empire had it been a reality. He was called a "wheat dreamer," but his dreams were highly practical. Perhaps without his great work the Kaw would not be the nation's granary today.

Mark Carleton was born in Jerusalem, Ohio, in 1866 and attended the country school there. When he was ten years old his family moved to Cloud County, Kansas. At that time Cloud County farmers were raising 350,000 bushels of wheat annually, mostly soft varieties. The year following his removal to Kansas Carleton witnessed the destruction of the wheat crop by disease. The black stem rust attacked the wheat and spread from field to field and from county to county. Whole fields were ruined. This disaster made a deep impression on the boy's mind. He began to wonder about the cause of the disease and how it could be prevented. It isn't right, he thought, for farmers to work hard all year and then have the chief source of their income wiped out in a few days' time. When he entered Kansas Agricultural College he specialized in botany, and by the time he received the Bachelor of Science degree he was an expert botanist—so promising that Wichita University employed him on their faculty as professor of natural history.

This professorship soon proved too limited in its possibilities for a man of his energy and inclinations. He was a born researcher and wanted to be out in the fields where he could squint through a magnifying glass at disease spots on leaves and dig into the black earth to see what it was made of. Consequently, he resigned his professorship and went back to the experiment station at Manhattan. As assistant in botany the opportunity to study grain rusts was his. As he put it, "From an economic standpoint, one of the most important fungus pests with which the farmers of Kansas come in contact is that which attacks grain causing the disease known as rust. The loss due to this disease in the United States in one year runs up into the millions of dollars. It is rare that a field of wheat is entirely free from it, and often a large portion of the crop is destroyed."

In those days the "utmost confusion existed as to the distribution of cereal rusts" and the "particular species occurring on any of the different cereals was only a matter of inference," he said. Practically everyone, including the botanists, believed that a rust parasite could travel from one cereal to another. Carleton decided to find out if this was true. He began his experiments in September, 1893. He sowed a plat of ground to wheat, oats, barley, and rye. Then he grew the rust. He smeared the rust on wheat plants and set them in the plat to bring about infection. The wheat rusted, but the oats and other grains were not diseased. He inoculated young oats with the rust and transplanted them. The "oats became somewhat rusted." The other grains remained healthy. He inoculated the other grains and blue grass with the rust parasite and obtained similar results. This series of experiments showed that the rusts were "probably physiological species" and did not jump from wheat to oats and from oats to some other grain; it proved that "wheat" was "infected by rust from wheat, but not by rust from oats, corn, or blue grass."

Carleton also inoculated several varieties of hard and soft wheat with rust. He discovered that all varieties suffered, but that hard wheat suffered the least. He concluded that the "breeding of varieties of grain which shall be rust resisting, the so-called 'rust proof' varieties," was the most promising solution of the rust problem.

These experiments made Carleton famous and secured for him a position with the United States Department of Agriculture. He began work for the department on March 1, 1894. Busy with various phases of the new job, he didn't resume the inoculation experiments for nearly two years. Meantime he continued to think about the rustproof variety. Somewhere in the world he was sure there was a wheat tough enough to resist rust and to withstand cold and heat and drought. He would find that wheat. He collected nearly a thousand varieties of wheat from all parts of the world and conducted a series of experiments during the seasons of 1895, 1896, and 1897.

He experimented at Garrett Park, Maryland, in 1895. He treated the soil with a fertilizer and then sowed the different varieties in alternate rows forty-eight feet long and twelve inches apart. The orange leaf rust was the only species attacking the plants, but it was abundant and gave an opportunity of testing the resistance of the different varieties.

This seemed too much like a hothouse experiment. The climate and the condition of the soil were too favorable. He decided to transfer the experiments out to the wheat area of the Great Plains where the plants would be subjected to the rigors of a severe climate and where stem rust as well as leaf rust was nearly always present. So he gathered up his bags of wheat and came out to Kansas in the fall of 1895.

He conducted the experiments on the farm of B. B. Stimmel near Salina the first year, and on State College land at Manhattan the second year. The winters were unusually severe in both localities. In the fall it was dry and the soil blew. There was a wide range in temperature. It got cold and froze. Then it warmed up and thawed. And for good measure a few Kaw blizzards were thrown in. The leaf rust and the stem rust both attacked the wheat plants. The slaughter was terrific. Hundreds of the imported varieties failed entirely, and only a small proportion of the whole number tested during the three seasons survived.

These experiments convinced Carleton that the ideal wheat for the plains was an "early maturing, hard, red, frost-resistant and drought-resistant sort." He found that some of Russian origin stood up better than others. He knew the Mennonites had brought Turkey wheat from Russia and were growing it successfully while their American neighbors failed with the soft wheats. He was certain he could find the ideal wheat in Russia. He must learn more about Russia and Russian wheats. He talked with the Mennonites. He read books. He studied maps. He collected a mass of information.

Then the big, gray-eyed wheat dreamer made up his mind to visit Russia. When he approached his superiors in Washington, they were cold to his request. They believed it was a wild notion of a wheat enthusiast, and an expensive notion for the department. He met their objections with an array of maps, facts, and figures. When they reminded him that he didn't know Russian he went home, bought some grammars, and learned the language.

Eventually he secured permission to go and left Washington on July 4, 1898. He spent some time with experts in St. Petersburg and Odessa, then went to Moscow where he ate some of the famous bread called "kalach" which he pronounced the best bread he had ever put his teeth into. They told him this bread was made from a kind of wheat grown by the Kirghiz and Turghai people on the Siberian border where it was impossible to grow ordinary wheats because of the extreme drought. "That's just the sort of wheat I'm looking for," he said to himself. "I must visit that land." So he pushed on and at last reached the Kirghiz steppes in western Siberia, which he describes as a "monotonous, unbroken expanse of treeless arid plains with a rainfall reaching less than ten inches." The dry heat of midsummer was so intense that mirages were frequent. A large proportion of the scanty rainfall occurred during the growing season, and the powdery soil absorbed it greedily.

He drove out on the prairie and looked at the wheat fields. He walked into a field, examined the plants carefully, and dug in the parched soil. Then he went on to other fields. He asked questions of the natives, using his hands when words failed to convey his meaning. He continued his search, riding down dusty roads and tramping through fields of grain. At last he found the Kubanka wheat, one of the toughest, most drought- and rust-resistant varieties known. The Kubanka is a durum wheat and has a bearded, compact head, yellowish-white chaff, and large, hard, light-amber colored kernels. The manufacturers of macaroni use this variety.

Carleton brought the Kubanka wheat back to America. He also brought the Arnautka, the Gharnovka, the Pererodka, and the Don, all hardy durum varieties. He said these wheats would grow best in the strip of territory extending from a few degrees east to a few degrees west of the 100th meridian and from Dakota to Texas, where wheatgrowing at that time was largely nonexistent because of the lack of drought-resistant varieties.

He went back to Russia in 1900 and discovered Kharkov wheat on the wind-swept plains of Starobyelsk. This district is farther north than the home of Turkey wheat and is characterized climatically by great drought and piercing cold winter winds. Kharkov was able, therefore, to withstand the weather farther west and north on our Great Plains.

The introduction of these new strains was only part of Carleton's job. There was no market demand for these varieties in America, and the durum wheats met with violent opposition from the millers and grain dealers. He had to educate the farmers and the millers as to the value of the new varieties. This, he said later, was a long, tedious process. The millers said that their mills wouldn't grind such hard wheats. Carleton told them the mills of Russia ground these wheats and made the best semolina in the world from Kubanka. The macaroni industry was undeveloped. Carleton wrote pamphlets on macaroni wheat, made speeches on macaroni, talked macaroni to the people and the cooks, and even ate macaroni as his chief article of food until he made the public macaroni-minded.

Mark Carleton was careless about his personal finances. He borrowed money from friends and acquaintances. Among others, he borrowed from a rich man of the opposite party. His superiors heard about this and dismissed him from his post in the Department of Agriculture. He went to South America, where he drifted from one job to another and paid part of his debts. On April 26, 1925, he died of acute malaria at Paita, Peru.

The Kharkov strain was accepted without much opposition. For some years it gave a better average yield than Turkey. In 1914, Carleton estimated that 80,000,000 bushels, or half the entire wheat crop of Kansas that year, was the Kharkov variety. Six years later the authorities estimated Kharkov at 20 per cent and Turkey at 60 per cent of the state's crop. In recent years the two strains have lost their identity to such an extent that no accurate estimate can be made.

The Kubanka wheat made progress more slowly. The durum seed introduced in 1898 was distributed to farmers as well as to experiment stations. The wheat was popular among the farmers because it was hardy and made a 30 to 50 per cent greater yield than other varieties. A crop of nearly 10,000,000 bushels was grown in 1903, and four years later the farm value of the crop was $30,000,000. The durum wheats were most successfully grown in the strip of territory from northwestern Kansas to North Dakota.

The development of this hard wheat area was the outstanding accomplishment of the wheat industry in the first decade of the present century. This was due in part to the influence of Mark Carleton, and in part to the increased demand for Kansas hard wheat.

About the time Carleton introduced the new strains, the federal government imported several lots of Turkey wheat from the Molochna district of Taurida and distributed the seed among the farmers. In 1901 the Kansas Millers and Grain Dealers' Association imported 15,000 bushels of pure Turkey seed wheat from central Taurida and sold it to farmers at cost. Carleton had recommended the source of this seed.

In the decade prior to the World War, farmers in central Kansas and elsewhere, hearing about the cheap land and good crops in the short-grass country, moved west and bought farms. They broke thousands of acres of grassland and planted wheat; the plow replaced the saddle; and immense fields of grain stood where herds of sleek cattle had recently grazed.

The population of every county in the area jumped. The aggregate wheat acreage increased from 572,201, or 13 per cent of the state's sowing in 1900, to 1,789,266, or 26 per cent, in 1910. In the latter year nine of the thirty-one counties produced more than a half million bushels each. That year Ford County stood first among the nine, producing 2,500,000 and ranked fourth in acreage and sixth in production among the counties of the state.

Theodore C. Henry, who raised soft wheats, was

the pioneer wheat king. The hard wheat era has had its large growers who could have claimed the title of king and others who might have rated among the lesser nobility. Several of these men have lived in the western part of the wheat empire. One of them, J. N. Fike, of Colby, Thomas County, was the largest wheatgrower in the Kaw country, and probaably the most extensive grower of hard winter wheat in the world, in 1910.

Fike was a pioneer settler in Thomas County and had raised wheat every year since he came to the county. He began large-scale operations in 1906 when he first used steam traction engines and sowed 1,600 acres of wheat. The following year he put out 2,500 acres; 4,000 acres in 1908; 10,200 in 1909; and 13,790 in 1910. He harvested a larger area of wheat on his Thomas County land in 1910 than was harvested in 1909 in the states of Maine, New Hampshire, Vermont, Massachusetts, Connecticut, Rhode Island, and Mississippi combined.

Fike's lands lay to the west and north of Colby. The 14,000 acres were not all in one field but consisted of tracts of 200 to nearly 4,000 acres each. The largest field lay nine miles west of Colby and consisted of 3,800 acres. The land was rolling with long, level stretches. The courthouse at Colby could be seen from his big wheat field.

Everything was handled on a large scale on the Fike farm. He employed 185 men in harvesting, 20 in threshing, and 30 plowing. He used 40 headers, five plows drawn by steam engines, and one pulled by a tractor. He owned one of the largest threshing outfits made. It threshed 2,400 bushels a day, the usual run being 2,000 bushels. The machine ran from six in the morning until sundown, every day the weather permitted, through August and September.

The harvesting and threshing of one crop and

preparation of the ground for the next year's crop went on all at the same time. In the words of a visitor who spent a day on the farm in 1910, "Thirty-seven headers were at work, with three or four others available within a day or two, one threshing machine was busy, one steam plow was going, four others were being put into commission, and one gasoline plow was also being put into condition. The steam plows, in addition to turning the soil, also dragged the straight or slant-tooth harrow, leveling and pulverizing the surface."

For many years wheat harvest on the Kaw has been an event of nation-wide interest. It requires an army of several thousand harvest hands from outside the state to garner the millions of bushels of grain. These men come from every state in the Union to rub elbows for a few weeks in Kansas wheat fields, and then they return quietly to their homes.

They represent scores of occupations, and various motives bring them—the city man on a vacation or out of a job, the experienced hand who returns year after year, the drifter willing to work for a few square meals and enough change to take him to the next town, the wayward youth trying to earn enough to get home, the college boy seeking experience or money for an education, and men attracted by the lure of the great outdoors and the desire for adventure. Whatever their motive, they come on foot, by rail, or thumb their way.

The army pours into the state from Oklahoma about the 20th of June and moves northward and westward.

As harvesttime approaches, the farmer is uneasy and he is happy. He is uneasy because of the many things he has to do in getting ready for harvest, and because the grain must be cut at the right time. A day or two sometimes makes a lot of difference. He is happy be-

cause the crop has come through safely, and there will
be a heavy yield. He smiles as he thinks of the things
he can do with the money. He will pay that note at the
bank and can send his boy to college in the fall, and
maybe there will be enough to take that trip to the
mountains he and his wife have talked about so many
times.

No time may be lost. Consequently, he rushes
around to get things in shape—arranges with his neighbors for wagons and teams, hires hands, repairs the machinery, gets extra parts for breakdowns, lays in a quantity of supplies, and watches the weather.

The farmer is not alone in the excitement of this
event. The hands have to be fed and the burden of this
falls on the women. Cooking for harvest hands and
threshers was quite a job a generation ago when bigger
crews were used, and it still requires plenty of work and
planning by the womenfolks. It is a matter of family
pride and neighborhood hospitality to feed the men
well, so they make it a festive occasion. The farmer's
wife and the neighbor women hustle about the kitchen
preparing great quantities of foods that represent their
supreme culinary effort. They stretch the table out full
length and get the seldom-used dishes off the top shelves
of the cupboard; and perhaps the neighbors supply
some. Then they place all the chairs in the house around
the table. Maybe they bring in a box or a keg or two to
fill in. If this doesn't make enough seats they put a plank
across a couple of kegs. Then they heap the table so high
with food it almost groans under the weight. The men
are in a jovial frame of mind and joke and banter each
other as they take their places and begin eating. How
harvest hands can eat! Huge platters of browned fried
chicken or roast beef, great dishes of mashed potatoes
with a puddle of melted butter in the center, several

kinds of vegetables, immense plates of bread or rolls, brown gravy, preserves, pie, cake, and coffee disappear into the mouths of these hungry men. Many farmers serve five meals a day—three regular meals at the house with lunches in the field forenoon and afternoon. "He eats like a harvest hand" is an expression commonly

used on the Kaw when reference is made to someone who can stow away an unbelievable amount of food.

In the western counties, where one man has thousands of acres of wheat, the fields may be miles from the farmhouse. He erects small one-story buildings in a corner of the field to be used during the harvesting, threshing and planting season. J. N. Fike provided a dozen or more cook shacks which were placed at points most convenient to the different gangs. These shacks were on wheels and were moved about the farm so that the men could reach them with the least loss of time.

On the eve of the World War, the Wheat Empire on the Kaw extended from the mouth to the farthest source of the river. Red Turkey shared the throne with Kharkov, his tough brother. During the war the wheat doctors at Manhattan sent forth a promising royal youth named Kanred whom they had reared by scientific methods at the experiment station. He could stand cold and resist rust better than Red Turkey; also he was ready for harvest three or four days earlier. Consequently, within a few years he occupied one-fifth of Turkey's territory. Then it was discovered that he had a weak straw and his popularity began to wane. Blackhull and other tough members of the family have taken over much of his and Red Turkey's domains.

16

A Blizzard of Seed Wheat

THE World War created a great demand for wheat. The need of more wheat to assist in winning the war was brought home to the farmers repeatedly. The propagandists told them it was a patriotic duty to raise wheat. "Wheat will win the war" was the slogan. The orators and newspapers urged them to grow more wheat, and government agencies assisted them in this program. The federal authorities lent them money to buy seed, and the Kansas Council of Defense helped them in every way possible to secure good seed, to take measures against damage by insects and disease, and to use the most efficient cultural methods.

The shortage of labor during the war forced the wheatgrowers to use machinery. They purchased tractors, combines, gang plows, and headers, and paid boom prices for them. Because of the large investments in equipment, the farmers had to put more acres into wheat to make it pay.

During the five-year war period the total production of wheat in Kansas amounted to 529,000,000 bushels. This was 100,000,000 bushels more than was produced in any other state in the same period.

The plains farmer learned during the war the advantages of the tractor over horses. It was powerful enough to pull more plows and make them cut deeper into the soil. It didn't have to stop under the hottest summer sun and could run all night if necessary. On semiarid land it was used to conserve moisture. Most of the rain fell in the spring and summer and was quickly evaporated by the hot sun and dry winds. If a rain came after harvest, the farmer, by using a tractor, could turn the soil over and store the moisture until seedingtime. The farmer also learned that if he plowed or listed a tract of land and then allowed it to lie idle a year it would produce more wheat.

When the war ended, the leaders urged the farmers to continue raising wheat to feed the people of the war-torn nations of Europe where farming had been neglected for four years. They didn't need much urging. Wheat was still bringing war prices, and that made it an attractive financial gamble. They purchased several hundred new combines, new tractors, and other equipment, and grew wheat on a scale never before attempted. Scores of farmers planted from 1,000 to 3,000 acres each. Others put in larger tracts. Many tenants became landowners, paying for the land and machinery in one year.

Several men enlarged their wheat acreages until each was planting thousands of acres. History records them as "wheat kings." Simon Fishman of Greeley was one of the largest growers in the state. He planted 10,000 acres or more annually. William Layton of Salina ranked high among the big individual producers. Albert Weaver of Bird City began raising wheat on a large scale before the war and has been a successful grower ever since. He located on the broad semiarid plateau in northwestern Kansas in 1906 and began growing wheat on summer-fallowed land in 1911. He increased his acreage until he got up to 5,000 acres a season. In 1922, with the use of horses, he grew 75,000 bushels of grain. He changed later to power machinery and has grown from 75,000 to 110,000 bushels of wheat annually the past twenty years without a single crop failure. It is common at harvesttime for him to have 40,000 to 50,000 bushels of wheat exposed to the sun in a drift 200 feet deep and covering a city block.

Other men organized wheat-farming companies which purchased vast tracts of land, huge quantities of machinery, and engaged in large scale operations. The Wheat Farming Company of Hays, Kansas, was the largest corporate producer in 1930. That year it worked 25,000 acres. The following year it planted 32,500 acres. The Sledd Farm Corporation, whose office was at Lyons, Kansas, farmed 25,000 acres located in eleven western Kansas counties.

Watching the success of these farmers and farm corporations, business and professional men scattered in cities and towns throughout the Middle West saw an opportunity to make money. Scores of them came to the plains country and bought wheat land. How extensively these "suitcase" farmers engaged in wheat-growing will be realized when it is stated that in northwest Kansas two businessmen owned and operated five times as many acres of land as the farm corporations.

Wheatgrowing was not all profit. Far from it. During the five high-price years, 1916-1920, there were two partial crop failures. Farmers went into debt to buy machinery and land and seed. In 1918 the federal government lent the farmers of western Kansas $3,000,000 for seed wheat. At the close of the war they had to pay $6.60 per day for ordinary harvest hands and $8 a day for tractor hands. Production costs ran around $20 to $25 an acre. In 1919 a banker in a western Kansas county estimated that the farmers of that county received $12,-000,000 for their wheat crop and owed $9,000,000 in mortgages and personal debts. When wheat prices fell in 1921, the growers continued to pay war prices for what they bought, and they had to meet inflated debts and taxes. It is said that between January, 1920, and March, 1923, over 10 per cent of the wheat farmers lost their farms. Another 17 per cent kept their farms through the leniency of the creditors. Scores of banks failed because farmers were unable to repay borrowed money.

When the grain is ripening, Kansas is literally a sea of wheat. As one writer puts it: "Anywhere in Kansas one may ride for miles and miles through wheat fields that stretch away to the rim of the horizon and he may ride on and on across county after county from the eastern end of the state to the western, from the northern to the southern borders, on any railroad or dusty highway, and yet there is no shore to the ocean of wheat." The Santa Fe Railroad is sometimes called "The Great Wheat Way" because it traverses a belt of wheat counties.

In pioneer times T. C. Henry's big wheat field east of Abilene was such a wonderful sight that trains on the Union Pacific stopped so that the passengers might see it, just as trains stop at Niagara Falls or the Grand Canyon. There has been so much wheat in Kansas in recent years that a man riding west on the Union Pacific one day said to his seat companion, "When you enter Kansas just take one squint out the window. You'll see nothing but wheat, and there'll be nothing else to see until you cross the line into Colorado; no use looking out but once."

As one stands in a field of tall, nearly ripe wheat when a breeze is blowing, the bending and rising of the grain make it seem as if one stood in the sea and watched the waves rolling forward.

The bearded husks, rubbing together, when the wind blows make a soft, rustling sound as if the voice of the wheat were whispering. In fact, the voice of the wheat does whisper. It has a message for all mankind. To the farmer and his wife it promises bread and butter and new things for the home. To the youth it speaks of a college education, of love and happiness. To one banker it sounds like the rustle of money, new crisp thousand-dollar bills pulling through his fingers. To one writer of poetic temperament it sounds like the rustling of a silken curtain; to another like shifting sands. To Harry Kemp, the Kansas poet, "The sound of the grain as it murmured . . . turned from the voice of the Prairie, into the roar of the sea." To the hungry millions it is God's answer to the Lord's Prayer.

In the days when headers were commonly used, the harvest crew usually consisted of six or seven men. Nowadays when the grain is combined three men are needed —the farmer and two helpers, one to drive the tractor and one the truck. The account given here pictures a scene typical of a Kansas wheat farm at harvesttime:

After breakfast the farmer and his two hands made their ways to the tractor and combine drawn up by the galvanized-tin shed which provided them shelter from the wet weather of winter and fall. The farmer started the tractor and let it warm up.

Out they pulled to the edge of the whispering wheat and down went the platform of the combine with its reel and canvas running empty, but not for long. The silken heads began to unfold evenly on the combine's platform as the driver steered the tractor with its trailing burden into the new-ripe wheat. The motor coughed, stumbled, and then took up its singing whine as the ripe heads were elevated to the smooth running cylinder. Like a devouring monster the combine hungrily swallowed the unthreshed wheat.

After adjusting the platform so that the sickle bar cut the wheat at just the right height so as not to miss any of the heads and yet high enough so that there would be a minimum of straw for the combine to handle, the farmer climbed carefully over the machine to adjust the draft to its proper position so that no chaff would be left in the wheat and yet no grain would be blown over the backboard of the combine.

Then he climbed to the grain tank. There it was. The golden grain rolling from the auger shaft in a stream as large as the brawny bulk of his forearm. He ran his fingers through the grain. It felt smooth and warm—almost too warm; this grain would go to the market where they could air it every day, for it was almost too warm for storage.

The sun was steadily climbing in the east now, and the tank was nearing the ninety-bushel mark. The farmer whistled to the boy driving the tractor, and then motioned to him to stop. As they came to a stop the man driving the truck drove over to the combine and backed up to the grain tank. The farmer twisted the wheel that released the wheat and out poured a stream of rich buff-colored grain. A short period of scooping the grain back in the truck bed, and the tank was empty, the door closed; they were ready to start again.

Two more truckloads, and it was dinnertime. Lifting the water jug from its resting place on the tractor the men rinsed their parched mouths, then cut the switches of the two motors. Heat rose in great successive waves from the steel machinery and it was hot enough on the galvanized-steel shell of the combine to blister one's unprotected hand.

Dinner over, they returned to the field. If the sun had seemed unbearably hot before the dinner hour it was a veritable inferno of heat waves as the sun seemed to hang suspended, motionless, over the tinder-dry world.

The machinery almost sizzled beneath the sun's rays; the combine was burning hot, and the cranks to the motors were hot against even a gloved hand.

They were started. The rounds became monotonous in a treadmill fashion—that is, until two-thirty in the afternoon when the farmer glanced over at the elevator shaft and discovered that the straw was piled up and overflowing.

With a shrill whistle to the tractor driver the farmer had thrown out the clutch and was down on the platform. The expensive cast-iron gear that had caused him so much trouble in the past four years had "cut out" again. This meant $12 and two hours of repair work if he was lucky and could get the gear at the local hardware store.

With instructions to the two men to tear down the machine and get ready for the new gear whenever he got back from town he crawled into his last year's model touring car and headed toward the village.

The local store had the gear. The farmer put it in his car and returned to the field, arriving late in the afternoon. Within an hour they had again started traveling around the section, which was becoming smaller and smaller with each round of the combine.

Evening came too early for the farmer who was eager to harvest the grain for which he had waited this long. They pulled the combine and tractor into one corner of the patch of wheat nearest the house as the wheat was dyed in the running colors of an inimitable western Kansas sunset.

The west was golden, the wheat field was golden, the wheat ricked in the corner of the field was golden, all for only a few moments. The more brilliant colors faded to blues and lavenders of early night as the men made their way to the house where already a yellow golden glow could be seen in the windows of the farm-house.

The plains farmers, during the war period, learned that by conserving moisture they could grow wheat on a rainfall that never before had produced wheat. This was especially true if they raised wheat on freshly broken sod. Wheat was bringing top price. So they added to their holdings in land and expanded their acreages of wheat. A mad race in a mad decade was on. They bought more machinery to raise more wheat to buy more land to raise more wheat. It became a vicious circle. There wasn't enough cultivated land to meet the demands of the resident farmers and take care of the needs of the farm corporations and the suitcase growers. So the "sod busters" broke more prairie. Each furrow brought the wheat area nearer the desert edge.

With thousands of acres of semiarid land in Kansas and neighboring states under cultivation, conditions were right for severe dust storms, if a long dry spell set in. The dry spell began in 1931. The annual rainfall dropped, reaching a low of eleven inches in 1934. Hard times resulted. The farming corporations went into re-ceivership. The suitcase farmers deserted their holdings. The cultivated ground became dry and powdery. After a year or two, there was no vegetable covering to hold the soil in place. It began to blow.

The agricultural authorities set up a program to stop dust blowing. By means of listing, strip farming, and other methods, they have pinned the soil down and are doing a good job holding it there. The Kansas wheat acreage shrank to 5,755,000 acres in 1933, but has again climbed to more than 10,000,000 acres. A blizzard of seed wheat is still sweeping over the Kaw, and from all appearances it will continue its annual descent on this area, but that it will be grown under conditions which will better protect the soil is almost certain.

17

The Nation's Breadbasket Goes Down The Kaw

An AUTHORITY on wheat recently said:

The Kansas farmer, when he hauls his wagonload of wheat to the nearest country elevator, knows no more than does the dealer who buys it to what far destination that wheat may go, nor into what form of bread it may be shaped before it is eaten. It may, perhaps, go no further than to the local mill, to return to the farmer's own flour bin; a larger chance is that it will take its way westward to be ground on the Pacific coast into flour which later will reach China; a still greater probability is that either the wheat or its product will find its way to Europe and reach ultimately the worker at Sheffield, the fisherman of Norway, children on the verge of starvation in the Balkans, or the torn and scattered tribes in Asia Minor . . .

It will probably never be known who transported the first wheat down the Kaw, or when or how he carried it. Maybe an Indian carried it in his canoe, or some French fur trader loaded it into his pirogue. Maybe a wagon train hauled it down one of the old trails that ran along the banks of the stream. It seems probable the steamboats that plied the Kaw transported the first grain raised by the early settlers.

Scarcely had Kansas Territory been opened to settlement in 1854, when steamboats flocked to the Missouri from all the rivers in the Mississippi Valley. Many of the small boats, and some of the intermediate in size, entered the Kaw and engaged in trade with the colonists. Steamers plied the Kaw until the close of the Civil War, when the railroads took over the traffic.

The *Excel*, a "stanch little stern-wheeler" with "remarkably strong engines," was the first steamer to ascend any distance up the Kaw. Charles K. Baker, an experienced riverman, was captain. The boat made its first trip in April, 1854, for the purpose of carrying materials to the site of Fort Riley. Major E. O. Ogden had selected a site at the confluence of the Republican and Smoky Hill rivers for a military post. After he had let contracts for foreign materials based upon wagon transportation, he found that water transportation was practicable. On her first trip the *Excel* carried 1,100 barrels of flour belonging to Perry and Young of Weston, Missouri, government contractors, from Weston to the site of the fort. The craft made the trip in two days and didn't hit a snag or sand bar. Captain Baker had to land several times a day to get firewood. The crew usually felled the trees and cut them up, though occasionally they appropriated rails from the Indians' truck patches. When Father John Duernick, second superior of St. Mary's Mission, heard the boat was coming he hauled up two loads of rails and had them chopped up by the time the boat arrived.

In October of that year the *Excel* made a trip up the Kaw, and upon reaching the mouth of the Smoky Hill, went a short distance up that stream. The size of the steamer prevented Captain Baker from venturing as far as he wanted to. On another trip the *Excel* ran from Fort Riley to Kansas City, a distance estimated to be 243 miles in twenty-four hours and made thirty landings. After a few months' service on the Kaw, the *Excel* went into the Missouri River trade.

The Kaw trade was taken over by the *Bee*, and later by the *Emma Harmon*, the *Financier*, and two-score other steamers, and a few flatboats. None of these boats was on the Kaw for more than a few months. Then some of them went into the Missouri or the Mississippi trade; some were burned; others were grounded and abandoned by their crews.

These boats carried the early settlers and their household goods, and undoubtedly had wheat and corn for seed on board. However, according to the Kansas City *Journal*, the *Silver Lake*, in 1859, transported the first shipment of Kansas corn down the Kaw. Here is the entry in the April 1st issue of that paper: "The steamer *Silver Lake* returned yesterday from Topeka after a most successful trip, loaded with corn and hides for Colonel Nelson, J. S. Chick & Co. It is gratifying to see the great piles of corn and hides piled up on the levee, the first shipment by steamboat ever made of the products of Kansas." On May 19th, the *Silver Lake* transported 2,300 bushels of corn from Lawrence, and on the next trip had 800 sacks of this grain on board.

Captain Willoughby, commander of the *Silver Lake*, was quite a character. He was noted chiefly for his vociferous profanity. He could outswear any of the rivermen, even the deck officers who uttered a profane oath with every breath. The captain was disliked by his associates. They called him "Old Willoughby." He distrusted his officers and refused to allow the clerk to touch the ship's money, preferring to stow it away in his own clothes. When last heard of Willoughby was down in Memphis, Tennessee, catching catfish for a living.

The *Col. Gus Linn* helped carry the Kansas crop down the Kaw in 1859. Captain B. F. Beasley built this boat at Pittsburgh, Pennsylvania, expressly for the Kaw trade, and it was called the "lightest-draft steamer ever built," drawing only eight inches light, was 135 feet long on deck, 28 feet beam, 2 feet hold, and carried 300 tons. She had fine accommodations for passengers.

A Pittsburgh newspaper announced that the *Col. Gus Linn* would go up the Kaw within 150 miles of Pikes Peak, where gold had been discovered. That would be in Colorado near the source of the Kaw's farthest tributaries where a duck would find it difficult to navigate. When the packet left for Kansas she carried a number of passengers bound for Pikes Peak at $130 fare.

The boat reached the Kaw in due time, and early in May began making regular trips between Kansas City and Junction City. The Kansas City *Journal* for May 22nd contained the following item: "The Kansas river packet *Col. Gus Linn*, arrived last night at seven o'clock with 41 passengers and 2,300 sacks of corn shipped from Junction City, fully demonstrating that the Kansas is navigable for boats of light draft in an ordinary stage of water." On May 26th the boat went up the river with a quantity of freight and a number of passengers, and made the trip from Kansas City to Fort Riley in five days. "Returning she took 2,200 bushels of corn at Manhattan and 500 sacks at Topeka, a portion of which she was obliged to leave on the bank to lighten over bars."

Captain Beasley planned to monopolize the Kaw trade and force his competitors to quit the river. Stories are told of his efforts to do this. He took all the freight

he could stow on his boat without sinking her, even if he had to unload part of it to get over the sand bars or to accommodate the next customer. On a trip upstream in July the boat ran aground just above Rising Sun, a town across the Kaw from Lecompton. The captain unloaded 1,500 sacks of flour in a pawpaw patch, and leaving a deck hand to guard it, he hurried up the river. Rising Sun was noted for its saloons. The deck hand spent most of his time in these joints, and a herd of razorback hogs belonging to the Delaware Indians took care of the flour. The pawpaw bushes looked as if they had been whitewashed.

On one of the last trips of the *Col. Gus Linn* from Manhattan to Kansas City, John Pipher was a deck hand. He said that the boat started from Manhattan with every pound of freight it could carry over the bars, but Captain Beasley took all that was offered at points below. He kept the boat moving, and to do this he pressed all the male passengers into service when the boat grounded, regardless of the fact that they had paid first-class fare. At Topeka he took several thousand bushels of corn aboard, and the boat went down to her guards. The passengers remonstrated, but Beasley headed the boat downstream. Above Tecumseh he landed this corn to make room for a consignment from that town, and this, in turn, he dumped on the bank above the Coon Creek bar to make room for a big consignment at Lecompton. When the steamer reached the wharf at Lecompton, the bank was piled high with sacks of corn, and George Zinn, one of the most important farmers in Douglas County, was there with a gang of men to load it on board. While these men were loading, the crew and passengers took in the town. Pipher remained at the boat and watched the loading of the corn.

When the boat was ready to sail, Beasley was in a

saloon uptown so drunk that he had to be assisted back to the packet. Coming to Pipher, who was sitting on the bank near the boat, the captain invited him to go to Kansas City as his "guest." The former, enjoying the joke, accepted the invitation. A few miles below town the boat grounded, and Beasley called on all the male passengers to help carry the freight ashore. He graciously approached Pipher and apologized for the necessity of asking him to assist in this task.

The ultimate fate of the *Col. Gus Linn* is unknown. She was still transporting corn down the Kaw in the fall of 1859. On September 20th she arrived at Kansas City with 1,300 bushels on board, and the officers reported there were at least 40,000 bushels at the wharves awaiting shipment.

There is a gap of four years, during the Civil War, in the records of steamboating on the Kaw. In 1865 a few boats were in service on the river. By that time the state legislature had chartered several railroads, and the Kansas Pacific was building its line westward up the Kaw valley. In 1864 the railroad companies had secured the enactment of a law by the Kansas legislature declaring that the Kaw and its four main tributaries were not navigable and authorizing the bridging of these streams. The last steamboat plied the Kaw in the spring of 1866. The floods had carried away the Kansas Pacific Railroad bridge at the mouth of the river, so the company chartered the *Alexander Majors,* a big sidewheeler, to run as far as Lawrence until the bridge could be rebuilt.

After that the Kansas Pacific and the Santa Fe handled most of the trade with the Kaw settlements and carried their agricultural products down the river valley to Kansas City. The Kansas City grain market had a small beginning but grew as the agricultural area ex-

tended westward. The earliest figures on the grain receipts at Kansas City are for 1871 and are supplied by
the Kansas City Board of Trade. The grain receipts
in bushels that year were: wheat, 687,000; corn, 350,-
000. Much of this grain had undoubtedly been grown on
Kansas farms and was sent to market by the Kaw
route.

In the seventies the amount of wheat shipped down
the Kaw fluctuated between good years and poor years.
The hard wheat became a factor in the market after
1880.

It is not known when the first Kansas wheat was
exported to a foreign country. Kansas hard wheat was
nameless in the world's great markets for several years
after it was first grown. For some time the millers mixed
the hard wheat with soft wheat and made flour for
Kansas housewives, or mixed it with hard spring wheat
and sold it as such.

At the turn of the century Kansas hard wheat
stood high in the world's leading markets. According
to a contemporary writer, "The peculiar qualities of
Kansas hard wheat are so well known in grain-and-
flour-importing countries of Europe that the value of
their home grown wheat is measured by the percentage of Kansas hard-wheat admixture required to produce a good bread-making flour." Another writer was
not entirely wrong when he said that the appearance of
a louse in the "fields of Kansas gives the Chicago wheat
bear a nervous shock," and that a "hot wind in Ellis
County puts Liverpool into a frenzy."

A considerable portion of the wheat grown in the
Southwest, in recent years as in pioneer days, has traveled down the Kaw to Kansas City. In 1900 the receipts
of wheat at Kansas City amounted to 34,000,000 bushels. The annual receipts gradually advanced until a high

of 125,000,000 bushels was reached in the early thirties. A sharp decline followed, from which the market has not fully recovered. However, the aggregate receipts for the thirty-nine years have amounted to nearly two and a half billion bushels. Kansas City is one of the largest terminal grain centers in the world.

The millers were largely responsible for sending the Kaw's breadbasket into distant lands and making a favorable name for it. C. Hoffman, who had built a mill on the banks of the Smoky Hill in pioneer times, was a stanch friend of Turkey wheat. He induced farmers to raise this variety and in 1880 remodeled his mill to handle it. He was one of the first millers to ship flour outside of Kansas. He made the first shipment in 1873; it consisted of three cars of flour consigned to a broker in Sherman, Texas. The Hoffman mill made the first shipment of export flour in 1882. It was consigned to a firm in Antwerp, Belgium. Two years later Hoffman put Kansas flour on the market in Paris, and the bakers of the city pronounced it the "only flour equal to Hungarian hard-wheat flour ever offered them."

By 1890 the annual capacity of the Kansas flour mills was 10,000,000 barrels. It takes ten million people to eat that many barrels of flour annually. Kansas had a population of less than a million and a half. The neighboring states had mills of their own, so the flour producers had to seek a foreign market. The Hoffman firm found markets in Belgium, France, Germany, Sweden, Great Britain, South America, and Cuba. Other merchants also found markets abroad for their products.

The demand for Kansas flour has continued to grow in recent years. Kansas City now ranks third among the cities of the country as a flour-milling center. Wichita, Topeka, Salina, and other cities have big flour mills. The state has ranked first in the milling industry part of the time in the past decade. Much of this flour has reached a market by way of the Kaw.

For years the Kaw has been the lane and Kansas City the gateway for the cattle kingdom. Even for a longer period of time the river has been the route, and the city the terminal, for the transportation of billions of bushels of grain and vast quantities of flour from the Agricultural Empire to all parts of the world.

18

The Early Farm Revolt

THE spirit of political unrest which disturbed
Kansas farmers after the Civil War was part of a general agrarian revolt against the established political
order. In Kansas the political upheaval was more pronounced than in other sections. Kaw farmers felt that
they had not received a square deal. They were fighters
and sons of fighters who resented injustice. Their leaders
expressed their resentment in violent language. Their
lusty voices were heard the length and breadth of the
land. This vehement outbrust on the Kaw gave character to the revolution.

There were several reasons for dissatisfaction on
the Kaw. The settlers were pushing into central and
western Kansas. Most of them didn't have much capital.
They bought a piece of land, paying all the money they
had on it and giving a mortgage for the balance, or
they filed on a homestead, and as soon as they proved
up they mortgaged it to raise some cash to make improvements. They were unfamiliar with farming on the
Great Plains where the normal rainfall was lighter than
in the East and where there were droughts, grasshopper
plagues, hot winds, and extremes in temperature. They
knew little about scientific farming and still less about

competition in the worlds' markets. The first families planted corn and soft wheats which were not adapted to this area. There were dry years and crop failures. There were periods of low prices and two panics. The farmers got deeply in debt and were discouraged.

In a survey of the unrest among Kaw farmers, it should be mentioned that a number of them had come to Kansas Territory to make it free. After slavery was abolished they looked for other public enemies. One leader estimated that six out of eight Free Staters were in the reform ranks. They were men of strong convictions who didn't compromise with injustice.

Prominent among the farm leaders who had fought slavery were Governor Charles Robinson and Colonel Samuel N. Wood. Robinson was a tall man with piercing blue eyes. He was the agent of the New England Emigrant Aid Company and selected the site of Lawrence for the first colony. He took a leading part in the Free State movement and was the first governor of the state. Sam Wood's parents were Quakers, and he was born in Ohio in 1825. He was admitted to the bar in 1854 and came to Kansas that year to help make it free. He was part owner of the *Kansas Tribune,* a Free State paper published at Lawrence, and was in the thick of every fight. He lived for some years in Chase County and represented his county in the legislature. Then he moved to Stevens County, founded the town of Woodsdale, of which he became mayor, and was a leader in the Populist movement. He took part in the bloody county seat war between Hugoton and Woodsdale and was shot and killed in June, 1891.

The farmers first expressed their dissatisfaction by forming agricultural organizations. The largest of these was the Patrons of Husbandry, commonly called the Grange. It originated in Washington, D.C., in 1867 and was founded by Oliver Hudson Kelley, a clerk in the Department of Agriculture, five other government clerks, and a fruitgrower. With an empty pocketbook and a heart filled with sympathy for the debt-ridden farmer, Kelley started out early in 1868 to organize granges. The order grew slowly. The first permanent local organization was in Fredonia, New York. In May of that year the farmers organized a grange at Newton, Iowa, and in September they established the North Star Grange in Minnesota. By the end of 1869 there were thirty-seven active granges in Minnesota. A year later, granges sprang up in Atlantic Coast states and as far south as Mississippi, but the heart of the organization was in Minnesota, Iowa, Wisconsin, Illinois, and Indiana.

Kansas farmers organized their first grange at Hiawatha in April, 1872. The organization of other granges followed rapidly. In the year 1874 the farmers established lodges at the rate of two or three thousand per month. They organized in every school district from one end of the state to the other.

In 1872 the members of the Workingman's party and other reform forces united with the Liberal Republican party and supported Horace Greeley for President. The Democrats fused with the Liberals in Kansas, as they did elsewhere in the country. The nominating convention met in Topeka on September 11th. On the motion of Sam Wood the convention nominated Charles Robinson as president. He was escorted to the chair, amid the applause of the delegates, and made a short talk. Other reform leaders made addresses, after which the convention nominated candidates for state offices, Congress, and presidential electors. In November the Liberal forces elected two state senators and fourteen members of the lower house and cut the Republican majority down from 40,000 to about 30,000.

The principles of the Liberal Republican party were too mild for these western reformers. Aside from the public land plank, the party platform contained little to attract Kansas farmers except a protest against corruption and extravagance in public office and inequalities in taxation.

They had more than one grievance on their chest. They were especially mad at the railroads. These corporations had received large grants of public land. In addition, the early settlers had voted hundreds of thousands of dollars in subsidy bonds to help build the lines. The farmers felt that, under the circumstances, the freight and passenger rates were too high and the railroad officials were too arrogant. A farm journal said that "one of the most satisfactory results of the uprising of the farmers" was the way in which the transportation question was being sifted. This paper called the railroads "one of our most grasping monopolies."

Then, too, they believed that the exemption of bonds, notes, and mortgages from taxation was an injustice to the farmers who as a rule didn't own tax-exempt securities.

The farm leaders held a state convention in Topeka in March, 1873, at which they expressed their dissatisfaction by setting forth a "declaration" of their "desires and purpose." They favored co-operative buying and selling, tax reforms, regulation of the freight and passenger rates of the railroads, economy in public expenditures, and the preservation of the public domain for actual settlement. They protested against the exemption of bonds, notes, and mortgages from taxation and declared that giving banks a "monopoly of the national currency" was "but little less than legalized robbery of the agricultural classes."

Following the lead of Illinois, where so many political gatherings were held on Independence Day, 1873, that it was referred to as the "Farmers' Fourth of July," Kansas farmers organized an Independent Reform party during the summer. They placed no state ticket in the field for the fall elections, but by means of local efforts elected enough members to the lower house of the state legislature to give the Democrats and Reformers twenty votes more than the Republicans had, and to elect ex-Governor James M. Harvey, a farmer and an Independent, to the United States Senate.

The granger movement reached its zenith in 1874 throughout the country. Early the next year the membership began to fall off. Many farmers had been attracted by the novelty of the order and soon lost interest. Others observed that the organization had accomplished little in the way of tangible results. Instead, the financial crash came in 1873, and conditions grew worse.

Failing in their attempt to obtain relief through the Grange and seeing the price of their crops and livestock steadily falling after 1873, the farmers decided that it would be better to raise the price of their products by increasing the amount of money in circulation, and pay their debts with this inflated currency. "Greenbacks that will pay debts, that will stop interest, that will employ the idle; is what the laboring man wants; this is what bankers and capitalists are striving to prevent," said a Greenback newspaper. "Every bushel of wheat the farmer is compelled to sell for forty cents ought to remind him that we once had better times and that our national legislature is responsible in the main for the great stringency in money matters."

The demand for currency inflation did not originate among the western farmers. Many people on many occasions had urged this remedy for financial ills, especially in periods of depression and in the poorer sections of the frontier. During the Civil War inflation was accomplished through the issue of "greenbacks." After the war the paper dollar declined until it was worth about half its face value in gold. The retirement of the paper money and the resumption of specie payments became political issues.

A fall in prices and widespread unemployment had accompanied the government's attempt to retire the greenbacks. The laboring men in the East said that this resulted from contraction of the currency. They organized the National Labor Union party in 1868 which declared itself in favor of inflation.

The western farmers didn't turn to Greenbackism until the granger organizations had failed to bring relief, and the panic of 1873 had intensified the agricultural depression.

In Kansas the Grange lodges went over in a body to the Independent party in 1874, which gradually came to be known as the Greenback party. The state convention of this party met at Topeka, August 5th. Their platform asked for the payment of the public debt according to the terms under which it had been contracted, for the repeal or reduction of the tariff on necessities, for the restoration of income taxes, for state and national legislation to protect the industrial and producing interests against all forms of corporate monopoly and extortion, and for the railroads to be made subservient to the public good.

The Greenback party began to decline after 1878, owing in part to the fact that the Republicans in Kansas adopted some of the leading Greenback principles and dissension occurred in the national organization, but mainly owing to the fact that times were getting better for the farmers. After 1878 the price of wheat, corn, and oats went up despite greatly increased acreages and much larger yields. Wheat rose from 57 cents in 1878 to $1 in 1881, corn from 19 to 55 cents, and oats from 16 to 38 cents.

With the improvement in economic conditions, the farmers began to lose interest in inflation. However, the Greenback party retained its organization until 1886, when the movement was practically spent. Thereupon, most of the Greenbackers joined the Union Labor party.

Kaw farmers suffered economic reverses in the eighties which caused widespread dissatisfaction and resulted in the Populist uprising. The inequalities in taxation, control of railroads, and other grievances of the seventies were mild as compared with the vicissitudes of the agricultural classes in the following decade. Conditions for the man on the farm grew worse each year. As times got harder, he became more bitter toward the established order and more eager to listen to the agitators who urged him to revolt.

The plight of the farmers in western Kansas was especially grave in the eighties. In 1878 and 1879 settlers poured into the high-plains area and took claims. They brought along corn and soft wheat and planted them. The whole region was scourged by a drought in 1880-1882. The dry air and hot winds destroyed the crops. This disaster, coming so soon after the settlement, discouraged the homesteaders, and all who could do so abandoned their claims and left the country.

Four years of rainfall followed the three years of drought. People came back to the country in droves, and all wanted farms. An immense crowd was always to be found in front of the United States Land Office at Garden City, where homesteaders filed on 50,000 acres daily. Land values began to pick up, and soon a boom took hold and carried real estate values skyward. Quarter sections that had been practically worth-less were accepted as security for loans of from $700 to $1,000. The moneylender and the real estate shark saw an opportunity to make handsome profits. Eastern men with money to invest made vast loans on western Kansas farms. The plains country was soon plastered with mortgages.

In 1887 the boom flattened out. Property values shrank. Hundreds of farmers were unable to meet their obligations, and the mortgages were foreclosed. Other landowners neglected to pay their taxes after the boom collapsed. By the foreclosure route and through the pur-chase of tax certificates, moneyed men became the legal owners of vast quantities of western Kansas land.

While the economic condition of the high-plains farmer was serious because of the newness of the coun-try, hard times hit other sections of the state, and the moneylender entered hundreds of homes in central and eastern Kansas and demanded his pound of flesh.

In the decade 1880-1890 moneylenders wrote more than 400,000 mortgages on Kansas property. A farm leader remarked, "They are plastered three deep over all this grand country."

"When these mortgages were put on," said a farm journal in 1888, "wheat was from $1 to $1.50 per bushel. Cattle were up, hogs were one-third higher than now, and the key to the whole problem is, twice to three times the amount of money was in circulation than is today. The farmer had to do something to improve his land so he could live. He placed a loan on the place trust-ing that at the end of three or four years the prices of his farm products would be equally as good as then."

Unfortunately, the price of farm products steadily declined after 1884. Wheat dropped from 78 cents in 1883 to 55 cents in 1889 and corn from 37 to 18 cents in the same period. To make matters worse, a record-breaking corn crop was raised in 1889, and the price dropped to 10 cents a bushel in some localities, the average being 14 cents a bushel. The corncribs were bursting, and the golden ears were piled high on the ground. Farmers found it cheaper to burn corn than to buy coal.

When the mortgages came due, the farmers couldn't pay them. Foreclosures followed, and thousands of people lost their homes. The Bureau of Labor estimated that for the five-year period 1887-1892 mortgages on 30,740 farms were foreclosed. By 1890, 43 per cent of the farming population of Kansas were tenant farmers.

These debt-ridden farmers didn't know which way to turn for relief. They stayed with the Union Labor party a short time, and then went over to the Order of Videttes. In the ritual the Videttes placed the cause of humanity above the cause of country. The opposition pronounced this the creed of a traitor. The order was in disrepute and after a brief period went out of existence. Next, they joined the Farmers' Alliance, a secret organization frequently called the Southern Alliance, which spread over Kansas in 1888. At the close of 1889 there were 130,000 members in the state.

In the fall election of 1889 the reformers placed tickets in the field in nearly all the counties under the name of Union Labor or Alliance.

In Cowley County, where the Alliance was especially strong, the Republicans split into two factions— city and farmer. The city faction controlled the county convention, so the farmers withdrew. After several conferences, the bolters appointed a committee to draft a plan for a people's ticket. The committee drew up a petition calling a convention in September. In the November election the People's ticket carried by an overwhelming majority. Commenting on this victory, the *American Nonconformist,* a reform paper published at Winfield, said:

Cowley County is redeemed! The grandest people's movement ever inaugurated on Kansas soil, scored its first victory last Tuesday. The grandest ever organized on Kansas soil, because in its work it contemplated no blood, no conflict of armed forces, no clang of musketry, no field strewn with wounded and dying butchered by their fellowmen.

When the reformers in other counties heard of this victory, they revolted. The movement spread like wildfire. In June of the following year representatives of the reform organizations held a convention at Topeka and organized the People's party, commonly called Populist party. A nominating convention met in Topeka, August 13th, and adopted a platform, put a state ticket in the field, and nominated candidates for Congress in all seven districts.

19

The Crusade of 1890

My country 'tis of thee,
Once Land of Liberty
Of thee I sing.
Land of the millionaire;
Farmers with pockets bare,
Caused by the cursed snare—
The Money Ring.

THUS ran the first stanza of a popular song
which the Populists sang at their rallies in the campaign
of 1890. This song expresses in a few words the chief
grievances of the debt-ridden farmers of Kansas.

They were fairly bursting with anger when they
entered this campaign. They felt they were victims of
gross injustice. They had sought relief by joining farm
organizations and by allying themselves with the reform
groups in politics, but the anticipated benefits did not
materialize. Times got harder and their pocketbooks became flatter each year. So these enraged farmers decided
not to compromise matters any longer and went on a
crusade against Wall Street, moneyed monsters, mortgage fiends, and all other dispensers of injustice.

The Populist party established headquarters in Topeka, and the campaign got under way.

Mary Elizabeth Lease, Jerry Simpson, Mrs. Annie
L. Diggs, Sam Wood, Judge W. A. Peffer, and many
others traveled up and down the state from Kansas City
to Weskan, and from the Nebraska line to the Oklahoma border, preaching the gospel of Populism.

Mrs. Lease and Jerry Simpson were the most prominent of the Populist speakers. They made quite a team.
Both had originally been Republicans and then had
joined the farm organizations. Mrs. Lease talked finance
and Simpson's theme was land. He was a single taxer
of the Henry George school.

Mrs. Lease, the "Lady Orator of the West," was
born in County Monaghan in the northern part of Ireland in 1853 and came to America with her parents
who settled at Ridgway, Pennsylvania, when she was a
child. She was educated in New York State and grew up
to be a tall, slender, good-looking woman. She came to
Kansas, and at the age of nineteen married Charles L.
Lease. Later she studied law and was admitted to the
bar. The family lived in Wichita. She made her first
public speech before the Union Labor Convention in
1888. She was a speaker for the Alliance until 1890 when
she joined the Populist oratorical brigade and is said to
have made 160 speeches during the summer and fall.

She was magnetic, possessed a ready wit, and had
an effective manner of stating things which brought the
truth home with a bang. She pointed from the starving
throngs in Chicago to the immense piles of corn in the
cribs and stacked on the ground in Kansas and said:

"What you farmers need to do is raise less corn
and more hell."

This remark fell on receptive ears and became the
rallying cry of the reformers. It was repeated over and
over at the campaign meetings that year.

Jerry Simpson, known to Kaw folks as "Sockless"

Jerry, was born in New Brunswick in 1842 and was of Scotch and English ancestry. He was largely self-educated. He served in the Union Army during the Civil War and then became a sailor on the Great Lakes, rising to the rank of captain. He came to Kansas with his family in 1878. After living for a time in Jackson County, he moved to Barber County and bought a cattle ranch near Medicine Lodge. A blizzard swept the plains and took most of his stock, leaving him in debt. T. A. McNeal, who was mayor of Medicine Lodge at the time, appointed him city marshal. He held this office when he entered the campaign of 1890.

Jerry was a tall, slender man. His friends said he was Lincolnesque, both in physical appearance and in manner of speech. His political enemies called him a clown and an ignoramus. As evidence of the latter, they pointed to the fact that he sometimes misspelled the name of his home town. Then Jerry would smile and drawl out the reply, "I wouldn't give a cent for a man who couldn't spell a word more than one way."

In a rough-and-tumble debate Simpson had few equals. His marvelous memory and natural mental alertness made him a formidable antagonist. Nothing pleased him better than to have his opponents fire questions at him. The faster they came the better it suited him.

As a public speaker, he entertained his audiences and kept them roaring with laughter. He was naturally witty and a past master of stinging sarcasm. The crowds expected to be entertained. His appearance on the platform was greeted by prolonged applause and shouts. He stood there for a few moments, looking at his audience, then his mouth widened into a "Simpson grin," and the crowd began to laugh with him—before a word was said.

He illustrated his speeches with a generous supply

of stories. His stories were not particularly new, but he told them well, and they caught the crowd. The Republicans were greatly alarmed over the Populist uprising, so they adopted a platform broad enough to catch everybody. Tom McNeal recalls a story Jerry told to illustrate the "sudden conversion of the Republican party," as he put it.

An Irishman and a Jew were out in a canoe. The canoe upset. The Irishman clambered into the boat. Then the Jew came to the top of the water, pretty much choked up, and wanted to be helped into the boat. The Irishman refused to let him in unless he was prepared to accept the Divinity of Jesus Christ and give up all of his Jewish theories. The Jew at first refused, and the Irishman pushed him back into the water. He came up again, more nearly drowned than ever, and the Irishman again put the question to him as to whether he was ready to accept all the Divinity of Christ. By that time, the Jew was nearly drowned, and in order to be saved he agreed to go back on his Jewish theology and accept anything the Irishman wanted him to accept about the Christian faith. Then the Irishman made this statement, according to Jerry, "Well, I am glad to know that you have accepted everything that a Christian ought to accept, but I am afraid if I let you into this boat you would recant if you get in, and therefore I am going to drown you now, so as to save your immortal soul."

Jerry was the Populist candidate for congressman from the southwest Kansas district—the "Big Seventh" —in 1890. His Republican opponent was Colonel James R. Hallowell, a distinguished corporation lawyer, a crack orator, and fastidious dresser. When the Republican press contrasted their party's polished candidate with the boorish Populist standard-bearer, the story runs that Jerry retorted by calling his opponent "Prince Hal." "This prince of royal blood," said he, "travels in his special car, his dainty person is gorgeously bedizened, his soft white hands are pretty things to look at, his tender feet are encased in fine silk hosiery, what does he know of the life and the toil of such plow-handlers as we are? I can't represent you in Congress with silk stockings—I can't afford to wear them."

Victor Murdock, then a cub reporter, wrote a story to the effect that the Populist candidate wore no socks at all, which was taken for the truth over the country. He was referred to as "Sockless Jerry," and the name stuck. Strangers came to Kansas and looked him up, expecting to see a barefooted tramp.

Simpson joined in the fun the crowds got out of the "sockless" story. His friends made the most of it, and the title proved an asset in the campaign. In the long parades there were always floats laden with girls knitting socks for Jerry. During the campaign he was presented with more than three hundred pairs.

The brigade of Populist "hell-raisers" stumped the state and talked to immense crowds. The discontented all came to hear them, and they made a striking assemblage. There were rough, bearded farmers whose calloused hands showed hard work and shabby clothes were evidence of hard luck; cattle herders wearing two-gallon hats and heavy boots; women clad in faded calico and with skins tanned to a dark brown by the hot winds and blistering sun; numerous barefooted, poorly dressed children; here and there a country merchant; a few newspapermen; and an occasional smooth-shaven, well-groomed resident of the metropolis who had probably come to see a "good show."

The rally at Winfield eclipsed all the big times of the past. The town never had entertained so many people. At one time four speakers were addressing all who could hear, besides the main stand where the candidates were talking.

"It was a paralyzer!" exclaimed a Populist paper. "A whole western cyclone! A regular cloud burst. Think of it, two thousand teams and vehicles, thousands of footmen and thousands of horsemen—and then they say the people are not in earnest!"

The Populists held a two-day encampment in Reno County; it was the grandest rally the county had ever known, fully 20,000 participating. There was a grand parade which took an hour to pass a given point. The wagons and floats carried banners on which were emblazoned "Down with Wall Street," "Give us Fifty Dollars Per Capita," and other Populist demands. Jerry Simpson was the leading speaker.

In Clay County the procession was three miles long double file. Mrs. Lease was the first speaker, and she held the audience two hours and a half while she scored the "petty politicians, little ten-cent editors, and the courthouse rings" unmercifully.

Out in Lane County the farmers began to pour into Lincoln Park in the morning, and in a short time the tabernacle was crowded, and many hundreds stood about the building. There were several short speeches. At noon the farmers and their families sat down to a picnic dinner. After dinner they repaired to the speakers' stand to hear Mrs. Lease. By this time hundreds more had arrived. The speaker held her audience spellbound. For four hours she stood there dealing out to the people "burning truths." Nearly everyone wept when she told how her father had died in Andersonville prison and her two brothers were killed on southern battlefields.

The meeting up in Brown County was a red-letter day for Hiawatha. A crowd of 10,000 gathered. They filled the amphitheater, the fences, the bandstand, and all other available space. Mrs. Lease spoke at one o'clock. Round after round of applause rent the air. She held the audience spellbound during the allotted time. As the last round of applause rent the air, they carried stand, speaker, and all amid the shouting throng.

At these meetings there were characterizations, playlets, songs, and cheers. Next to oratory, singing was the leading feature of the rallies. Every Populist who wasn't an orator was a poet, so there was no dearth of songs and song leaders. The words were set to well-known tunes. H. and L. Vincent, owners of the radical press at Winfield, published a paper-backed song book, of which thousands were sold at ten cents a copy.

Perhaps these farmers opened their singing with "The Mortgaged Farm."

Maybe they began with "The Kansas Fool" sung to the tune "Beulah Land":

> We have the land to raise the wheat,
> And everything that's good to eat;
> And when we had no bonds or debt,
> We were a jolly, happy set.

> Oh, Kansas fools! Poor Kansas fools!
> The banker makes of you a tool;
> I look across the fertile plain,
> Big crops—made so by gentle rain;
> But twelve-cent corn gives me alarm
> And makes me want to sell my farm.

Or, they sang "The Farmer's Daughter":

Oh, here we are as thus you see,
Each one a farmer's daughter
We know just when to legislate
And when we had not oughter.

So we won't have any of your banker's sons
To kneel to us and bow, sir;
For we can do without a man
If he can't follow the plow, sir.

The partisan spirit ran high, and as the campaign progressed the feeling not only became more bitter, but it also became personal. It reached the point where friends couldn't discuss political questions without quarreling. Populists and Republicans wouldn't speak to each other. Neighbors who had been friends for years engaged in heated arguments and ceased to be on speaking terms. Families even split along party lines. The children carried the ill feeling of their elders to school and called each other ugly names and taunted one another with rhymes:

Rats, rats, and pickled cats,
Are good enough for Pops and Democrats.

When the crusade ended and the votes were counted it was found that the Populists had elected their candidate for attorney general; he had received the support of the Democrats. The Republicans had elected the other state officers, but by greatly reduced majorities. The Populists had elected five congressmen; a huge majority in the lower branch of the state legislature; and two members of the upper house.

The majority in the state legislature enabled the reformers to choose the man to succeed John J. Ingalls in the United States Senate. They selected William A. Peffer, editor of the *Kansas Farmer,* and proud owner of a beard that came down to his waist. He was an able man. The Populists pointed to his excellent qualifications, while the Republicans, in a legislative resolution, stated that his "chief recommendation was his luxuriant whiskers." The defeat of Ingalls pleased the Populists. He was president of the Kansas Loan and Trust Company which made him a "mortgage fiend de luxe." Mrs. Lease and other Populist orators attacked him, while the Republican press pointed out that his was the only loan company in Kansas that had extended overdue mortgages from year to year and had furnished seed wheat to needy farmers.

The Populists in the lower house began by trimming legislative expenses and filling the hopper with reform bills. Only a dozen or so bills of minor importance passed both houses and were enacted into laws. The Republican Senate blocked the measures regulating railroad rates, providing for a mortgage moratorium, placing a severe penalty on usury, and other major legislation. If measured in terms of enactments on the statute books, Kansas didn't gain much from this crusade.

20

The Legislative War of 1893

THE Populists of Kansas held their state convention at Wichita in 1892, adopted a platform embodying the chief principles contained in the national platform with certain additions of local significance, placed in the field a full slate of Congressional nominees, and a state ticket with Lorenzo D. Lewelling of Wichita as candidate for Governor. These candidates received the support of the Democratic party.

The campaign in Kansas was largely a repetition of the crusade of 1890, but was carried on by candidates for state and local offices, while the prominent orators spent their time preaching the Populist gospel in other states. With the help of the Democrats, they elected the entire state ticket, 25 of the 40 State senators, 58 of the 125 representatives, 5 of the 7 congressmen, and the congressman-at-large.

The inauguration of the state officers took place on Monday, January 9, 1893, and it was indeed a gala day for the disciples of reform. Thousands of people had come to Topeka to witness the event. Populists of all shades of belief and of all ages were there. They ranged in years from the pioneer reformers who had become gray in the service to the beardless youths who were scarcely old enough to cast their first vote. They and their families had come to see the triumphal march of the forces of justice.

The day's program opened with an elaborate parade in which the party chiefs of Kansas and the Populist bigwigs from distant states took part. Mrs. Lease had purchased a new silk dress and a new bonnet for the occasion and rode in the triumphal procession.

John W. Breidenthal, chairman of the Populist State Committee, presided at the ceremonies and remarked that this was the inauguration of the first People's party on earth. The retiring governor, Lyman U. Humphrey, made a brief valedictory address, after which Governor Lewelling was introduced. He reviewed the long struggle of the poor and downtrodden against the rich and powerful and urged the people of Kansas to array themselves on the side of justice and protect the interests of all citizens.

Then the incoming governor took the oath of office, followed by the other state officers. The crowd called for Jerry Simpson, who made a few remarks. Next they called for Mrs. Lease, who said a few words. When they asked for other speakers the chairman shut them off and dismissed the meeting. That evening the Populists held a "camp meeting" in Representative Hall. The crowd called for one after another of the orators, and the gabfest ran on late into the night.

It is well that they made the most of the day, for on the morrow trouble broke. There followed days of bickering, name calling, sharply worded resolutions, fist fights, threats of armed violence, and the rattle of swords.

The Populists had elected 58 members of the lower house. There were three Democrats and one Independent. The Republicans held 63 election certificates which would have given them a majority had no contests been brought. Determined to control the lower branch, the Populists and Republicans went into caucuses on the evening of the inaugural and held all-night sessions. The Populists decided to contest eighteen seats, while the Republicans contested seven. The former nominated a slate of officers with W. H. Ryan of Crawford County for temporary chairman and J. M. Dunsmore of Neosho for speaker, and planned to exclude the holders of contested seats from voting at the election. The latter nominated J. H. Cubbison of Kansas City for temporary chairman and George L. Douglass of Sedgwick County for speaker. The Republican strategy was to go ahead with the organization of the House. If the Populists objected, the party would let the courts settle the matter; there they hoped to get a favorable decision from Republican judges.

The legislature convened at noon, January 10th. Long before that hour a crowd of visitors had filled the galleries.

By twelve-thirty all the legislators were in their seats, the Republicans occupying the south side and the Populists the north side of the hall. At 1:20 the secretary of state, R. S. Osborn, entered the chamber, walked to the speaker's stand, and called the House to order, stating that it was his duty to place before that body its roll of membership but that he would not act as chairman pending organization without the unanimous consent of the members. Representative Douglass immediately entered an objection, stating that the secretary of state had no authority to be presiding officer except by unanimous consent and that the Republicans did not consent. Representative Dunsmore rose and said the fact that the Republican leader had recognized Osborn gave him the right to be considered the temporary chairman.

Then Douglass rose and asked Osborn to read the roll, but denied the right of anyone to address him with an objection since he was not the presiding officer. The Populists wanted no such restrictions, as they intended to enter objections to seating certain men. At that moment W. L. Brown entered the room with a message from the Senate and addressed the secretary of state as the presiding officer. Half the Republicans rose to their feet, and all shouted their objections at the same time. Osborn said he would not deliver a certified list of members until the House had selected a presiding officer; then he walked rapidly out of the chamber, taking the roll with him.

No sooner had the secretary of state left the speaker's stand than R. H. Semple of Franklin County, a Populist, walked hurriedly up to the desk and picked up the gavel. Thereupon Douglass jumped to his feet and moved that Representative Cubbison be elected temporary speaker. Cubbison sprang from his chair in the second row back and rushed to the speaker's stand, while his nomination was being made and seconded and the vote taken by the Republican side of the House. He picked up another gavel, and both chairmen rapped for order. The Republicans worked swiftly. Representative E. W. Hoch nominated J. B. Remington of Miami County for temporary secretary. The motion was put. Chairman Cubbison declared it carried. Chairman Semple decided it was lost. Without an instant's delay, the Republicans elected C. C. Clevenger, sergeant at arms, adopted the rules of the last session, and called the roll. Then they swore in the members and elected George Douglass as speaker. They did all this so quickly as momentarily to daze the Populists, who had expected to control the organization through the secretary of state. The Populists quickly recovered and elected W.

H. Ryan temporary speaker, whereupon he took the chair. Then they proceeded to elect J. M. Dunsmore permanent speaker, and Ben C. Rich chief clerk. Dunsmore took his place beside Douglass on the speaker's stand. Amid the noise and the babel of voices on the floor and in the galleries, each entertained and put the motions of his respective "House."

Things became quieter by three o'clock. As no one had had any lunch, the Populists sent for sandwiches. After serving their own group and the two speakers, they handed the remainder to the Republicans. Evidently "Pop" sandwiches tasted good even if they couldn't "stomach" Populist principles.

After lunch the Populist body notified the secretary of state that the House was organized with J. M. Dunsmore as speaker. That official appeared and presented the Populist chairman with a certified roll of members, which was the signal for tremendous cheering by the Populists. A roll call was ordered. The fifty-eight Populists answered to their names, but the Republicans, the three Democrats, and one Independent did not respond. As the roll was called, the Populists challenged the names. They threw out the eighteen members whose seats they had contested and seated the claimants, ten of whom were present. The Independent then joined the Republicans, but the three Democrats decided not to take sides.

As it was late in the afternoon, the rival groups transacted no more business that day. Neither side trusted the other, so no adjournment was taken and the session lasted all night. At two o'clock in the morning the speakers reached an agreement whereby they could obtain some rest. With gavels in their hands, they lay down on the floor back of the desk facing each other and slept under the same blanket until six o'clock. The adage that politics makes strange bedfellows was literally true on this occasion.

About ten o'clock in the morning the Douglass House adjourned and immediately reconvened, and an hour later the Dunsmore House did the same thing. At half past twelve a conference committee composed of leaders of the hostile groups and of citizens met with the governor. They reached an agreement that both houses would adjourn until nine o'clock Thursday, the 12th, and referred the matter to a committee representing the three political parties.

The committee met in the evening and continued in session all night. Each party submitted a plan which was rejected by the other two, so the committee adjourned without accomplishing anything.

Nothing of note occurred until about two-thirty in the afternoon, when the three Democrats joined the Republicans, and amidst the cheers of that group, filed their oaths of office. Late in the afternoon the governor sent a message in which he recognized the Dunsmore House, and the hall resounded with cheers from the Populists. The next day, Friday, the Senate received Ben Rich, the Populist chief clerk, who read a message. Formal recognition followed on Saturday.

On Saturday both houses adjourned until four o'clock Monday afternoon to allow time in which to formulate plans of action.

The Populists were feeling quite secure. Speaker Dunsmore selected his permanent committees and sent notice to the Republicans to cease obstructing the operations of the legal house and to disband and work with the Populist organization. An exchange of letters took place between the two speakers, and by the first of February they had reached an agreement that each house was to defer to the other in the putting of motions and in transacting business.

Things ran smoothly enough, and to all appearances amicably, until February 9th, when the Republicans introduced a resolution to vacate the Populist seats and fill them by election if the members did not claim their right of membership by February 21st. Then the Populists decided to let the courts act and passed some appropriation bills.

The Populists claimed that back of this resolution lay a plan to unseat the whole administration and set up a provisional government with Speaker Douglass in charge. They were sure that such a move was on foot when an unusual number of strangers appeared on the streets on Friday and Saturday, February 10th and 11th, some of them armed with guns. Rumors were current that these strangers planned to arrest or assassinate the governor, tear down the State House, and commit other violence. The Populists charged that the railroads had brought these men in to assist the Republicans in their scheme to overthrow the government.

On Monday, the 13th, the Dunsmore House passed a resolution in which they referred to the Republican body as "that lawless rump House on the south side of this House," and instructed the sergeant at arms to throw these "disorderly persons" out of Representative Hall in order that the work of the legislature might go on uninterrupted.

Then the Republicans went into action. They adopted a resolution instructing Sergeant at Arms Clevenger to arrest L. C. Gunn, a clerk in the office of the Missouri, Kansas, and Texas Railway Company at Parsons, for failure to appear before the Douglass House in an election contest case. Clevenger started at once on this mission. The following morning the Douglass House called up the resolution to vacate the Populist seats and just before noon passed a resolution to arrest Ben Rich for continually interrupting the proceedings by "loud and boisterous language and unlawful and unusual noises without legal excuse or justification therefor." Rich had anticipated this action and was absent. Three deputy sergeants, W. H. Young, L. B. Clogston, and A. C. Jordan, went out to find him.

They found him at the Dutton House on the corner of Kansas Avenue and Fourth Street. He refused to submit to arrest but said that he planned to go to Representative Hall after dinner and the deputies could accompany him if they would wait. While he was eating, Chairman Breidenthal and other Populists assembled at the hotel to accompany him to the capitol. Rich left the hotel in custody of both groups and followed by several citizens. As the party went down Kansas Avenue, the crowd increased in size. At the corner of Ninth Street Rich tried to turn west to the State House, while the deputies attempted to take him across the street to the Copeland Hotel, and a fist fight ensued. Ryan hit Deputy Clogston on the jaw, knocking him down, and then straddled his neck, while Breidenthal and Scott went for the other two deputies. Populist fists crashed against Republican flesh. The deputies got in a few blows but were soon knocked out. The Populists then proceeded to Representative Hall and were welcomed by the Dunsmore House with shouts and applause.

Fearing trouble, the governor asked Sheriff Wilkerson to provide as many peace officers for the capitol as might be necessary to preserve order. Speaker Dunsmore sent the sheriff a similar request. Wilkerson refused to comply on the ground that he didn't know which was the legal House. Governor Lewelling then instructed H. H. Artz, the adjutant general, to take charge of the Populist guards and preserve order. That night the Populists remained in Representative Hall and locked the doors. The guards were on duty all night.

The next morning, when the Republican door-keeper went to Representative Hall, he was confronted by armed guards who refused to let him enter the room to assume his regular duties. On learning this, the Republican members assembled at the Copeland Hotel. They formed in line, with Speaker Douglass and Ed Hoch at the head of the column, and marched to the State House. Douglass carried a massive sledge hammer, and others in the party were armed with guns and clubs. When they reached the foot of the main stairway they found it lined with armed guards. After a struggle with these guards they forced their way up the stairway. At the upper landing they were confronted by more guards who stood with guns pointed at them, ready to fire. At that moment J. Ware Butterfield who had forced his way into the hall from the stairway at the west end and had hurried across the hall and through the doors, called loudly to the guards:

"For God's sake, don't shoot! Don't shed innocent blood!"

Since none but Populists were supposed to be in the hall, the guards hesitated and turned toward Butterfield. Before they could turn again, the rapidly advancing Republicans were upon them and they could not use their weapons effectively had they intended to do so. His intervention may have prevented bloodshed. The Republicans forced the doors with the sledge hammer and entered the chamber. Fifteen or twenty Populist guards, in charge of the hall inside, beat a hasty retreat. The Republicans, amid shouts and tumult, took possession of the hall, the offices, and the committee rooms. The Populist members withdrew to the corridor.

In the afternoon the governor instructed General Artz to assemble the state militia. He called out nine companies. The first company, composed of fifteen men, arrived about four-thirty.

That evening a committee of citizens urged the governor not to call out any more of the militia and invited him to go to the Representative Chamber for a conference. He asked the Republicans to vacate the hall and leave it in his care for the night. It is said that they refused to do this, saying they would "surrender only to the militia and then only after they were conquered by bloodshed."

The besieged Republicans passed a long, sleepless night. Several women who belonged to a suffrage lobby were present. They had to make the best of it. Unfortunately, one lady was suffering from severe injuries she had received by getting too close to a fist fight between some deputy sheriffs and a group of state auditors. They passed the night with speechmaking and cardplaying.

Thursday morning, February 16th, the leading newspapers in the West came out with large headlines stating that Kansas was in a state of civil war and bloodshed was momentarily expected.

During the day the militiamen arrived and went into camp about the capitol grounds. The Wichita battery brought their Gatling gun with them. When the men set it up and trained it on Representative Hall, they found that it lacked the firing pin.

Conferences with the governor consumed most of the afternoon, and the hostile camps awaited the outcome before starting war. The committee considered several proposals but could reach no agreement, so declared a truce until nine o'clock the following morning. In the night a genuine Kaw blizzard, which had been threatening since the night before, struck with all its fury, and before morning a foot of snow had fallen. Many of the men were lightly clad, and in the face of this wintry blast they shivered and their teeth chattered. There would have been much suffering had the reliefs not been frequent. By morning, the storm had cooled the hotheaded leaders off some and had taken most of the fighting spirit out of the men.

Conferences with the governor, which had been going on all night, continued through the forenoon. At noon they reached an agreement acceptable to both sides. The militia and the force of the deputy sheriffs were to disband and go home. Each house was to return to its status prior to the arrest of Rich; the Republican House was to have Representative Hall and the Dunsmore House was to meet elsewhere until the courts acted. The Populists fitted up the south wing of the basement of the Stormont Building for their sessions.

Two cases were before the Supreme Court. The court handed down the decision on Saturday morning, February 25th. The majority of the court upheld the legality of the Douglass House.

The Populists met behind closed doors to consider their next move. They deliberated from one-thirty on Saturday afternoon until Monday night, when they decided to submit to the court decision, presented Speaker Dunsmore with the chair he had occupied and gavel he had used, and then marched in a body, behind a standard-bearer carrying the American flag, to Representative Hall and took their seats.

The Populist victory at the polls in November turned into a sickening defeat. When the courts decided in favor of the Douglass House, the measures which had been passed by the Populists were outlawed. The only plank in the Populist platform that became a law was the resolution to submit the equal suffrage amendment to the people.

21

The Silver Campaign

WHEN the news reached Kansas that the Populist convention at St. Louis had nominated William Jennings Bryan for president, one Populist newspaper exclaimed:

"Mr. Bryan is better than his platform—in fact, he is a Populist platform within himself."

Another party journal said:

"The nominations give general satisfaction, and we think the ticket could not be improved. With the brilliant, gallant young giant of Nebraska and the undaunted, invincible young Georgian, at the head of our ticket, we are prepared to go into battle to win, and we are sure to come out of the fray with victory perched upon our banners."

The Democratic State Convention met at Hutchinson, August 4th, and the Populist convention at Abiline, August 5th. The Democrats nominated a set of presidential electors and then adjourned for a day, while a committee carried a message to the Abilene convention. The Democrats proposed that their party should nominate the presidential electors and the Populists should name the state ticket. The latter agreed to the arrangement. They nominated the same electors the

Democrats had chosen and then selected their state ticket. The Democratic convention reconvened and accepted the Populist nominees. The leading candidates on the ticket were: John W. Leedy, for governor; A. M. Harvey, for lieutenant governor; Frank Doster, for chief justice; and J. D. Botkin, congressman at large. The fusion completed, the campaign was soon under way.

A week later four thousand people witnessed the funeral of the silver craze at Garnett. The Republicans had been "proclaiming from the housetops so loudly and so long that the silver craze" was dead that the friends of the white metal decided it was about time for the funeral. Wednesday, August 12th, was selected for the obsequies. The weather behaved perfectly. Early in the morning farmers and their families began coming in buggies and wagons. They continued to come until noon. The trains also brought crowds.

The funeral services began at ten o'clock. The crowd shed no tears. Enthusiasm ran high, and good feeling prevailed. The services opened with short speeches. Jerry Simpson, Ed Little, a Silver Republican, and M. S. Peters, an advocate of the white metal, arrived on the afternoon train. Peters made a short speech. Then Jerry Simpson was introduced and talked for three hours. His speech was full of wit and trite sayings. Little followed Jerry on the platform. When he finished, the crowd insisted on another speech from Jerry.

The campaign began in earnest when the Bryan supporters held a big rally at Blue Mound late in August. The candidate for governor spoke to a large audience in the afternoon. In the evening there was a torchlight procession with two hundred torchbearers in line. A meeting at the opera house was scheduled to follow the parade. The building wouldn't hold the crowd, making an open-air meeting necessary.

The fusion forces waged an intensive campaign which continued full blast up to the eve of the election. The men organized silver clubs, and the women formed Bryan clubs. The candidates and other speakers traveled up and down the state and addressed huge audiences. Mrs. Lease stirred up sentiment for free silver in Minnesota and returned to Kansas in October taking her place on the campaign platform.

Many of these rallies were all-day affairs. Bryan and free silver were on everybody's lips and filled hundreds of newspaper columns. The fusionists shouted loudly for the Commoner and his platform, while their opponents pointed to the dangers of putting Populist principles into effect. A Populist paper said that the Republicans were traveling up and down the country telling the people that if "Free Silver is adopted the country will go to the devil as if greased for the occasion."

Music was a prominent feature of the rallies. The local bands led the processions and entertained the crowds until the speakers arrived. A Topeka quartet, the Quenemo Glee Club, and other musical organizations furnished special numbers. The campaign managers supplied printed songs which were set to tunes that caught the public ear. The halls resounded and the woods echoed when the crowds turned loose on these political gems.

Below is one stanza and the chorus of a fusion song.

> Rally for Bryan and Sewall, boys
> And rally for Doster, too,
> Shouting the battle cry for Leedy.
> Harvey for his running mate,

John Madden for congressman too,
Shouting the battle cry for victory.

Chorus—
Union forever, hurrah, boys hurrah,
Down with McKinley
And old Hanna too;
And we'll send them up salt river,
We will send them, good and strong,
And there we will pickle them down with Bryan.

The silver forces tried to capture the old-soldier vote with a song:

Come, my good old soldier boys as we were long ago,
But now our heads are very few and getting white like snow,
But our recruits are very speedy and anxious for the show,
To get to vote for Bryan and our Leedy.

Hurrah, Hurrah, the battle now is on
Hurrah, Hurrah, the battle now is won;
Now with Bryan and Leedy, boys, we are sure to win the day,
While we are marching in Kansas.

The Republicans seasoned their songs with campaign spice as the following stanza will indicate:

We want an honest dollar, so we do,
We want an honest dollar, so we do,
We want an honest dollar and for it we will holler,
If we have to burst our collar—
Now will you?

Thomas E. Watson of Georgia, the Populist candidate for vice-president, came to Kansas in September and threw a monkey wrench into the machinery. One writer relates the incident:

Having gained a position of advantage as the Populist nominee for the second place on the ticket, he insisted that Sewall must withdraw in his favor, as the price of the Populist support for Bryan for President. After making a speaking tour of the southern states, preaching this doctrine, he transferred his activities to Kansas.

The Populists wanted to elect Bryan, and gave little encouragement to the Georgia malcontent, but Watson would not be silenced. He made three speeches in Kansas—at Erie, Abilene, and Iola—denouncing the Democratic party and Mr. Arthur Sewall of Maine. The Republican press was in high glee and gave him much publicity. The fusion campaign seemed wrecked. "The Populist party in Kansas is just on the rocks," said the *Capital*. "If Tom Watson could prolong his stay in the state a few more days, he would probably leave the party in ruins."

A shrewd move by John Breidenthal, state chairman of the party, offset any damage Watson may have done. On the eve of election, a letter from Breidenthal to a party worker appeared in print. In this letter the chairman stated that the Republicans had plenty of funds and workers and were gaining ground every day, while the Populists lacked both money and workers and were quarreling among themselves. "Only a miracle can save us," he said. This letter was "confidential" and had fallen into the hands of the Republicans "by a piece of political good luck."

The Republicans swallowed the letter hook, line, and sinker, and gave it wide publicity, with the result that their workers relaxed their vigilance, while the silverites redoubled their efforts. The election resulted in a sweeping fusion victory. Then the Republicans discovered that the letter had been a hoax.

22

The Grass Roots Are Converted

THE election campaign of 1896 was the last flare of the Populist revolt. The party, torn by internal dissension, grew weaker after the election and was in bad shape for the campaign of 1898. The Republican press, that year, commented on the disrupted condition of the party. The Emporia *Gazette* went so far as to publish "An Ode to the Departed," which was reprinted in other newspapers.

While it was true that the Populists were "drowned in the deluge of prosperity" which the country enjoyed at the turn of the century, there were other reasons for the death of the party. The breakup had begun in 1893. The legislature war that year demoralized the party and damaged its prestige. The governor was unfortunate in his appointments and had to remove some of his appointees for incompetence or disloyalty. The antiadministration faction put up a middle-of-the-road ticket in the next election. The Populists also split on the question of fusion. One faction believed in fusion with the Democrats, while the other wanted the party to make an independent fight.

The Populists had obtained complete control of the state government in the election of 1896. The rank and file expected much of the party, but were disappointed. The legislature enacted twenty reform laws, but failed to pass the three measures nearest the Populist heart— the initiative and referendum, reduction of interest rates, and the railroad bill.

As a result, a large number of Populists deserted their organization and went over to one of the old-line parties. During the campaign of 1898 the Hays *Republican* said that was the first year the Populist party "could not get up a meeting in this city" and predicted that the Populists in the county would vote the Republican ticket.

Mrs. Lease was among those who joined the Republican party. She retired from active politics, and a few years later removed to New York.

Jerry Simpson served three terms in Congress, being elected for the third term in 1896 on a fusion ticket. He was defeated in 1898 and retired to private life. He lived in Wichita for a time, and published *Jerry Simpson's Bayonet* from May, 1899, until September, 1900. In 1902 he removed to New Mexico, partly because of ill-health. When his health grew worse he returned to Wichita, where he died in 1905.

When the Populists returned to the old-line parties, they continued their demands for political and social reforms and influenced the action of both parties. The historian of the third party puts it even stronger:

The Populist doctrines had so permeated the consciousness of the masses, that although the Republicans succeeded in defeating the party, the people had turned Populist and believed in the Populist program, and in order to keep down the party of that name the Republicans were compelled from time to time to give the people measures which they had learned to think of as their right.

About the time the Populist party went on the rocks, Theodore Roosevelt became president and started his campaign for clean politics and against the "malefactors of great wealth." Before long reformers bore the stamp of respectability. Reform measures grew in popular favor. Office seekers found it advisable to put progressive planks in their platforms and shout for reform in their campaign speeches. If they sought re-election, they had to show a record in favor of reform.

In Kansas the Republicans wrested the control of the state government from the Populists in 1898, and with the exception of eight years, they have been in power since that date. In these forty-odd years the legislators have enacted reform laws galore. Some of these measures originated in Populist demands. Others have taken care of new problems arising out of a changing social order.

The regulation of railroads confronted the first Republican administration. The Populist governor had convened the legislature in extra session, at the close of his administration, to enact a railroad law. The lawmakers abolished the Railroad Commission and created a Court of Visitation which was empowered to hear cases and fix rates. The Supreme Court declared the law unconstitutional before it had a fair test. The Republican legislature of 1901 created a new board. Subsequent legislation provided for the uniformity of freight rates, regulated the working hours of railroad employees, and did away with free passes.

Next the state tried its hand at "trust busting." The independent oil companies complained that the Standard Oil Company was forcing them to the wall by a price war. They asked for a state-owned refinery and wanted the Railroad Commission to control the pipe lines. The issue was before the legislature of 1905. A leading newspaper called the Standard Oil a "Bull Octopus." "It is useless," this paper said, "to parley with the fact that Bull Octopus has its clutches on Kansas." The governor gave the state refinery plan a pat on the back in his message to the legislature, and the solons enacted the necessary laws to curb the illegal activities of Bull Octopus. The Supreme Court declared the state refinery act unconstitutional. The other legislation survived the scrutiny of the courts and has stood the test of time. The antidiscrimination law, which was general and applied to the prices of numerous articles besides oil, has been especially beneficial. Antitrust laws, good and bad, have been passed, until today the legislation relating to monopolies and unfair trade fills quite a section in the volume of *General Statutes*. Referring to these enactments, one writer says, "We no longer recognize the divine right of wealth and cussedness."

The first law relating to primary elections was passed back in Populist days. Succeeding legislatures made amendments and additions. In 1908 the lawmakers passed an act providing for the "nomination of all candidates" by the electors, and repealing all acts in conflict with it.

Women were granted the elective franchise in this era of reform. The right to vote at school elections was extended to women in 1861. The legislature of 1867 submitted a constitutional amendment for full suffrage. A Negro suffrage measure was before the voters at the time, so they turned both of them down. The legislature of 1893 submitted an amendment to the electors. The Populists endorsed the plan, while the old-line parties refused to back it. This made it a party measure and caused its defeat. The women's organizations continued the fight until 1912, when the people adopted an amendment granting them equal rights and privileges with the

men at the polls. Kansas was one of the first six states
to ratify the nineteenth amendment making woman
suffrage a national matter.

In addition, Kansas has enacted child-labor legislation, established juvenile courts; improved the laws
governing the collection of debts and the foreclosure of
mortgages; done away with bucketshops; provided for

the recall of "every public officer holding either by election or appointment" at the will of a majority of the
voters; and ratified the amendments to the national
constitution providing for the election of United States
senators by direct vote and for Prohibition, by an almost unanimous vote.

Kansans were strong for the progressive movement
which ended in a schism in the Republican ranks and

the formation of the Bull Moose party in 1912. One historian says that Theodore Roosevelt "polled several million of votes on a platform that was more populistic than Populism itself. His following was especially strong in Kansas, among the Philistines who had persecuted Samson." Woodrow Wilson carried the election, with Theodore Roosevelt close second, while William Howard Taft received only twenty-two per cent of the votes. After the battle, the Topeka *Capital,* in an editorial entitled "What of Roosevelt?" said,

"It has been the greatest democratic campaign in the largest meaning of the word ever conducted in the nation, and it has fixed certain genuinely democratic ideas and ideals in men's minds."

While Kaw folks were passing reform laws and raising millions of bushels of wheat and corn, they looked to the education of their children. They have dotted the prairies with elementary and high school buildings, and they have raised the educational requirements of the teachers. In order to provide the children in the poor districts with educational advantages equal to those enjoyed by pupils in the wealthy districts, they recently established a state equalization fund. They have also built up their institutions of higher learning. The growth of the state schools illustrates the yearning of Kaw youths for college education. In 1900 there were three state schools. In a few years two more schools were added: Fort Hays State College, in western Kansas, and a State Teachers College, in southeastern Kansas. Four times as many students are enrolled in these schools as were enrolled at the opening of the century.

23

Soldiers of the Pen

THE Indians were the first authors in the Kaw
country. They didn't write books, but they did have an
oral literature. They had their legends and traditions,
and they made up poems. They sang of arms and heroes,
of love and of nature, and they sang their babies to sleep.

The early explorers and travelers wrote about the
Kaw or had some one with them who could flourish a
pen. Coronado was the first white man to visit the Kaw
region. He and four of his companions wrote accounts
of the expedition. The conquistador's description of
the land sounds much like the sales talk of a modern
real estate man. In a sense it was a sales talk. He was selling his king the idea that he had discovered a great
territory with soil "very fat and black," in the place of
the province rich in "yellow dirt" which he had set
out to find.

A partial narrative of the journey was put in print
in the decade following the expedition. Hakluyt provided readers with an English translation a half century
later.

The Kaw had newspapers as soon as it had anything.
The Leavenworth *Herald* was the first newspaper in
Kansas Territory. The first issue of this paper was

printed September 15, 1854, by a hand press under an elm tree on the bank of the Missouri River. The printing outfit was moved into the first house erected on the townsite. The first issues of the two pioneer papers at Lawrence were printed in the East: one at Medina, Ohio, the other in Pennsylvania. One writer tells us that the Leavenworth *Herald* was printed before it had an office and the *Herald of Freedom* was printed before it had a town.

The opening of Kansas Territory to settlement resulted in war over slavery. People everywhere were eager to learn about the struggle. Noted correspondents of great eastern dailies came to Kansas to write it up. Writers pushed their pens hard and fast, and printing presses worked overtime to supply interested readers with partisan literature.

The early settlers were too busy fighting and making both ends meet to wield their pens and use their imagination at the same time. However, they wrote some verse and a few novels.

Most of the books of the period were historical and descriptive in nature. Among these were a score of books written by the correspondents of eastern newspapers. One of the best in this group is *The War in Kansas* by George Douglas Brewerton, correspondent of the New York *Herald*. He uses the dialogue method extensively. This is good, especially when he puts it in the dialect of Kaw folks.

A type of native poetry peculiar to territorial Kansas made its appearance early. This was the border song. The best examples are in Tomlinson's *Kansas in 1858*. A stanza bearing the title "Border Song" is used as the heading for each chapter, and the "Song of Montgomery's Men" is printed in full in one chapter. Tomlinson gives credit for the song to a youthful member of the company commanded by Free State Captain James Montgomery, though the composition indicates more than one head in the making, the first stanza being more regular and finished than the rest. The first stanza and the chorus are given here:

> One morning bright, by early light,
> Word ran from youth to age,
> That Brocket then, with all his men,
> Was on the Little Osage.

> O, the Little Osage,
> The Little Osage,
> We'll fight the foe where'er they go,
> Up on the Little Osage.

The outstanding singer of the period was Richard Realf. He produced verse of finish and real beauty, and according to one authority, "manifested more of a natural gift of poetry than any one of all who have attempted to sing in Kansas." His residence in the territory was brief, but his interest in Kansas and his devotion to the principles for which Kansas stood give the state ground for claiming him as her own.

Realf was born in England and was publishing verse when he was seventeen. In the spring of 1856, at the age of twenty-one, he arrived in New York and six months later came to Kansas. Shortly after his arrival, he wrote a descriptive poem entitled "The Defense of Lawrence." "Kansas," written the same year, is the first of a series of poems of tribute to the state. During his short residence in Kansas he wrote at least twenty-five of his best lyrics.

The Civil War marked a break in the literary history of Kansas. The border wars had ceased and with them passed the most fruitful source for literary effort. The correspondents of the eastern papers went to the war front. With the writers gone and the material out of which literature is created lacking, little writing was done.

The war over, men put down their guns and went home to their farms and shops. The next quarter of a century was a period of remarkable economic growth and prosperity. But during that period the people were too busy raising cattle and corn to make outstanding contributions to Kansas culture.

A group who felt that writers should be encouraged founded the *Kansas Magazine* in 1872. A periodical equal to the *Atlantic* was the standard set by the founders. The magazine was short-lived, ceasing publication in October, 1873, but during its brief existence it contained some of the best contributions made to Kansas literature.

Henry King, a Topeka newspaperman who was an excellent judge of good literature, was editor the first year. James W. Steele and John J. Ingalls were leading contributors. Much of Steele's best writing appeared in the magazine. He is noted for his sketches through which runs a vein of refined humor. Ingalls contributed essays of high artistic form. "Blue Grass" is best known, though "Catfish Aristocracy" was popular and is still read. It is said that the author owed his seat in the United States Senate to the attention attracted by his essays. These essays, his orations, and the poem "Opportunity" which is a classic in the English language, give him a high place among writers.

The impulse given by the *Kansas Magazine* and the writings of the men who contributed to it did much for the advancement of literature in the state. More than a score of attempts have been made to run literary periodicals, most of which have failed. The short story, unknown in the war period, made its appearance in 1872. Kansas novels, poetry, and short stories became a distinct part of the state's history.

Topeka has been the center of much of the literary activity in the state, which is evidence that politics and poetry do mix. It has been the home of more than a score of the state's novelists, to say nothing about the poets, short-story writers, journalists, and historians who have lived there.

Eugene Fitch Ware, called the "Poet Laureate of Kansas," lived for several years at Topeka. His pen name is Ironquill. His first poem to attract attention was "Neutralia" and was published in chapters in 1871. His *Rhymes of Ironquill* passed through many editions and have been read with wide interest in both England and America.

He was a loyal Kansan. He sang of Kansas and her history, the abundance of her harvests, the beauty of her prairie, the strong character of her pioneers, the wild animal life, droughts, cyclones, and grasshoppers. He expresses his stanch loyalty to the Jayhawker State especially well in the poems "Quivera," "John Brown," "The Three States," and "Ad Astra Per Aspera."

It was not alone of Kansas that he sang. His themes are diverse. "Today," "The Washerwoman's Song," "The Protest," and "Frauds" are examples of his diversity of interest.

The element of cheer and enthusiasm is prominent in Ironquill's verse.

Ware was honored during his lifetime. He was twice elected to the state senate. In 1888 he served as presidential elector at large for Kansas. He was appointed commissioner for the state to the Yorktown Centennial and later to the Washington Centennial. He delivered, on invitation, his poem "Decoration Day" at the Arlington National Cemetery before an audience of several thousand people, which included the president, his family and cabinet, and many high officers of the army and navy.

One of the best known Kansas writers missed being a resident of the Kaw valley by some miles. This is Edgar Watson Howe, whose home was in Atchison for sixty years. He came to Atchison in 1877, and with a capital of less than $200 established the Atchison *Globe*, a daily paper of one sheet. The first few weeks he used the space to poke fun at himself and the paper "to save the people that trouble." He distributed the sheet free the first two weeks. The townfolks laughed at his jokes and subscribed for his paper.

He built a home by and by and called it "Potato Hill," to give it a name not used by other homeowners. He was generally known as the "Sage of Potato Hill."

Howe was a writer of fiction, philosophy, and travel. His first book, *The Story of a Country Town*, published in 1888, brought him wide recognition. He wrote the book by the light of a kerosene lamp on the kitchen table after his day of labor on the *Globe*. He wrote with pen and ink in a ruled daybook with a paper back. When he completed the manuscript he couldn't find a publisher, so he published it himself at the *Globe* office. He issued 1,500 copies and had to give several away to get the book in circulation.

The book is largely the author's own story written out of the bitter experiences of his childhood days. The idyllic pictures of village life which sweetened the literature of his period irritated him. He knew they were inaccurate. So he wrote his novel to show up the sham, the barren religion, the prejudice, the petty jealousies, and the backwardness of the small town. The story is his masterpiece of fiction and is one of the most effective pictures of a western town ever drawn.

The book is noted for the personality of the characters. They seem to be people of flesh and blood and not creatures of his fancy. The author says, "I meet Jo Errings every day, . . . I have known several John Westlocks . . . and troops of Mrs. Westlocks." Likewise, the reader who grew up in a small town of the Middle West knew a John Westlock or a Jo Erring, in his youth, and when one of the characters appears in the story he visualizes an old acquaintance, perhaps a next-door neighbor.

The Country Town was the first of the *Main Street* books, but it came out too early to be fully appreciated. Had it appeared thirty years later it would have created as much of a stir as the books of iconoclasts of village virtues made early in the present century. Although some complained of the bitterness in the novel and wanted more cheer in their fiction, the story attracted wide notice. The public bought the book, and the publishers who had rejected it clamored for the right to publish it. Fifty editions were run off, and for more than a half century the author received royalty checks regularly.

Other books followed, especially books of travel and stories. Howe also wrote short stories for leading magazines, and was noted for his paragraphs. They were humorous, cynical, and tinged with satire.

In 1911 he turned the *Globe* over to his son, and in a short time began publishing *E. W. Howe's Monthly, Devoted to Information and Indignation.* Writers throughout the world quoted this four-page journal.

Ed Howe died in October, 1937, at the age of eighty-four.

For many years Emporia, on the Neosho River,

was the home of Walt Mason, the self-educated humorist and poet. He was born in Canada and came to the United States in 1880. He was connected with the Atchison *Globe* for a brief period and later on farmed and did newspaper work in Nebraska. Discovering that pigs and poetry wouldn't mix, he came to Kansas in 1907 and and went to work for William Allen White on the Emporia *Gazette*. Here is the story of his employment:

It was one of those lazy September days back in 1907 in Emporia. Things were pretty quiet in the *Gazette* office. The cub reporter gazing idly out of the window saw a queer vehicle draw up in front of the office. It was an odd affair, a topless phaeton, with one of the back wheels almost spokeless. Hitched to it was a small bay horse.

The occupant of the strange rig rolled out. He was a big round man, and there was a worried expression on his face when he tapped on the door of the *Gazette* editorial room. Going to the one typewriter the office possessed he took off his felt hat, revealing a head of short, curly hair, and began to write on the machine.

When he had finished writing his piece, which turned out to be a prose poem, he handed it to William Allen White and said:

"I'm Walt Mason. Does the *Gazette* pay for this flapdoodle?"

The *Gazette* wanted that "flapdoodle." His prose poems became a regular feature of the paper and attracted considerable attention. He wrote on a wide range of subjects, and the homey philosophy of his genial jingles appealed to the cities as well as the countryfolks. Like Ware, he wrote on commonplace subjects and in simple language. However, he is more optimistic and sentimental than Ironquill. Three of Mason's poems gained world-wide notice. They are "The Little Green Tents," "The Journeys," and "The Eyes of Lincoln." For years more than two hundred daily newspapers in the United States and Canada published his rhymes regularly.

Walt Mason published six books of poems. These had heavy sales and all six were out of print at the time of his death, June 22, 1939.

Emporia is also the home of William Allen White. He was born there and in 1895 purchased the Emporia *Gazette,* which paper he has owned and edited to the present time. He has made the paper one of the most famous small-town dailies in the country. An editorial "What's the matter with Kansas?" brought him his first wide notice. It was quoted all over the United States. He couldn't find much wrong with Kansas then, and in the forty-odd years that have passed since that writing he hasn't found anything seriously wrong with the state. In fact, he is strong for Kansas.

He is author of a dozen books and has contributed numerous stories to leading magazines and newspapers. His speeches and essays on political questions have attracted attention, but he is probably best known for his editorials. They are quoted in the leading newspapers of the country. He wrote *The Real Issue and Other Stories* in 1896. This was followed by *The Court of Boyville,* and other books. He is author of a biography of Woodrow Wilson and one of Calvin Coolidge. He has contributed more of real worth to biography than any other Kansan of the period.

White is skillful in depicting political characters and noted for his boy characters. His boys are not sissies, nor are they rowdies. They are live American youngsters.

His writings contain vivid descriptions of life in the

small town of the Middle West. He knows the people of these towns. While he appreciates their sterling qualities, he is not blind to their shortcomings. His shorter stories as well as his novels are rich in actualities.

The Kaw has a wealth of material available for writers of literature. A number of them have used these sources, but none has risen to real greatness. The great Kansas novel remains to be written.

24

This Is the Kaw

THIS is the story of the Kaw. It is the story of early wagon trails across the "prairie ocean," of bloody border wars, cattle drives, wheat, and the revolt of farmers against injustice. It is the story of the building of a prairie empire.

The Kaw is still flowing. But the blight of seven years of drought is on it. The blue thirties have left their scar. The stream is shallower and runs more slowly than formerly. The country through which it flows has been hard hit. This is especially true of the high-plains area. Here, many farm homes need paint and repairs. Some have been abandoned by their owners, while others have been lost by foreclosure. A thin growth of grain now covers fields which in good years raised bumper crops. The range grass has become thin through years of over-grazing and neglect. However, the comeback of the Buffalo grass in western Kansas is almost unbelievable. By using methods approved by the experts, industrious farmers have improved the condition of their grasslands. Pastures which a few years ago would not support a few head of goats are coming into their own.

Leaving the high plains, the tributaries of the Kaw flow through one of the rich oil districts of the country.

For miles one sees long rows of steel derricks, unpainted shacks, new stores, supply houses, lumberyards, machine shops, and big piles of pipe.

The value of the state's income from mineral wealth approaches that from her agricultural products. Petroleum produces over half the mineral wealth. About twenty per cent of the people of Kansas are affected by the oil industry. Some counties are nearly solidly leased. Thousands of farmers whose income from agriculture is low receive substantial amounts in the form of royalties or lease rentals.

Those who vision the future say that Kansans will depend more and more on the mineral resources and industries as their chief source of income.

In central Kansas the Kaw's tributaries enter an area that hasn't been hit so hard by the dry years. Here the fields and pastures are greener and the farm homes generally are in better repair than those farther west.

At Junction City, where the Republican and the Smoky Hill unite and form the Kaw, the effects of the drought are scarcely visible.

In the late spring the valley of the Kaw from Junction City to Kansas City reminds one of a vast tapestry patterned by green fields of wheat, corn, and potatoes, green meadows, truck patches, orchards, wooded tracts, and verdant hills.

The valley is still growing the tall corn, big potatoes, and delicious melons for which it is famous. It is also noted for its leadership in culture and industry.

The two largest state schools, the State University and the State College, are located on the banks of the Kaw; Washburn College, the Congressional school, is in a river town, while Baker University, a Methodist institution, missed the stream by a few miles.

A number of Kansas writers live in the valley and

several of the state's leading newspapers and periodicals
are published here.

Topeka, in the heart of the valley, is not only the
mecca of the politically minded of the state and the
home of several Kansas authors, but it is quite an industrial city. The main offices of the Santa Fe Railroad are
located here. The products of Topeka's industries are
diversified and range from flour and steel to the publication of farm papers.

Likewise, Kansas City, at the mouth of the river, is
a leading industrial center and the gateway through
which the grain and livestock of the Southwest pass on
their way to the world markets.

The hard times have shaken the people and disturbed their political thinking. The effort made by the
New Deal to bring about social justice appeals to Kaw
folks. When the New Dealers talk along that line they
are talking the language Kansans understand. This is the
thing Kansas people have stood for and fought for since
the first families settled on the Kaw.

As in the past, they do not agree on the best method
of bringing about social justice. In pioneer days the victims of unjust laws bolted their party and went on a
crusade. Their children are a little more conservative.
However, enough of them left the party of Alf Landon
in 1936 to swing the state to the Democratic standard-
bearers.

This means that Kansans are still alert on questions
of social well-being and place principles above party, and
will leave their party when they decide the party doesn't
represent their views.

The dry years have caused some to lose faith in Kansas. They have decided that the country was never intended for white men and have moved to other parts.

But the vast majority carry on. They won't give

up. Many of these persistent individuals are grizzled veterans of the plains who have lived through other depressions and have overcome seemingly unsurmountable obstacles. In fact, some of them haven't seen much but hard times. They don't know when they are whipped. They are determined to win this bout with nature, or "bust a hame string" in the effort.

The children and grandchildren of these pioneers have inherited their faith in Kansas and their determination to stick it out. An illustration recently came to the writer's attention. On a dusty day, when everyone was choking on the flying real estate, a college girl was talking with the writer.

"I don't see what anyone wants to live in Kansas for," she remarked as she choked on the dust.

"Are you leaving the state as soon as you graduate?" the writer asked.

"No, sir! I'm staying right here in Kansas," was her firm reply.

These young people possess the optimism of youth and have a faith in the future that would excite the admiration and envy of any oldster. No matter how dark things look they see a glimpse of brightness. One of them is the writer's secretary. When she enters the office her smile is as cheering as a ray of sunshine on a gloomy day. They are the products of the Kaw, and are the finest crop any river can produce. Maybe the clatter of livestock marching to market will grow fainter in lean years. Perhaps the belt of golden grain will become thinner. What does it matter? With this crop of splendid boys and girls as its product, the Kaw will flow on, carrying them with it, to the far corners of the world.

Acknowledgments

FIRST of all, I wish to thank Dr. Myrta McGinnis, Gwen Lane Funston, and Gwendolyn Dimmitt, of Fort Hays Kansas State College; Thelma Hruza, of George Peabody College; George Thompson, of Iowa University; the staff of the Kansas Historical Society, the library staff of the University of Kansas; and Elizabeth Davis, Reference Librarian, State College, Manhattan.

I thank Colonel Jack Potter, of Santa Fe, New Mexico, an Old Trail driver and author of *Lead Steer,* for putting me straight on trail and cattle history, and my uncle, H. W. Prouty, who was a pioneer on the Kaw, for help on early-day events.

I am grateful to Chapman and Grimes, Publishers, of Boston, for permitting me to use sources I used in *Prairie Trails and Cow Towns.*

I appreciate the help of many other persons whom I cannot mention by name because of lack of space.

I have written a large part of the Kaw story from original sources. I searched newspaper files and government publications and dug dust-covered manuscripts out of the basements and attics of county courthouses and city buildings.

I have listed the sources in the bibliography. Naturally some sources yielded more information than others and deserve special mention. The state histories by Spring, Connelley, and Isely and Richards, the massive volume of details published by Andreas, and the State Historical Society's volumes have been helpful in several chapters. In fact, Kansas school children are fortunate in having the little book by Bliss Isely and W. M. Richards for a text.

The following sources have been quite useful for the chapters mentioned: Root and Connelley's *Overland Stage to California* and Inman's *Old Santa Fe Trail*, for the second chapter; Clifford Miller's thesis on social life in Kansas Territory, for the third chapter; Cordley's *History of Lawrence*, contemporary volumes by eastern newspapermen, and books on John Brown, for Bleeding Kansas; Glenn Bradley's *Story of the Santa Fe*, for the railroads; Hunter's *Trail Drivers of Texas*, McCoy's *Historic Sketches*, and Jack Potter's writings, for the cattle chapters; Mark Carleton's writings, agricultural reports and bulletins, and articles in periodicals, for the wheat story; Annie Diggs's *Story of Jerry Simpson*, and the histories of Populism in the Historical Society's volume and in Connelley's state history, for the farm revolt; and manuscript theses and histories of literature, for the survey of Kansas writers.

Bibliography

Books and Pamphlets

Alliance and Labor Songster, The, Winfield, Kans.: H. & L. Vincent, 1890.

BALL, CARLETON R., and CLARK, A. J., *Experiments with Durum Wheat.* Washington: U.S. Dept. of Agriculture, Farmers' Bulletin No. 618, 1918.

BECKER, CARL, *Kansas.* Reprinted from *Turner Essays in American History.* Copyright, 1910, by Henry Holt & Company, New York.

BELL, WILLIAM, *New Tracks in North America* (2 vols.). London: Chapman and Hall, 1869.

BENTLEY, O. H., *History of Wichita and Sedgwick County, Kansas* (2 vols.). Chicago: C. F. Cooper and Co., 1910.

BLACKMAR, FRANK W., *Kansas; a Cyclopedia of State History* (2 vols.). Chicago: Standard Publishing Company, 1912.

BLANCHARD, LEOLA HOWARD, *Conquest of Southwest Kansas.* Wichita, Kans.: The Wichita Eagle Press, 1931.

BLANKENSHIP, RUSSELL, *American Literature, as an Expression of the National Mind.* New York: Henry Holt & Company, 1931.

BOWLES, SAMUEL, *Across the Continent.* Springfield, Mass.: Samuel Bowles & Co.; New York, Hurd & Houghton, 1866.

BRADLEY, GLENN DANFORD, *The Story of the Santa Fe.* Boston: Richard G. Badger, 1920.

BREWERTON, GEORGE DOUGLAS, *The War in Kansas.* New York: Derby and Jackson; Cincinnati, H. W. Derby, 1856.

Bryan and Leedy Free Silver Song Sheets. No imprint.

BUCK, SOLON J., *The Agrarian Crusade; a Chronicle of the Farmer in Politics.* New Haven: Yale University Press, 1921.

BURCH, JOHN P., *Charles W. Quantrell. A True History of His Guerrilla Warfare . . .* As told by Captain Harrison Trow. Vega, Texas.

CARLETON, MARK ALFRED, *Basis for the Improvement of American Wheats.* Washington: U.S. Dept. of Agriculture, Division of Vegetable Physiology and Pathology, Bulletin No. 24, 1900.

———— *Cereal Rusts of the United States; a Physiological Investigation.* Washington: U.S. Dept. of Agriculture, Division of Vegetable Physiology and Pathology, Bulletin No. 16, 1899.

———— *Emmer: A Grain for the Semiarid Regions.* Washington: U.S. Dept. of Agriculture, Farmers' Bulletin No. 139, 1901.

———— *Lessons from the Grain Rust Epidemic of 1904.* Washington: U.S. Dept. of Agriculture, Farmers' Bulletin No. 219, 1905.

———— *Macaroni Wheats.* Washington: U.S. Dept. of Agriculture, Bureau of Plant Industry, Bulletin No. 3, 1901.

CARRUTH, WILLIAM HERBERT, *Kansas in Literature.* Part I, Poetry; Part II, Prose; with a Historical Sketch and a Bibliography. Topeka, Kans.: Crane and Company, 1900.

CONNELLEY, WILLIAM ELSEY, *John Brown.* Topeka, Kans.: Crane and Company, 1900.

———— *Quantrill and the Border Wars.* Cedar Rapids, Iowa: The Torch Press, 1910.

———— *A Standard History of Kansas and Kansans.* Chicago and New York: Lewis Publishing Co., 1919.

———— *Wild Bill and His Era; the Life and Adventures of James Butler Hickok.* New York: Press of the Pioneers, 1933.

COOLIDGE, DANE, *Fighting Men of the West . . .* New York: E. P. Dutton & Company, 1932.

CORDLEY, RICHARD, *A History of Lawrence, Kansas, from the First Settlement to the close of the Rebellion.* Lawrence: E. P. Caldwell, 1895.

CUTLER, WILLIAM G. (Editor), *History of the State of Kansas.* Chicago: A. T. Andreas, 1883.

DAVIDSON, WILLIAM, *Selections from Ironquill.* Topeka, Kans.: Crane and Company, 1899.

DE KRUIF, PAUL, *Hunger Fighters.* New York: Harcourt, Brace & Company, 1928.

DIGGS, ANNIE L., *The Story of Jerry Simpson.* Wichita, Kans.: Jane Simpson, Publisher, 1908.

EBBUTT, PERCY G., *Emigrant Life in Kansas.* London: Swan, Sonnenschein and Company, 1886.

FISHER, H. D., *The Gun and the Gospel . . .* (2nd ed.). Chicago and New York: Medical Century Company, 1899.

GREGG, JOSIAH, *Commerce on the Prairies* . . . (2 vols.). New York: Henry G. Langley; London: Wiley and Putnam, 1844.

Hard Red Winter Wheat Varieties. Washington: U.S. Dept. of Agriculture, Farmers' Bulletin No. 1806, December, 1938.

HENRY, STUART, *Conquering Our Great American Plains.* New York: E. P. Dutton & Company, 1930.

HITCHCOCK, A. S., and CARLETON, MARK ALFRED, *Preliminary Report on Rusts of Grain.* Manhattan, Kans.: Kansas State Agricultural Experiment Station, Bulletin No. 38, 1893.

———— *Second Report on Rusts of Grain.* Manhattan, Kans.: Kansas State Agricultural Experiment Station, Bulletin No. 46, 1894.

HOWE, E. W., *The Story of a Country Town; with an Introduction by Carl Van Doren.* New York: Albert and Charles Boni, 1926.

HUDSON, J. K., *Letters to Governor Lewelling* . . . Topeka, Kans.: The Topeka Capital Company, 1893.

HUNTER, JOHN MARVIN (Compiler and Editor), *The Trail Drivers of Texas.* (2nd ed. rev. 2 vol. in one.) Nashville, Tenn.: Cokesbury Press, 1925.

INMAN, COLONEL HENRY, *The Old Santa Fe Trail; the Story of a Great Highway.* Topeka, Kans.: Crane and Company, 1899.

ISELY, BLISS, and RICHARDS, W. M., *Four Centuries in Kansas.* Topeka, Kans.: State Printer, 1937.

KANSAS LEGISLATURE, *House Journal, 1872-1939.* Topeka: State Printer, 1872-1939.

KANSAS LEGISLATURE, *Senate Journal, 1872-1939.* Topeka: State Printer, 1872-1939.

KANSAS LEGISLATURE, *Session Laws, 1861-1939.* Topeka: State Printer, 1861-1939.

KANSAS STATE BOARD OF AGRICULTURE, *Report, 1872 to 1937-38.* Topeka: State Printer, 1873-1939.

KANSAS STATE CHAMBER OF COMMERCE. *Yearbook, 1937-1938.* Topeka, 1938.

KANSAS STATE HISTORICAL SOCIETY, *Collections,* Vols. I-XVII. Topeka: State Printer, 1881-1928. *The Kansas Historical Quarterly,* Vols. I to VIII. Topeka, 1931-1939.

KANSAS CITY BOARD OF TRADE, *Annual Report.* Kansas City, Mo., 1871-1938.

KANSAS CITY STOCK YARDS CO., *Annual Live Stock Report, 1924-1938.* Kansas City, Mo., 1925-1939.

McCoy, Joseph G., *Historic Sketches of the Cattle Trade of the West and Southwest*. Kansas City, Mo.: Ramsey, Millett & Hudson, 1874. Reprinted, Washington, D.C., The Rare Book Shop, 1932.

Nimmo, Joseph, *Report in Regard to the Range and Ranch Cattle Traffic in the Western States, Made to the Secretary of the Treasury, February, 1885*. U.S. 48th Congress, 2nd Session, House Executive Documents, Vol. 29, No. 267.

Phillips, William, *The Conquest of Kansas, by Missouri and Her Allies*. Boston: Phillips, Sampson and Company, 1856.

Potter, Jack, *Cattle Trails of the Old West*. Clayton, N. M.: Laura R. Krehbiel, 1939.

———— *Lead Steer and Other Tales*. Clayton, N. M.: The Leader Press, 1939.

Powell, Cuthbert, *Twenty Years of Kansas City's Live Stock Trade and Traders*. Kansas City, Mo.: Pearl Printing Co., 1893.

Redpath, James, *The Public Life of Captain John Brown*. Boston: Thayer and Eldridge, 1860.

Richardson, Albert D., *Beyond the Mississippi* . . . Hartford, Conn.: American Publishing Co.

Ridings, Sam P., *The Chisholm Trail; a History of the World's Greatest Cattle Trail*. Guthrie, Okla.: Co-operative Publishing Co., 1936.

Root, Frank A., and Connelley, William Elsey, *The Overland Stage to California*. Published by the Authors, Topeka, Kans., 1901.

Sanborn, F. B., *The Life and Letters of John Brown*. Boston: Roberts Brothers, 1885.

Shippee, Lester Burrell, *Recent American History*. New York: The Macmillan Company, 1924.

Speer, John, *Life of Gen. James H. Lane* . . . Garden City, Kans.: John Speer, Printer, 1896.

Spring, Leverett, *Kansas; the Prelude to the War for the Union*. Boston: Houghton Mifflin Company, 1885.

Sterling, Wilson (Editor), *Quarter-Centennial History of the University of Kansas, 1866-1891*. Topeka, Kans.: Geo. W. Crane and Company, 1891.

Thayer, Eli, *A History of the Kansas Crusade; Its Friends and Its Foes*. New York: Harper and Brothers, 1889.

Tomlinson, William P., *Kansas in Eighteen Fifty-Eight* . . . New York: H. Dayton; Indianapolis: Dayton and Asker, 1859.

U.S. COMMISSIONER OF AGRICULTURE, *Annual Report, 1871.* Washington, 1872.

U.S. COMMISSIONER OF INDIAN AFFAIRS, *Annual Report, 1839 to 1843.* Washington, 1839-1843.

U.S. DEPT. OF AGRICULTURE, *Yearbook, 1896 to 1937.* Washington, 1897-1937.

VAN DOREN, CARL, *Contemporary American Novelists, 1900-1920.* New York: The Macmillan Company, 1922.

VILLARD, OSWALD GARRISON, *John Brown, A Biography Fifty Years After.* Boston and New York: Houghton Mifflin Company, 1910.

WALTON, W. M., *Life and Adventures of Ben Thompson.* Republished in *Frontier Times,* Bandera, Texas, Vol. 3, No. 10 to Vol. 4, No. 3, July-December, 1926. First Published in 1884.

WARE, EUGENE FITCH, *Some of the Rhymes of Ironquill.* (13th rev. ed.) New York and London: G. P. Putnam's Sons, 1909.

WARMAN, CY, *The Railroad* (2 vols.). New York: Federal Publishing Society, 1898. (Builders of the American Nation Series.)

WRIGHT, ROBERT MARR, *Dodge City, the Cowboy Capital . . .* Wichita, Kans.: Wichita Eagle Press, 1913.

Newspapers and Periodicals

Abilene *Chronicle,* 1870-1876.

American Nonconformist, and Kansas Industrial Liberator, Winfield, 1886-1889.

American Review of Reviews, 1903.

Atchison *Free Press,* 1865.

Country Gentleman, August, 1919; June, 1924; May, 1933.

Dodge City *Times,* 1876-78.

Ellis County Star, Hays, 1876-1882.

Ellsworth *Democrat,* 1892.

Ellsworth *Reporter,* 1871-1876.

Farmer's Advocate, McPherson, 1874.

Ford County Globe, Dodge City, 1878-1885.

Greenback Headlight, Frankfort, 1879-1880.

Harpers Monthly Magazine, 1875, 1935.

Harper's Weekly, 1874.

Hays *Sentinel,* 1876-79.

Herald of Freedom, Lawrence, 1854-1858.

Junction City *Tribune*, 1896.
Junction City *Union*, 1868-1873.
Kansas Agitator, Garnett, 1890, 1896.
Kansas Farmer, Topeka, 1875-1890.
Kansas Greenbacker, Emporia, 1878.
Kansas City *Journal of Commerce*, 1867-1873.
Kansas City *Star*, 1903-1939.
Kansas City *Times*, 1918-1940.
Kansas Tribune, Topeka, 1857-1859.
Missouri Commonwealth, Independence, July, 1850. Extract on file in Kansas Historical Society Library, Topeka; quoted in Root and Connelley, *The Overland Stage to California;* and Inman, *The Old Santa Fe Trail.*
MUSE, R. W. P. "History of Harvey County, Kansas," in *Arkansas Valley Democrat*, June 1, 1883.
Nation, 1926.
Newton *Kansan*, 1872-1900.
Ottawa *Journal and Triumph*, 1872, 1890.
Republican, Hays, 1890-1898.
Rocky Mountain News, Denver, 1859-1865.
Saturday Evening Post, 1933.
Scribner's Magazine, 1892.
Scribner's Monthly, 1880.
Survey, 1923.
Thomas County Cat, Colby, 1886.
Time, 1931.
Topeka *Capital*, 1893-1939.
Topeka *Commonwealth*, 1869-1880.
Wichita *Eagle*, 1872-1930.

Manuscripts

ABILENE CITY COUNCIL, *Minutes*, 1870-1872.
ALBRECHT, ABRAHAM, *Mennonite Settlements in Kansas*. Master's Thesis, University of Kansas, 1925.
DODGE CITY COUNCIL, *Ordinance Book*, 1876.
ELLSWORTH CITY COUNCIL, *Minutes*, 1873.
ELLSWORTH COUNTY CORONER, *Papers*, 1873.
ELLSWORTH POLICE COURT, *Docket Book*, 1871-1874.
FOX, MAYNARD, *Book Length Fiction by Kansas Writers*, 1915-1938. Master's Thesis, Fort Hays Kansas State College, 1939.

GUY, MRS. LEILA M., *Studies in Kansas Poetry.* Master's Thesis, University of Kansas, 1914.

HARPER, J. B., *A Survey of the Kansas Short Story.* Master's Thesis, University of Kansas, 1915.

HENRY, MRS. M. C., *A Glance at the Kansas Novel.* Master's Thesis, University of Kansas, 1915.

JOHNS, VERNON O., *Development of the Flour Milling Industry in Kansas.* Master's Thesis, University of Kansas, 1926.

KANSAS DISTRICT COURT, *Papers,* 1873-1877.

KANSAS STATE BOARD OF AGRICULTURE, *Original Schedules of the Census,* 1875, 1885, 1895.

LONG, E. F., *Kansas Literature: a Historical Sketch to 1875.* Master's Thesis, University of Kansas, 1915.

MEEKER, JOTHAM, *Diary, 1833-1834.*

MENNONITE HISTORICAL LIBRARY, North Newton, Kans., Collection of material on introduction of wheat into Kansas.

MILLER, CLIFFORD DWIGHT, *Social Conditions of Territorial Kansas.* Master's Thesis, Fort Hays Kansas State College, 1936.

NEW ENGLAND EMIGRANT AID COMPANY, *Minutes, 1855-1856.*

NEWTON CITY COUNCIL, *Minutes,* 1872-73.

NEWTON CITY COUNCIL, *Ordinance Book,* 1872-73.

SEIBERT, VICTOR C., *History of the Kansas Mennonites with a Study of Their European Background.* Master's Thesis, Fort Hays Kansas State College, 1936.

TAYLOR, REBECCA WELLS, *Some Lost Towns of Western Kansas.* Master's Thesis, Fort Hays Kansas State College, 1935.

THOMPSON, GEORGE G., *Bat Masterson; the Dodge City Years.* Master's Thesis, Fort Hays Kansas State College, 1939.

U.S. BUREAU OF THE CENSUS, *Original Schedules of United States Census,* 1870, 1880.

WICHITA CITY CLERK, *Ledger,* 1874.

WICHITA CITY CLERK, *Warrant Record,* 1874-1875.

WICHITA CITY COUNCIL, *Minutes,* 1870-1875.

WICHITA CITY COUNCIL, *Ordinance Book,* 1870-1875.

Index

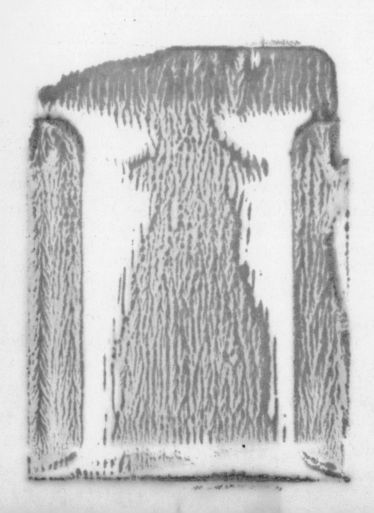